PEACE ON THE LAKES – CANADA AND THE RUSH-BAGOT AGREEMENT

PEACE ON THE LAKES – CANADA AND THE RUSH-BAGOT AGREEMENT

Peter W. Noonan

Magistralis
Ottawa, Canada

Library and Archives Canada Cataloguing in Publication

Noonan, Peter W. (Peter William), 1956-, author
Peace on the Great Lakes : Canada and the Rush-Bagot agreement / Peter
W.Noonan.

Includes bibliographical references.
Issued in print and electronic formats.
ISBN 978-0-9683534-3-1 (hardback).–ISBN 978-0-9683534-1-7 (paperback).–
ISBN 978-0-9683534-2-4 (html)

1. Neutrality–Great Lakes (North America). 2. United States–Foreign
relations–Great Britain. 3. Great Britain–Foreign relations–United States.
4. United States–Foreign relations–Canada. 5. Canada–Foreign relations–
United States. I. Title.

FC249.N65 2016   971.3   C2016-903886-6
C2016-903887-4

CONTENTS

PREFACE

The Rush-Bagot Agreement is the oldest formal arms limitation agreement in the world. Originally entered into by Great Britain and the United States after the conclusion of the War of 1812, it was intended to avoid the ruinous effects of the naval arms race on the great interior lakes of North America that had already begun in the late stages of the war. By limiting the naval forces that each country could construct and maintain on the Great Lakes it was also intended to lessen tensions along the maritime border between what was then the British Empire, and the young independent republic that had broken free of the empire. Later, the Rush-Bagot Agreement was inherited by Canada when Canada began to enter the family of nations during the late nineteenth and early twentieth centuries. It has been the foundation for the mutual efforts by the Canadian and American governments to moderate the risk of a militarization of their common border.

Although the Rush-Bagot Agreement was often breached, in its early days particularly, it has survived rebellions, insurgencies, and the threats of war to sustain the long peace between Canada and the United States. Many diplomatic agreements have since been entered into between Canada and the United States and the relationship between the two countries is now amongst the closest of relationships between any two states in the world. Long bereft of its practical impact due to a close military alliance between Canada and the United States, the Rush-Bagot

Agreement has nevertheless acquired a greater role as a symbolic expression of the firm intention of those two North American countries to establish and maintain a perpetual peace across the longest international border in the world.

I write these words in the 200th year of the Rush-Bagot Agreement, a diplomatic achievement that will mark its bicentennial in April 2017. The Rush-Bagot Agreement remains a monument to peace, and a concrete expression of a thought expressed by former Prime Minister Lester B. Pearson in his Nobel lecture in December 1957: "The best defence of peace is not power, but the removal of the causes of war, and international agreements which will put peace on a stronger foundation …." For Canada and the United States, the Rush-Bagot Agreement has pointed the way to that goal in North America, and it is to memorialize that purpose that this effort has been conceived as a study of the Rush-Bagot Agreement from a Canadian perspective.

Ottawa, Canada

June 2016

INTRODUCTION

1600 - 1750 THE GREAT LAKES

The Great Lakes of North America, a marvel of nature, constitute the largest reserve of freshwater in the world. Comprising a combined area of 95000 square miles, and extending across a drainage basin of 291,680 square miles, each of the five main lakes is the equivalent of an inland sea[1]. Together they hold approximately 20% of the world's total volume of freshwater. The Great Lakes were created at the end of the last ice age, around 10,000 years ago, when the great Laurentides Ice Sheet which had covered the continent as far south as 40 degrees north began to recede[2]. As the great ice sheet withdrew the weight of the glaciers was lifted from the land, and the compression which the land had previously been subjected too began to reverse. As it did so, the lakes created by the scour of the retreating glaciers began to conform to the approximate shape and size of the Great Lakes as we know them today.

The five major lakes form a tiered chain of freshwater seas with the water from Lake Superior, the highest and largest of the lakes by volume, spilling into Lakes Huron and Michigan, the next lowest lakes, and the water from Lake Huron dropping into Lake Erie. Subsequently, the water drops more than 360 feet over the Niagara Escarpment from Lake Erie into Lake Ontario forming

1. Don Courtney Piper, *The International Law of the Great Lakes: A Study of Canadian-United States Co-operation* (Durham (North Carolina): Duke University Press, 1967) 5.
2. Pierre Berton, *The Great Lakes* (Toronto: Stoddart Publishing, 1996) 35.

Niagara Falls, one of the wonders of the North American continent.

Lake Superior is the largest, deepest, and uppermost lake with a volume of water so great that it exceeds the water volume of the other four Great Lakes combined. It is 31,700 square miles in area and reaches a depth of 1333 feet. Water flows from Lake Superior into Lake Huron, and from Lake Huron water crosses into the adjoining Lake Michigan. In hydrological terms Lake Michigan and Lake Huron form one lake although they are geographically distinct. Lakes Superior, Michigan, and Huron are considered to be the upper lakes in contrast to Lake Erie and Lake Ontario which are considered to be the lower lakes (i.e. closer to the sea level in elevation).

Lake Huron is 23000 square miles in area (including Georgian Bay) and reaches a depth of 750 feet. It is connected at its southern end to the St. Clair River which takes water from Lake Huron into Lake St. Clair, a small shallow lake lying between Lakes Huron and Erie. From the southern end of Lake St. Clair water flows into the Detroit River which is really a strait, as its French name implies, before exiting into Lake Erie, which is the shallowest of the five great lakes.

Lake Erie has an area of 9910 square miles and reaches a depth of 210 feet. Water from Lake Erie flows into Lake Ontario, which is the smallest of the Great Lakes at 7340 square miles in area, although it is deeper than Lake Erie reaching a depth of 802 feet. From Lake Ontario water flows east into the St Lawrence River, where it flows a further 744 miles downstream before the water enters the Atlantic Ocean.

Downstream of Montreal the St. Lawrence River is joined by the Richelieu River which flows 106 miles north from Lake Champlain to reach the St. Lawrence. Lake Champlain is also a large, deep freshwater lake 125 miles in length and up to 14 miles wide, although it does not match in size any of the five Great Lakes. Nevertheless, it is of great importance from the standpoint of military history since its north-south orientation made the Lake Champlain and Richelieu river system a preferred invasion route, north or south, during the eighteenth and nineteenth centuries.

Today, the St. Lawrence River and the Great Lakes combined provide a water transportation route deep in the continent extending more than 2347 miles from the ocean, allowing oceangoing vessels to reach as far inland as Duluth, Minnesota. Although the lakes form an essential water transportation corridor, they can be dangerous to navigate. Violent storms can overtake mariners on any of the Great Lakes. Ninety-foot waves have been recorded on Lake Superior, and the relatively shallow Lake Erie can be particularly dangerous in a storm[3].

For centuries, the Great Lakes were the abodes of the aboriginal peoples of North America. However, in the sixteenth and seventeenth centuries the major European powers embarked on a massive project to take possession of the Americas, often by co-opting the indigenous aboriginal peoples into political and military alliances, or undertaking their outright subjugation. In the case of North America the European advance consisted of two prongs. On the eastern coast settlements were established by the Spanish, British, French, Swedes, and Dutch, while on the edge of the Pacific Ocean the Spanish moved up the coast after their conquest of the Aztecs in what is now Mexico.

On the eastern coast the Swedes and Dutch[4] were relieved of their colonies by the British, who established hegemony along the eastern seaboard of what is now the United States of America with the exception of Spanish Florida. The British also

3. Berton, *The Great Lakes*, 129.
4. Denmark was also present in Greenland, the large island lying off of the northeastern coast of North America. The Danes also conducted voyages of exploration into Hudson Bay.

penetrated into Hudson's Bay and established littoral trading posts under the control of a great monopoly combine, the Hudson's Bay Company. In the territory north of the British-American colonies and west of the island of Newfoundland the French established a great inland colony centred on the lands along the St. Lawrence River and the Great Lakes, which became the fault line for a century and a half of conflict between France and Great Britain for the control of the eastern half of the North American continent.

Initially, the British hugged the eastern seaboard while the French ranged further afield in search of furs, particularly beaver pelts, which proved to be the most valuable commodity that could be extracted from the new continent during the early period of colonization. The French territory was known as Canada, a word corrupted from the language of the aboriginal people settled around what became the fortress city of Quebec.

For the purposes of political organization the French established their colony along the St. Lawrence River under the name of New France. From their base at Quebec the French moved into the interior in search of furs. Tough French men known as *coureur du bois* (runners of the forest) mastered the aboriginal art of paddling canoes into the interior and made first contact with many of the inland tribes.

Canoes were a marvellous nautical invention perfectly suited to transportation on Canadian rivers and on the Great Lakes. Made of birchbark on a wooden frame and sealed with spruce gum, a canoe of the standard length of sixteen to eighteen feet could easily carry two men and a small freight cargo enormous distances. Later, the colonial government would build larger eight-man canoes called *canot de maitre* for the fur trade at Trois Riviere, which both the Hudson's Bay Company and its competitor, the North West Company, adopted[5].

Canadians of this era also used bateaux, a catch all term for a durable long, double-ended, shallow-draft boat that could surmount the rocks in Canadian rivers and moved through the water under sail or oar power, or was pulled against the river currents with shore-based tow lines and onboard poles[6]. These craft were the equivalent of modern commercial motor vehicles, moving cargoes around the country on the lakes and rivers in the absence of roads. A bateaux could carry three to five tons of cargo or passengers but it was still capable of being physically carried by its crew if necessary. They ranged in size from between fifteen and thirty feet in length and were rowed by at least four men. Steering was rudimentary, through the use of a steering oar. When rigged for sailing the bateaux carried one square sail on a mast. The bateaux was a common sight for a century and a half, providing much needed water transportation for the fur trade and commerce generally.

The main French Canadian water and land transportation route into the interior led from Montreal along the Ottawa River and through Lake Nippissing into Lake Huron, and then across that lake into Lake Superior and Lake Michigan. Thus, it was some time before the early colonial regime in Canada fully explored Lake Ontario, or even became acquainted with Lake Erie. It was not until the coming to Canada of Robert Cavalier Sieur de La Salle that true marine penetration of the Great Lakes began. La Salle was an impatient and energetic nobleman marked by an intensity of temperament[7], who sought personal glory in addition to financial gain[8]. La Salle dreamed of an inland empire secured by a system of forts and ships using the Great Lakes as a natural transportation route into the interior[9]. His great

5. Stephen Leacock, *Canada and the Sea* (Montreal: Alvah M. Beatty Publications(1943) Ltd., 1944) 26.
6. Ibid, 37.
7. Thomas B Costain, *The White and the Gold* (1954; repr., Toronto: Popular Library,1965) 323, 335.
8. Ibid, 336.
9. Berton, *The Great Lakes*, 28.

vision was a maritime transportation system joining the Great Lakes and the Mississippi River system into an interconnected transportation network joined by a series of inland fortified posts, a bold vision for maritime transportation on North America's inland seas that was considerably ahead of its time.

La Salle built a brigantine-rigged ship of 10 tons burden on Lake Ontario and took passage in it with a party of men to the Niagara peninsula in November 1678, arriving at the Seneca village located there on December 7th[10]. At Cayuga Creek above the falls La Salle built a 65-ton burden barque, modelled on a Dutch galleot to accommodate the shallow lakes, and christened it the *Griffon*[11]. On August 7, 1679, the *Griffon* departed from Niagara and sailed into Lake Erie, reaching the Detroit River on August 10th and entering into Lake St. Clair, the small lake that lies between Lake Erie and Lake Huron, on the 12th. By August 27th the *Griffon* had reached Lake Michigan where it eventually stopped at Green Bay[12].

The *Griffon* was, no doubt, a marvel to the aboriginals who viewed it sailing serenely through the Great Lakes where no marine vessel had ever trespassed before. Indeed, the great size of the vessel as it was being built engendered fear in the natives, and prompted some members of the Mohawk First Nation to threaten to burn it[13]. At Green Bay, La Salle was able to obtain a valuable cargo of furs but he elected to leave the ship at that point in order to travel overland to explore the Illinois country for the possible future locations of inland forts. The *Griffon* was sent back to Niagara with its crew and cargo but somewhere along the way disaster overtook the first vessel to sail on the Great Lakes. After departing on September 18, 1679, the *Griffon* was

10. Pierre Berton, *Niagara: A History of the Falls* (Toronto: McClelland & Stewart,1992) 25.
11. Leacock, *Canada and the Sea*, 26.
12. Ernest J Lajeunnesse, *The Windsor Border Region: Canada's Southernmost Frontier* (1960 repr. Toronto, Essex County Historical Association, 1972) xxxv.
13. Costain, *The White and the Gold*, 337.

never seen or heard from again, and its ultimate fate remains a mystery[14]. The loss of the *Griffon* was a grievous blow to La Salle and underscored the dangers of marine navigation on the Great Lakes. Thereafter, no ship sailed the waters of the upper lakes for almost a century – until after the British conquest of Canada[15].

14. Lajeunnesse, *The Windsor Border Region*, xxxv.
15. Ibid, xxxvi.

PART ONE - WAR AND PEACE
1750 - 1836

1750-1763 GREAT BRITAIN AND COLONIAL AMERICA CONQUER CANADA

Throughout the late seventeenth and early eighteenth centuries France consolidated its hold on Canada, extending its reach west and south to link New France with the Louisiana colony via the Illinois Country. A vast arc of French control and influence extended from the mouth of the St. Lawrence River all the way to New Orleans on the coast of the Gulf of Mexico. In the meantime, the British consolidated their hold along the eastern littoral of the continent, extending their frontier from Spanish Florida north to Maine (which was then a political dependency of the Bay Colony of Massachusetts) and encompassing all of the lands lying east of the Appalachian mountain chain. Several small wars[1] punctuated the relations between the two colonial powers vying for control of North America, usually as the result of a European conflict spilling over into the new world, but none of those wars ultimately threatened the political control that France or Britain exercised over their colonial possessions in North America.

The strategic position of Canada during this early period of competition and conflict in North America was quite favourable. The country was heavily forested to the south where the British-American colonies were located, and the lines of communication

---

1. The wars included King William's War 1688-97; Queen Anne's War 1702-13; and King George's War 1744-48. All of those were the colonial by-products of European wars, generally involving the European politics of royal succession.

between the French colonies in the north and the British colonies to the south were poor. Only the rivers provided natural highways into the interior of the country for an invading army. The most direct route from the south to the capital at Quebec, on the St. Lawrence River, lay along the Chaudiere River but that route proved to be a difficult traverse for any potential invasion force[2]. The Chaudiere is a fast-flowing whitewater river and invading forces required experience in transporting men and materiel through rapids and fast water, a skill less likely to be formed in the British-American colonies than in Canada. A better invasion route from the south lay along the north-south route through Lake George and Lake Champlain, which led in turn into the Richelieu River south of Montreal. That route formed a natural invasion route although if certain portages and other natural strong points along that route were properly fortified and defended the strong-points could be held against superior forces[3].

However, Canada had two weaknesses in its natural defences. The first weakness was the St. Lawrence River itself, which gave access into the center of the country from the ocean including its capital and main fortress at Quebec. The St. Lawrence was also the main transportation route for essential military supplies from metropolitan France. Thus, France's control was predicated upon maintaining a sufficient naval force to allow for re-supplying the colony from the mother country. That proved problematic during an era in which the British invested heavily in the Royal Navy as the main bulwark of defence for its island kingdom, which also gave it command of the seas. In contrast,

2. William Wood, *The Fight for Overseas Empire:The Declaration of War* in Adam Shortt and Arthur G. Doughty, eds., *Canada and Its Provinces, Vol. 1* (Toronto:Glasgow, Brook & Company, 1914) 246-254; repr. C. Belanger, *L'Encyclopedie del'histoire duQuebec/The Quebec History Encyclopedia*, (Montreal:Marianopolis College, 2005) http://www.faculty.marianopolis.edu/c.belanger/quebechistory/encyclopedia /TheSevenYearsWar-FrenchandIndianWar-DeclarationofWarin1756.htm. (Accessed May 21, 2015).
3. Ibid.

European geography had always dictated that France must be a major land power and, accordingly, France invested heavily in its land forces. The French navy was a secondary consideration for the imperial government in Paris, which left its overseas colonies in a precarious position in the event of a war with Great Britain.

The second potential weakness facing Canada was the Great Lakes, where a loss of French control could impede or even sunder its long interior lines of communication into the *Pays d'en Haut*[4] and the Illinois Country[5]. For the colonial government in Canada the control of the Great Lakes, and of Lake Ontario in particular, was essential. The loss of naval control on Lake Ontario would allow an enemy to bring forces from that lake to invest Montreal, with the potential to conquer all of Canada from that direction.

The active defence of Canada rested with the colonial government which was organized with a Governor as the most senior civil official. The Governor, who was appointed by the King in Paris, was also the commander in chief of the French armed forces within Canada. Next in importance to the Governor was the Intendant, a senior administrative official who was charged with responsibility for the finances of the country, and who was directly responsible to Minister of Marine within the imperial government in Paris. Also highly influential was the Bishop of Quebec, who was in charge of the affairs of the Roman Catholic church, the state church in Canada under the French regime.

In the mid-eighteenth century, when the prospect of a great conflagration in North America began to loom large, the main

---

4. The *Pays d'en Haut* was a huge dependent territory of New France lying west of Montreal and extending as far west as the eastern portions of the Prairies. It included all of the Great Lakes, and the land surrounding the lakes, and it was administered from Quebec.
5. The Illinois Country incorporated lands in what is now the American states of Illinois, Indiana, and Missouri, in the area of the upper Mississippi River basin. It was administered from Quebec until 1717, and thereafter it was administered from Louisiana.

strength of the military in Canada rested upon the regular French army troops, the *troupes de la terre*. The regular force was made up of a professional class of soldiers who were equal to the skill of their opponents in the regular forces of the British army. By the time war broke out in the 1750's, France would have approximately five thousand *troupes de la terre* in Canada[6].

Next in importance to the regular force were the *troupes de la marine*, which consisted of companies of colonial regulars largely drawn from the ranks of the local militia. This force was trained in the arts of asymmetrical, or camouflage warfare, practised by both the aboriginal peoples and the European settlers in North America. The *troupes de la marine* numbered perhaps two thousand in the 1750's. A force of naval troops was also available for the defence of Canada. Their numbers ranged from one thousand to fifteen-hundred, not counting those seamen stationed at Fortress Louisbourg in Acadia.

However, the main strength of the armed forces in Canada in the mid-eighteenth century was the colonial militia, which included all able-bodied men in the colony of New France. In number, the militia could potentially field upwards of fourteen-thousand men on the eve of the Seven Years War. While the militia could move and fight well in asymmetrical combat it was not a useful force in the set-piece battle formations used in formal eighteenth century European-style combat.

Finally, the colonial government had available to it warriors from the aboriginal nations allied to France. Aboriginal forces never exceeded three thousand effectives but their skillfulness (and fearsomeness) as warriors exaggerated their impact in the minds of their opponents, and magnified the psychological advantage of the colonial forces over the British-American militia. All in all, the colonial government probably had something in the order of

6. Ibid.

twenty-thousand troops available to it for the defence of Canada in the mid-eighteenth century[7].

Trouble on the North American continent had been brewing since the end of King George's War, fought between 1744-48. In the war's aftermath, the hold of the Iroquois Confederacy on the Ohio country west of the Appalachians began to diminish[8]. Hitherto, the Iroquois Confederacy had perfected a delicate diplomatic balance between the French in Canada and the British along the American seaboard. Now, with their influence in the Ohio Country lessening, the French were emboldened to penetrate this territory and establish forts to better secure the lines of communication between the colony of New France, and the colony of Louisiana, through the Illinois Country. As a result, the colonial government in Canada began construction of forts in the *Pays d'en Haut* at Presque Isle on Lake Erie and further south along French Creek, a tributary of the Allegheny River, and, ultimately, at the forks of the Ohio River, which would give strategic control of the Ohio Country to the authorities in Canada[9].

Naturally, the developing French control in the interior raised alarms in British America and in London. The British government instructed the Governor of Virginia, Robert Dinwiddie, to contest French encroachments but not to do so as an aggressor. Rather, Dinwiddie was encouraged to adopt a defensive strategy to prevent encroachments on British territory. The difficulty with that strategy however, was that it was unclear where the boundaries of one empire intersected with those of the other. In fact, both empires were vying for control of the interior of the North American continent. Thus, the Seven Years War, unlike the wars which preceded it in North America, did

---

7. Ibid.

8. Fred Anderson, *Crucible of War: The Seven Years War and the Fate of Empire in British North America, 1754-1766* (New York: Vintage Books, 2001) 24.

9. Ibid, 32.

not begin as the result of European politics but rather began as a contest for territory in North America. Ultimately, the war would inflame not only the North American continent but would spread to Europe and Asia becoming, in effect, the first world war. It would lead to the permanent collapse of the French regime in Canada and briefly establish British hegemony over most of the North American continent before internal dissent led to the sundering of British rule over its thirteen littoral American colonies.

Governor Dinwiddie, in conformity with his instructions, decided to send an emissary to make contact with the French officials who were active in the Ohio Country. Dinwiddie made an unusual choice in selecting a man to undertake this task. He chose an ambitious young twenty-one-year-old major in the colonial militia, George Washington. Washington came from a Virginia family of some relative prominence, though not of the most aristocratic upper layer in Virginian society[10], and in light of his youth he was inexperienced in both military combat and diplomacy. Eager to make his mark in life however, Washington, with 160 Virginian militiamen and some additional aboriginal warriors under his command laboured up the Ohio valley seeking out the French interlopers. Near a place called Great Meadows he established a camp and while at this location he received word of the approach of a French force. The French had heard of the British advance into the Ohio valley and had sent an officer, Ensign Jumonville, together with a small force to intercept the British, and to dissuade them from contesting French control over the Ohio Valley.

Washington advanced his force towards the approaching French force and the result was a confused engagement near Great Meadows, at the Battle of Jumonville Glen, which resulted in the death of the French commander and a number of his troops

10. Ibid, 42.

during his attempt to read out a declaration of French sovereignty in the Ohio River valley. It has been suggested that Washington, who was experiencing his first combat engagement, may have lost control of the situation and that a number of French troops may have been killed by the aboriginal warriors accompanying Washington's troops after surrendering. However, the historical picture is incomplete and like many such skirmishes the true facts were obscured by the shock of the engagement[11]. Nevertheless, Washington hastily retreated back to Great Meadows where he completed a small palisaded fort, which he called Fort Necessity.

Having learned of Jumonville's fate the French dispatched a more powerful force from Fort Duquesne to drive the Virginians out of the Ohio Valley. Washington, now hunkered down at Fort Necessity with around 300 effective fighting men, waited for the French attack which came on July 3, 1754. Fort Necessity was aptly named, as it was a hastily constructed edifice which offered little shelter from the elements and only limited protection from enemy fire. During the prolonged French attack many of the Virginians were killed or wounded and discipline began to falter. Undoubtedly, the fort would have been taken and the defenders possibly massacred by the aboriginal warriors accompanying the French force but the French commander, believing that honour had been served, and Jumonville's death avenged, offered terms to Washington. Washington wisely accepted the French terms and surrendered Fort Necessity, retreating back into Virginia with heavy losses and defeated and dispirited troops[12].

From these minor collisions in the Ohio back country the tinder would begin to burn, and a wider conflagration now became inevitable. Although the war known as the Seven Years War would not be formally declared until May 15, 1756[13], both Great

---

11. Ibid 50-59.
12. Ibid, 65.
13. In the United States the war is known as the French and Indian War.

Britain and France began to reinforce their military forces in North America, and to plan for a war of territorial aggrandizement.

Canada's security behind its riverine and lake frontiers required that it maintain sufficient naval forces to control both the natural invasion route running south of Montreal along the Lake Champlain axis, as well as control of Lake Ontario. For this purpose the colonial government had constructed small fleets to maintain naval superiority over the British. On Lake Champlain the first warship built by the colonial government was the *St. Frederic*, a 45-ton sloop built at Fort Frederic (Crown Point) in 1742, which was used mainly to resupply the Canadian forts established on the lake[14]. In the early stages of the war the colonial government used a variety of galleys, barges, bateaux and even canoes, as well as the *St. Frederic*, to resupply the military establishments at Fort St. Frederic, *Point a la Chevelure* (Chimney Point) and Fort Carillon (Ticonderoga)[15].

Between 1757 and 1759 the colonial government constructed several more vessels of war for the defence of Lake Champlain. A 10-gun schooner was built and named *La Vigilante* as well as three sloop-rigged xebecs christened *La Musquelongy*, *La Brochette* and *L'Esturgeon*, each armed with eight guns[16].

On Lake Ontario the colonial government established a more powerful fleet at its principal base at Cataraqui, or Fort Frontenac, which is now Kingston, Ontario. Between 1749 and 1756 the colonial government built the *La Marquise de Vaudreuil*, a 20-gun topsail schooner of 120 tons, the 14-gun *La Hurault*, also a topsail schooner of 90 tons, *La Louise*, a six-gun gaff-rigged schooner of 50 tons, and *Le Victor*, a 4-gun sloop of 40 tons[17]. In

14. "French and British Military Conflict (1664-1763)," Lake Champlain Maritime Museum http://www.lcmm.org. (Accessed May 21, 2015).]
15. Ibid.
16. Ibid.
17. Victor Suthren, *The Island of Canada: How Three Oceans Shaped Our Nation* (Toronto: Thomas

addition, the colonial government also constructed a number of auxiliary flatboats for transport purposes.

With this fleet, the colonial government intended to exercise effective control over Lake Ontario. A Canadian officer, Captain Rene Hippolyte LaForce, was appointed to the command of both the flagship, *La Marquise de Vaudreuil*, and of the squadron itself. LaForce had been a merchant seaman before the war, and engaged in the coasting trade between Canada and Acadia[18] but by 1754 he found himself with the army, attached to Ensign Jumonville's ill-fated efforts to engage George Washington in a diplomatic discourse in the Ohio backwoods. Taken a prisoner by the British-Americans, he was sent to Virginia and it was upon his release in 1756 that he was appointed to the naval command on Lake Ontario.

Control of Lake Ontario by the colonial government of Canada would not go unchallenged by British America. The British-Americans were alarmed at the prospect of unfettered control of Lake Ontario by Canada, and embarked on a strategy to wrest away control of the lake from the Canadian force. To counter the naval base at Cataraqui, the British Americans in New York penetrated the wilderness and established a foothold on the Great Lakes at Oswego, on the southern shore of Lake Ontario. A fort was constructed in 1727 replacing a more modest post built earlier, and over the succeeding decades a number of forts would be built under various names in its general vicinity.

In the 1750's the British-Americans began constructing warships at Oswego. Two schooners, the *Oswego* and the *Ontario* were

Allen, 2009), 222. In Leslie Hannon, *Forts of Canada: The Conflicts, Sieges, and Battles that Forged a Great Nation* (Toronto: McClelland and Stewart, 1969), 161, *La Marquise de Vaudreuil* is reported to have had 24 guns. In Robert Malcomson, *Warships of the Great Lakes 1754-1834*, (Annapolis: Naval Institute Press, 2001) 10, *La Marquise de Vaudreuil* is reported as having 24 guns, *La Hurault* as having 12 guns, and *La Louise* and *Le Victor* were each armed with 6 guns.

18. Yvon Desloges, "LaForce, Rene Hippolyte," *Dictionary of Canadian Biography, Vol. 5*, (Toronto: University of Toronto/Universite Laval, 1983).

built and armed with six four-pounder cannons and 10 swivel guns, and two 20-ton schooners, the *Vigilant* and the *George*, were also constructed and armed with swivel guns[19]. Royal Navy officers were placed in command of the ships and seamen from New England, New York, and Pennsylvania were hired to crew them[20]. Lieutenant Housman Broadley of the Royal Navy was placed in overall command of the British-American squadron[21]. Later, both the *Oswego* and *Ontario* were converted to sloops, as Lieutenant Broadley felt that a sloop rig provided better handling[22]. In 1755, the British-Americans, at the urging of Governor Shirley of Massachusetts, the commander-in-chief of British America, commenced the construction of the 12-gun sloop *Mohawk*, the 18-gun brigantine *London*, and the 18-gun snow *Halifax*, as a result of intelligence reports which stated that the Canadians were building at least one and possibly three large vessels at Cataraqui[23]. Eventually, the Royal Navy squadron at Oswego consisted of 11 vessels together with a large number of auxiliary craft[24]. In this first shipbuilding war the British-Americans sought to gain naval supremacy on Lake Ontario, which was the key lake necessary for the control of the Canadian interior.

The unusually mild winter of 1755-56 permitted the colonial government to maintain naval operations during the winter, particularly operations to resupply Fort Niagara, while the British Americans had laid up their ships for the winter and were thus unable to challenge the Canadian vessels[25]. However,

19. Malcolmson, *Warships of the Great Lakes 1754-1834*, 9. Suthren, *The Island of Canada*, 223, states that *Oswego* and *Ontario* were armed with 5 guns each.
20. Carol MacLeod, *The Tap of the Garrison Drum: The Marine Service in British North America 1755-1813* (Ottawa: Parks Canada, unpublished, circa 1974), 14, 22.
21. Malcolmson, *Warships of the Great Lakes*, 8.
22. MacLeod, *The Tap of the Garrison Drum: The Marine Service in British North America*, 14.
23. Ibid, 17.
24. Donald Bamford, *Freshwater Heritage: A History of Sail on the Great Lakes* (Toronto: Dundurn Press, 2007), cited in Suthren, *The Island of Canada*, 223.
25. MacLeod, *The Tap of the Garrison Drum: The Marine Service in British North America*, 19.

by the spring the British-Americans had their squadron back in the water, and were prepared to challenge French Canada for the naval supremacy on Lake Ontario.

On June 27, 1756, Lieutenant Broadley took part of his squadron, consisting of *Oswego* and *Ontario*, together with one of the small schooner-row galleys, on a cruise into the lake. It so happened that Captain LaForce was also at sea with his squadron at the same time and the two met in a short and indecisive engagement on the lake. Perceiving himself to be at a disadvantage in comparison to the Canadian squadron, Lieutenant Broadley elected to break off contact with the superior enemy force and he returned to Oswego. LaForce gave chase with his squadron and Broadley, realizing that his smaller schooner (it was either *Vigilant* or *George*) could not maintain the pace of his two larger vessels, ordered it to detach itself from the squadron and to proceed on its own. LaForce also detached vessels from his squadron to pursue and capture the enemy schooner, which the Canadian ships succeeded in doing. In the meantime LaForce, realizing that he would not be able to overtake the *Oswego* and the *Ontario* before they reached safety at the port of Oswego, broke off his chase.

Thus, the only engagement on Lake Ontario during the Seven Years War resulted in a minor Canadian victory. Louis Antoine de Bougainville, then serving in Canada as an aide to the French army commander, the Marquis de Montcalm, recorded in his diary this "petty victory" although he also acknowledged that the forced retreat of the British squadron and the acquisition of a British prize at least confirmed French naval superiority in the eyes of the aboriginal population[26]. The opposing squadrons did not meet again before Montcalm, striking swiftly from Canada, marched a substantial force into upper New York and invested the British-American fortifications at Oswego. Using siege

26. Louis Antoine de Bougainville, *Journal*, cited in Suthren, *The Island of Canada*, 224.

artillery, Montcalm began a bombardment of Fort Ontario on August 12th which rendered the fort uninhabitable after two days of shelling. The British-Americans abandoned Fort Ontario, retreating into neighbouring Fort Pepperell, and Fort George, both of which quickly came under withering fire that forced their capitulation. After the surrender, Montcalm levelled the British-American fortifications and base facilities at Oswego.

While the siege was occurring, unfavourable winds had prevented Lieutenant Broadley from escaping into Lake Ontario with his squadron. The quick capitulation which followed the conquest of the forts also prevented him from firing his ships, and thereby depriving the French-Canadian fleet of their use. In the result, when LaForce arrived with his squadron after the land battle had concluded he was able to augment the French-Canadian fleet on Lake Ontario by adding the British-American ships to his own[27]. Canada now had complete control of Lake Ontario and thus preserved its lines of communication into the *Pays d'en Haut* and the Illinois Country. For the British-Americans the loss of Oswego and the British squadron was a bitter defeat that damaged morale and led to recriminations among some of the responsible actors[28].

For two years Canada retained clear naval control on Lake Ontario. Meanwhile, action occurred on a number of fronts in Acadia and Canada following the formal declaration of war between Great Britain and France, which occurred on May 18, 1756. Ever so slowly, the British, despite reverses, tightened the noose around the French empire in North America, using the naval superiority that Britain's Royal Navy provided. With resupply from metropolitan France jeopardized by the Royal Navy's command of the Atlantic Ocean, the French and Canadian forces were increasingly left to shift for themselves as

27. Malcolmson, *Warships of the Great Lakes*, 13.
28. MacLeod, *The Tap of the Garrison Drum: The Marine Service in British North America*, 25.

the titanic struggle for supremacy in North America approached its apex.

A critical blow fell on August 27, 1758, when British-American Lieutenant Colonel John Bradstreet (a Nova Scotian) with three thousand men returned to Oswego and crossed Lake Ontario in bateaux to successfully mount an attack on Fort Frontenac, which protected the Canadian naval force. Fort Frontenac had been depleted of its troops to reinforce Fort Carillon on Lake Champlain. As a result, the elderly French army commandant, Pierre-Jacques Payen de Noyan et de Chavoy, felt he had no option but to surrender the fort on the 28th, after a short bombardment by Bradstreet's forces.

During the siege Captain LaForce attempted to escape with his ships but his escape path was blocked by British-American small-craft and artillery fire which forced him to ground his vessels. LaForce and his crews escaped into the forests surrounding the battle site and a total of nine vessels in LaForce's squadron were subsequently surrendered with the fort[29]. Bradstreet proceeded to destroy Fort Frontenac and to sink all of the Canadian ships except for two which he used to transport captured booty back to Oswego. There, Bradstreet burned his two prizes and then fell back on New York[30]. It seems strange that Bradstreet should have burned the remaining warships, as their presence would have given the British-Americans naval supremacy on Lake Ontario. It appears that he may have acted in haste, and before orders from General Abercromby to preserve the vessels could reach him[31].

The loss of Fort Frontenac together with the naval squadron on Lake Ontario was a significant blow to French Canadian fortunes in the west. It increased the vulnerability of the western

29. Ibid; Hannon, *Forts of Canada*, 162.
30. Malcolmson, *Warships of the Great Lakes*, 14.
31. MacLeod, *The Tap of the Garrison Drum: The Marine Service in British North America*, 35.

posts, although it was still possible for the colonial government to maintain its line of communication with the *Pays d'en Haut* and the Illinois Country via the Ottawa River and Lake Huron, even without naval control of Lake Ontario. In any event, the schooner taken from Broadley's squadron in June 1756 was not at Cataraqui when Fort Frontenac was taken and, though small, it provided the colonial government with the only remaining active warship on Lake Ontario. (The schooner was subsequently retaken by the British following the Battle of Fort Niagara in July 1759[32].) In the meantime, in April 1759, the colonial government also built two new warships at *Pointe Baril* on the St. Lawrence River, the *Iroquoise* and the *Outouaise* to keep open the colonial government's lines of communication on the western St. Lawrence River and Lake Ontario to Niagara[33].

Fortress Louisbourg, the great east-coast bastion on *Ile Royale* (Cape Breton Island), also fell to British regular troops in 1758, and the Royal Navy thereafter exercised control over the sea approaches to Canada. With the start of the campaign season in the spring it was clear that the year 1759 would be decisive with respect to the outcome of the war in North America. The British planned three major offensives against Canada in 1759. The first and most powerful would be a thrust against Quebec from the east via the St. Lawrence River. Major General James Wolfe commanded an army of mostly British regulars supported by major ships of the Royal Navy under the command of Admiral Charles Saunders. A second thrust by a force consisting of British regulars and British-American provincial forces under the command of Major General Jeffrey Amherst planned to follow the traditional invasion route via Lake George and Lake Champlain against Montreal. A third thrust by a mixed force of regulars and British-American provincial troops would be made

32. Ibid..
33. Ibid, 37.

34

from Oswego against Fort Niagara to fully secure control of Lake Ontario.

The colonial government's squadron on Lake Champlain (*La Vigilante*, and three sloops, *La Musquelongy*, *La Brochette* and *L'Esturgeon*) assured the government of control of that lake in the absence of a British-American naval force. The French-Canadian force was commanded by Joseph Payant St. Onge who had held the command of the Canadian naval forces on the lake since 1742[34]. *Vigilant* was a former merchant vessel armed with ten guns, and the three sloops were armed with eight 4-pounder guns. St. Onge also had two row galleys under his command, the *Grand* and the *Petit Diable*[35]. In recognizing the need to challenge the Canadian authorities for control of the lake, the British assigned a New England sea captain, Joshua Loring, to construct new warships in America under a navy commission[36]. He built a 20-gun brig, the *Duke of Cumberland*, the 16 gun sloop *Boscawan*, the seven gun radeaus *Ligonier* and *Ticonderoga*, and three row galleys, as well as auxiliaries (bateaux and canoes)[37].

As General Amherst advanced, the commander of the colonial forces, the Chevalier de Bourlamaque, received orders to hold a line at the north end of the Lake. Leaving a small but an effective garrison at Fort Carillon to slow the British-American advance, Bourlamaque withdrew his regular and colonial forces northwards. The garrison at Fort Carillon held out for several days against Amherst until the latter deployed his siege artillery, which made short work of the fort's defences and forced the garrison to withdraw[38]. Bourlamaque decided to forego a substantial effort to hold Fort Frederic given the obvious power

---

34. Malcolmson, *Warships of the Great Lakes*, 15.
35. MacLeod, *The Tap of the Garrison Drum: The Marine Service in British North America* 43.
36. Ibid, 27.
37. "French and British Military Conflict (1664-1763)," Lake Champlain Maritime Museum http://www.lcmm.org. (Accessed May 21, 2015) 15.
38. Daniel Marston, *The French and Indian War 1754-1760*, (Oxford: Osprey Publishing, 2002) 53.

of Amherst's siege artillery, and abandoned the fort shortly afterwards, retreating to the fortified base at *Isle aux Noix*[39].

The most significant naval action on Lake Champlain occurred on October 11, 1759, when Captain Loring cruised with his squadron and sighted *La Vigilant*. He chased the ship but *La Vigilant* eluded him and his ships subsequently grounded in a narrow channel through which *La Vigilant* had bolted. After refloating his ships Loring sighted the three French xebec sloops and two longboats which he chased into and trapped in Cumberland Bay. The longboats escaped but the xebecs were not so lucky and the crews were forced to scuttle or disable them before escaping by land back to *Isle aux Noix*. Captain Loring took the French sloops as prizes[40] before entering winter quarters at Fort Ticonderoga (formerly Fort Carillon).

Meanwhile, Fort Niagara had fallen to the British-American forces on July 26, 1759, severely impeding the colonial government's lines of communication to the Illinois Country and Louisiana. Upon taking Fort Niagara, the British-American commander, Sir William Johnson, took two prizes, the small schooner-row galley that Captain Broadley had lost to Captain LaForce in 1756, and an unfinished sloop. Johnson renamed the schooner the *Farquhar* and armed it with six guns while the sloop was named *Mississauga* and armed with ten guns taken from the fort[41]. However, they were still inadequate to challenge the *Iroquoise* and the *Outouaise* for the control of Lake Ontario. Therefore, Johnson proceeded with the construction of two snows at Oswego under shipbuilder Peter Jacquet of Philadelphia. However, the British-Americans suffered from a lack of skilled tradesmen, which delayed construction, and the

39. Ibid, 54.
40. Malcolmson, *Warships of the Great Lakes*, 16; "French and British Military Conflict (1664-1763)," Lake Champlain Maritime Museum http://www.lcmm.org.(Accessed May 21, 2015)
41. MacLeod, *The Tap of the Garrison Drum: The Marine Service in British North America*, 41.

first vessel, named *Mohawk*, was not available until November 1759[42].

Finally, after laying waste to the lands around Quebec through the summer of 1759, General Wolfe found a way up the cliffs near Quebec and put his army before the city on the Plains of Abraham. On September 13, 1759, Wolfe's army confronted General Montcalm and his French and Canadian forces in the European style of battle that ultimately decided the future of North America. Although the battle lasted a mere 15 minutes, the result was a decisive loss for the French and Canadian forces. Both General Wolfe and General Montcalm were killed, and heavy losses were suffered by the French and Canadians which caused their commanders to abandon the city to the British Army, and to retreat with the colonial government to Montreal.

For the victorious British army the winter was long and desperate as the British forces were cut off from the outside world by the freezing of the St. Lawrence River, and the withdrawal of the Royal Navy's major warships. Winter quarters were harsh for the British and to some extent the reason for that lay with the long British summer siege of Quebec which had severely damaged the city. Although they had captured the capital city, the British hold on Quebec was tenuous and their victory would depend on which flag would be displayed by the warships which first appeared in the St. Lawrence River in the spring of 1760.

In April 1760 the colonial government's land forces advanced from Montreal and the British army deployed to meet them. A significant battle occurred near the village of Sainte Foy and the British army was defeated in the field and was only saved from disaster by its commander's timely orders to retreat back into the city. However, on May 15, 1760, a forest of masts appeared in

---

42. Ibid, 42.

the river and when flags were unfurled from the warships it was the British standard that appeared. The arrival of the Royal Navy lifted the colonial government's siege of the occupied capital and the French and Canadian forces retreated west towards Montreal.

In the west, following the sacking of Fort Frontenac, the colonial government had taken steps to retrieve the naval situation on Lake Ontario. After the construction in the winter of 1758-59 of the schooner-rigged *Iroquoise*, and the brig *Outaouaise*, Captain LaForce took command and used this small squadron to support the garrison at Fort Niagara when it was invested by British forces under Brigadier Prideaux in the summer of 1759[43]. However, LaForce's shore bombardments were ineffectual and failed to prevent the surrender of the fort on July 25, 1759.

In the meantime, General Amherst was attempting to secure a naval force to support his column proceeding along the Lake George-Lake Champlain invasion route. Captain Loring arranged for the construction of new warships to be used on Lake Ontario and the upper St. Lawrence River. The British-Americans had lost the *Farquhar* and *Mississauga* to storms in December 1759, but had built two new snows, the 16-gun *Mohawk*, and the 18-gun *Apollo* (subsequently renamed *Onondaga*) at Niagara, as well as a sloop (named *Mississauga II* after initially being christened as the *Ontario*) at Oswego. Captain Loring undertook a cruise with the two new snows and sought battle with Captain LaForce's squadron but although Captain Loring sighted the Canadian squadron, the British-American captains had little knowledge of the east end of the lake or the islands of the St. Lawrence River, and a fog prevented Loring's ships from engaging the Canadians, who escaped down the river to Fort Levis[44].

43. Malcolmson, *Warships of the Great Lakes*, 16.
44. MacLeod, *The Tap of the Garrison Drum: The Marine Service in British North America*; Malcolmson, *Warships of the Great Lakes*, 18.

Fort Levis was a hastily constructed post established at Chimney Island on the St. Lawrence River. By early 1760 it lay in the direct path of General Amherst and his column moving east from Oswego to besiege Montreal. Another British column moved north up the Richelieu while a third column moved upriver along the St. Lawrence from Quebec.

On August 10, 1760, the western column got underway, with a flotilla of bateaux escorted by row galleys carrying the British-American forces east from Oswego. Captain Loring had gone forward with an army detachment under General Haldimand to sound the passages in the river, and to hopefully trap one or more of the Canadian ships. They encountered *Iroquoise* near Wolfe Island and the Canadian ship was damaged beyond repair after grounding on a shoal while attempting to evade Loring. *Iroquoise* was permanently beached at Fort Levis. At the outset of the Battle of the Thousand Islands which followed, the British devised a cutting out expedition to take *Outaouaise*, which they undertook to do on August 17, 1760. After heavy fighting the ship's commander, La Broquerie, was forced to strike his colours and he and his crew were made prisoners. *Outaouaise* was taken as a prize and put into Royal Navy service (after being renamed *Williamson*) against Fort Levis, which came under siege by General Amherst on August 19th.

The *Williamson* was joined by the *Mohawk* and the *Onondaga* as the siege progressed but the French gunners knew their trade and *Williamson* and *Onondaga* were sunk after the fort's defenders severed their cables with gunfire and pounded them into submission. The *Mohawk* was also put out of action. However, no relief of Fort Levis was possible and the French commandant was forced to surrender on August 25, 1760. The British subsequently salvaged the *Mohawk*, *Iroquoise* (renamed *Anson*) and *Williamson*, and continued to use them to patrol Lake Ontario and the St. Lawrence River. *Onondaga* was ruined and after salvaging the ironworks it was burned by the British[45].

In the South, the advance along the traditional invasion route via Lake Champlain was renewed. On August 11, 1760, a British advance on the Lake began which was led by the brig *Duke of Cumberland*, the sloop *Boscawan*, and the radeau *Ligonier*, together with the three captured French xebec sloops and the two captured radeaus, as well as two long boats, three galleys, 263 bateaus, 41 whaleboats and 12 canoes[46]. This substantial fleet which carried the British-American forces north to the Canadian base on *Isle aux Noix* suffered from a lack of experienced Royal Navy officers, which prompted Amherst to appoint an officer from a Highland Regiment who had previously served as a midshipman in the navy, Alexander Grant, to the command of the fleet. While the radeau and the galleys bombarded the base, the invading army constructed batteries on land. The British succeeded in capturing *Vigilant* and the remaining French naval vessels on August 25, 1759. Faced with insurmountable odds, the French garrison abandoned and burned the fort on August 28th, and retreated towards Montreal, ending Canadian naval control on Lake Champlain.

The situation that now faced the colonial government in Montreal was dire. The capital at Quebec had been lost and a British regular column was advancing on Montreal from the east. To the south, the chain of forts along Lake Champlain had been taken by the British-American forces and the naval squadron had been seized by the invaders. A substantial land force now approached the temporary capital from the south. To the west, naval control of Lake Ontario had been lost with the destruction of Fort Frontenac. The ability of Canadian forces to challenge the Royal Navy for control of the Lake with the new ships constructed at *Pointe au Baril* had been lost when the remaining Canadian warships were sunk, or taken, by the enemy at the

45. MacLeod, *The Tap of the Garrison Drum: The Marine Service in British North America*, 57.
46. Malcolmson, *Warships of the Great Lakes*, 20; "French and British Military Conflict (1664-1783)," Lake Champlain Maritime Museum http://www.lcmm.org. (accessed May 21, 2015)

Battle of the Thousand Islands. The colonial government still held its western posts at Detroit and Michlimackinac, and communications between those points and Louisiana through the Illinois Country still remained possible, but in the decisive theatre along the St. Lawrence River the strategic position was grim.

With no prospect of reinforcements from metropolitan France, or from the remaining French forces in the *Pays d'en Haut*, and with supplies dwindling and facing certain defeat, Governor General Vaudreuil entered into negotiations with General Amherst for the capitulation of Canada. On September 8, 1760, the Governor General surrendered Canada to the British, and the French colonial government in Canada collapsed. By November 29, 1760, when the British-American Royal American Rangers took possession of Detroit pursuant to the Montreal capitulation, the Great Lakes were firmly controlled by the British[47].

The conquest was an existential shock to the country and for the next three years while the country remained under British military rule, and the Seven Years War played out in Europe and Asia, a hope remained that French rule might be restored through diplomacy. Ultimately, however, the war ended on conditions that were favourable to Great Britain. France accepted the return of its Carribean sugar islands of Guadalupe and Martinique in lieu of the return of Canada, which Voltaire had memorably characterized as "a few acres of snow." As part of the peace negotiations Spain received western Louisiana from France (the eastern portion went to Great Britain) and the final result of the Seven Years War was the elimination of France from North America. All that remained of the once great French empire in North America were the tiny islands of St. Pierre and

---

47. Hannon, *Forts of Canada*, 248.

Miquelon off the coast of Newfoundland, and the French fishery rights on the Newfoundland coast.

From a military perspective, the Seven Years War showed how essential European naval supremacy was for the control of the colony. If France had possessed a sufficiently strong naval force to resupply Canada, the outcome could have been much different, given the natural defences available to the colonial government. Without that naval supremacy, or at least the ability to challenge the Royal Navy in the Atlantic, the position of France in Canada remained vulnerable. Furthermore, the war showed plainly that the defences of Canada required the colonial government to maintain naval superiority on the lake barriers against invasions from the south. Thus, control of Lake Champlain and Lake Ontario were vital for the defence of the country. Those valuable lessons would be assimilated by the new masters of the country.

1763-1783 THE AMERICAN REVOLUTION AND THE REBEL INVASION OF CANADA

With the signing of the Treaty of Paris in 1763 the fate of Canada passed from France to Britain. For the first (and only) time in history Canada and the American colonies were united under the crown of Great Britain, and British America now stretched from the gulf coast of British Florida to Hudson's Bay, and from the eastern seaboard to the Mississippi River. Control of the vast new territories added to the British Empire compelled the (now British) colonial government in Canada (which the British renamed as the province of Quebec) to maintain a sufficient marine presence on the major lakes to protect the empire's lines of communication into the interior.

Captain Loring was assigned responsibility to develop a marine service for this purpose. Unfortunately, he was wounded at the Battle of the Thousand Islands and during his long convalescence it was his subordinate, Lieutenant Robertson, who established a Crown dockyard at Navy Island, near the brink of the falls on the Niagara River. By the time Captain Loring turned over his command of the lake forces to Lieutenant Alexander Grant in 1765, the squadron consisted of *New Brunswick*, a schooner deployed on Lake Ontario, *Charlotte*, a sloop stationed on Lake Erie, *Gladwin*, also a schooner, posted to Lake Huron, and finally the sloop *Musquelongy*, previously seized from the former French colonial government, which was located on Lake Champlain[1]. The ships were employed in communications with the western forts, including Ogdensburg, Oswego, Niagara, Detroit and Michlimackinac[2].

The need for a squadron of ships to maintain secure communications with the western forts became readily apparent at the end of the Seven Years War, when an uprising by the aboriginal peoples in the west broke out. In Pontiac's Rebellion of 1762 the western aboriginal people sought to take Detroit from the British. The fort was besieged and Colonel Gladwin, the post commander, used schooners at Detroit to bombard the aboriginal encampments, prompting Chief Pontiac to attempt unsuccessfully to seize the schooners. The rebellion petered out as the French withdrew from North America[3]. General Amherst departed Canada in November 1763 without putting the marine service on a firm footing, even though the isolated western garrisons were dependent on water-borne resupply, an omission for which he has been criticized[4].

The new commander-in-chief, General Gage, attempted to put the organization of the marine service on a firmer footing by issuing orders for its establishment in December 1764, and preventing army officers from interfering with operational matters. Seamen were to follow the law and customs of the navy but vessel masters would still take their orders from the local army post commanders. Both officers and seamen were prohibited from taking an interest in any trade goods transported by the marine service[5].

Gage found himself constrained by the need to obtain authorization for expenditures from the imperial government

1. Robert Malcolmson, "Not Very Much Celebrated: The Evolution and Nature of the Provincial Marine, 1755-1813", *The Northern Mariner/Le Marin du nord*, No. 1,January, 2001 25 at 28.
2. Malcolmson, *Warships of the Great Lakes*, 23.
3. Hannon, *Forts of Canada*, 250.
4. MacLeod, *The Tap of the Garrison Drum: The Marine Service in British North America*, 74.
5. Ibid, 83.

in Britain, and by the costs of maintaining the military infrastructure in British America. In 1765 he estimated that a proper marine service would cost approximately five thousand pounds per year. As well, there was an immediate need for a new ship, and new storehouses and wharfs, all of which would constitute an additional substantial one-time cost in addition to the cost of maintaining the army in North America[6].

Captain Loring retired in the autumn of 1765 and wrote a parting memorandum in which he cited the obvious need for an effective marine transport service on the lakes both for military resupply and for the fostering of trade because commercial traders preferred the security of sending their cargoes on military ships. As well, the marine service was necessary to maintain law and order, both on the lakes and in connection with the aboriginal population. Loring felt that the marine service should be placed under the Royal Navy and should be expanded into Lake Superior[7].

Both Gage and Loring's views fell upon deaf ears in London where the imperial government was still focussed on reducing the cost of its military infrastructure in the New World. To reduce its costs, the imperial government outsourced the management of its lake fleets to a private contractor, John Blackburn of London, who had some experience in carrying out provisioning contracts for the armed forces in North America, an activity that brought him useful contacts with influential people such as Sir William Johnson, the Superintendent of Indian Affairs[8]. Blackburn employed the ship's officers and crews and maintained the ships[9], with a promise to return them to the control of the colonial government should war break out. The

6. Ibid, 85.
7. Ibid, 86.
8. Ibid, 90.
9. Certain specified perils including loss due to fire, storm, or enemy action were excepted from the contractor's responsibilities under the contract.

ships remained subject to army orders and the army was responsible for arming them. Blackburn committed to maintain one ship on each lake and in 1767 the imperial government transferred the four existing vessels to him.

Contracting out services, especially for provisions, had a long history so it was not such a large leap for the imperial government to consider contracting out the marine service, given that its primary function was marine transport and only secondarily provided a means for imperial coercion. The contract did not provide Blackburn very much in the way of profits. He received three thousand, and two hundred pounds per year but the estimated maintenance costs for 1767, for example, was three thousand one hundred pounds[10]. Blackburn also sought to use the ships to carry commercial goods on the lakes. Although at first some question was raised concerning the propriety of this approach, the Board of Trade ruled in 1768 that the ships of the marine service could carry the goods of British subjects as cargo. That decision greatly increased the prospect for profits, and it led the incipient Provincial Marine into its true vocation as an auxiliary armed transport service[11].

Cargoes transported by the Provincial Marine were usually large quantities of freight goods, although passengers were also carried from time to time. For the army the basic requirement was for vessels that could carry provisions (e.g., pickled beef or pork, fresh meats such as beef, lamb, or poultry, peas, rice, flour, butter etc.) and military supplies such as guns, shot and powder, medical supplies, and baggage and bedding. The marine service was also used to transport troops between the main centres at Niagara, Detroit and Michlimackinac[12].

For private merchants the cargoes carried included commercial

10. MacLeod, *The Tap of the Garrison Drum: The Marine Service in British North America*, 91.
11. Malcolmson, "Nature of the Provincial Marine", *Northern Mariner*, 29.
12. MacLeod, *The Tap of the Garrison Drum: The Marine Service in British North America*, 313, 319.

products such as furs, wagons, horses, and oxen, as well as hay supplies for the animals, and other trade goods[13]. For commercial firms, the Provincial Marine offered a safe carriage service for any cargoes that firms wished to transport on the Great Lakes. From 1763 to 1777 the Provincial Marine was essentially the most significant marine transport service on the lakes[14].

The transport vocation of the vessels under Blackburn's management failed to forestall the growth of private marine companies however. Beginning in 1769, private enterprise entered the picture with the construction of the sloop *Enterprise*, built at the Detroit shipyard of Richard Cornwall who established his yard in 1767[15]. Alexander Grant had been retained by Blackburn to superintend the Provincial Marine's ships and Grant also entered into the marine trade on his own account, building four trading vessels between 1769 and 1771. Nevertheless, despite the low profit margin on the contract itself, and the private competition, Blackburn was sufficiently incented to seek and obtain renewal of his contract in June 1770, and March 1773[16].

Although British-American colonists still required the protection of the imperial government, such as during the serious aboriginal rebellion led by Chief Pontiac and others from 1763-66, relations between Great Britain and the British-American colonists deteriorated after 1763. No longer did the threat of a common enemy lying across the English Channel, or northwards across the St. Lawrence River, focus the loyalties and energies of the British and their American colonists. Great differences in attitude and outlook had formed across the passage of years and those differences could no longer be

13. Ibid, 314, 319.
14. Ibid, 324.
15. Ibid; Malcolmson, *Warships of the Great Lakes*, 24.
16. MacLeod, *The Tap of the Garrison Drum: The Marine Service in British North America*, 94, 98.

papered-over. Increasingly, Britons and British-Americans found that they were no longer a common people.

After the Seven Years War the imperial government decided that the American colonies should bear a greater portion of the expense of maintaining troops in the colonies sufficient for their protection, and that the system of collecting customs revenues should be improved so as to prevent smuggling and to increase Crown revenues[17]. Those initiatives prompted a reaction in the seaboard colonies, particularly in the New England provinces, which suffered economic dislocation following the conclusion of the Seven Years War as a result of the removal of a great deal of government spending from the economy. By the mid-1760's there were severe recessionary conditions in British America.

Within the littoral colonies south of Nova Scotia there was great interest in penetrating the western frontier in search of new land and economic opportunities. However, the imperial government decided that the interior should be reserved for the aboriginal population and in the *Royal Proclamation of 1763*, British Subjects were expressly forbidden from obtaining title to land from the aboriginal people in the interior, or from undertaking surveys that could derogate from the aboriginal title to the western lands. While forts were established in the interior to foster the fur trade, as well as to provide for defence, further settlement was discouraged and no formal governmental structure was planned for the interior. Most British-Americans could not understand this policy, which carved out an immense area of land from settlement that metropolitan Britain, together with British America, had just fought a war to obtain. Land speculators, in particular, were aggrieved. Without royal permission, colonial subjects began moving into the back country. A fundamental

---

17. A series of *Navigation Acts* enacted by Parliament maintained a mercantilist economic model between Great Britain and its colonies by preventing direct foreign trade. The effect was to enhance the economic vitality of Great Britain and retard the economic development of its colonies.

breach between the imperial government in London and some, though not all, British-Americans began to loom closer.

British-Americans began to frame their political conflicts with Great Britain using the lens of English liberties. The crystallizing issue was the extent of parliamentary sovereignty in British America. While Britain maintained that it had an unrestricted right to legislate for the colonies the colonists demurred, and thus the expression, no taxation without representation, became a political touchstone for the British-American population's growing disenchantment with Parliament. As the sixties turned into the seventies the political environment became toxic. In the Boston Tea Party, a public protest, colonists destroyed tea cargoes which were subject to a special tax. In response, restrictive legislation known as the *Coercive Acts*[18] greatly reduced the powers of colonists in the Massachusetts Bay colony to administer their own affairs. At the same time, Parliament also sought to rein in a growing desire on the part of the colonies to access new lands west of the Appalachian mountains by greatly expanding the existing boundaries of Canada (i.e., the Province of Quebec). The effect of the *Quebec Act* was to hem in the British American colonists along the eastern seaboard, which was anathema to them.

The colonists and their mother country were now proceeding down separate paths. However, there were many intelligent and well-meaning people on both sides of the Atlantic that sought to lower tempers and to make the necessary effort and compromises to hold the empire together. Their failure to do so must be attributed to divergent public opinions among the elites on either side of the Atlantic, and to larger forces of history that could not be restrained.

On the eve of rebellion by the British-Americans the situation in

18. In the thirteen colonies this legislation was known as the *Intolerable Acts*.

Canada was calm. The province of Quebec, unlike the seaboard colonies, did not have a legislature and the still recent collapse of French rule left the inhabitants psychologically cowed and unwilling to challenge Great Britain politically. The role of the Roman Catholic church remained paramount in Canadian society and the church was a conservative institution and disinclined to ally itself with the political agitation prevalent in the English-speaking protestant colonies to the south. The linguistic and cultural barriers also served to insulate Canadian society from the ferment to the south. However, there were British-American traders in Montreal and those merchants did send an observer to the Continental Congress which convened in Philadelphia in 1776[19], an action which caused the Governor General to increasingly mistrust them.

Nova Scotia, by contrast, was English-speaking and had a mixed population of immigrants from both Britain and the colonies to the south. The political concepts that were being articulated in the other colonies resonated with at least a portion of the Nova Scotian population but Halifax was the main Royal Navy base in the Americas, and there was a strong presence there by the Royal Navy and British regular army troops. Many Haligonians profited by providing for the needs of the armed forces stationed in the province, and thus they had economic reasons to support the continued imperial tie. In any event, the powerful forces stationed in Nova Scotia tended to dissuade those who might desire to foment agitation against the Crown[20]. The neighbouring colony of St. John's Island (later Prince Edward Island) retained strong links to Great Britain and was seemingly immune to the political ferment taking place in the south.

Newfoundland was more remote than the other colonies and distance also tended to insulate it from political developments in the other North American provinces. Further, there was no

---

19. MacLeod, *The Tap of the Garrison Drum: The Marine Service in British North America*, 137.
20. A brief uprising by a few colonists in Nova Scotia in 1776 was suppressed by the army.

provincial assembly in Newfoundland and, as in Nova Scotia, the Royal Navy maintained a prominent presence. The continuation of the imperial tie made sense in Newfoundland since the navy could protect the offshore fishery which was the colony's major source of income. Lastly, distant Rupert's Land was an unsettled wilderness loosely administered for profit by the Hudson Bay Company and penetrated only by itinerant fur traders.

The outbreak of the rebellion in the spring of 1775 led the colonial government in Canada to take actions to protect the southern river and lake barrier. Captain LaForce, who had commanded colonial naval forces under the French regime was recalled to duty and began patrols of the St. Lawrence River between Sorel and Quebec[21]. In May, rebel forces under Ethan Allan and Colonel Benedict Arnold seized Fort Ticonderoga and Crown Point from the colonial garrison. At this time there was only a single guard ship on Lake Champlain, *Betsy*, launched in 1771 as a 50-ton sloop. On May 10, 1775, Colonel Arnold and 50 men made a daring raid on Fort St. Jean on the Richelieu River just north of the northern tip of Lake Champlain and took the *Betsy* and four bateaux as prizes, burning five remaining bateaux[22]. The rebels thus obtained naval control on Lake Champlain.

Having lived through successive wars with French Canada, the rebellious British-American colonists were well aware of the potential military threat from the north. In an effort to consolidate colonial opposition to the British government the Continental Congress, urged on by George Washington, authorized a military assault on the province of Quebec by rebel forces. The offensive against Canada was two-pronged. A force under General Montgomery proceeded from Ticonderoga north along the traditional invasion route with the intention of taking

21. Desloges, "LaForce, Rene Hippolyte," *Dictionary of Canadian Biography, vol. 5.*
22. Gardner W Allen, *A Naval History of the American Revolution, vol 1,* (New York: Houghton Mifflen Co, 1913) 162.

Montreal before moving east to invest the capital at Quebec. In the meantime, Colonel Arnold would take a second force north along the Chaudiere River directly towards Quebec to join in the siege of the capital. At the time there were only a few hundred British regulars in the province of Quebec and Arnold, who had previous business dealings in Canada, thought that the French-speaking population would side with the rebel forces.

On Lake Champlain, the rebels had put together a marine force consisting of *Betsy* (now renamed *Enterprise*), a private schooner renamed *Liberty*, and two newly constructed gunboats[23]. A force of twelve-hundred men proceeded under an escort up the lake and invested Fort St. Jean, which fell on November 1, 1775. A newly constructed 14 gun schooner, the *Royal Savage*, was taken by the rebels in that assault. The rebels then proceeded to haul their two gunboats over the Richelieu River rapids to escort the armed force north in the assault on Montreal, which fell on November 13, 1775[24]. Governor General Sir Guy Carleton barely escaped from the rebel net at Montreal. He evacuated on an armed private schooner owned by merchant marine Captain Jean Baptiste Bouchette, but winds forced the ship to shelter at Sorel leaving the Governor General exposed to rebel capture. Bouchette then took Carleton and his aide by a small boat down the river, evading the rebels and successfully reaching Quebec[25].

Meanwhile, Colonel Arnold had struggled up the Chaudiere River route and arrived on the St. Lawrence with his troops in poor condition. In December, Montgomery's forces joined with Arnold's and by December 9th they had begun to bombard the city, which Carleton defended with a mixture of British army regulars, provincial militia, and seamen[26]. Montgomery and

23. Malcolmson, *Warships of the Great Lakes*, 26.
24. Ibid, 27.
25. W A B Douglas, "Jean-Baptiste Bouchette", *Dictionary of Canadian Biography, 5* University of Toronto Press/Les Presses de l'universite Laval, 1983.
26. Yvon Desloges, *From a Strategic Site to a Fortified Town*, (Quebec: Septentrion,2001) 12.

Arnold launched a major assault on the capital on December 31, 1775. The attack failed and Montgomery was killed and Arnold wounded. Carleton had recognized the danger of attempting to meet the rebel forces on the open field and so he kept his forces behind the walls of Quebec. The rebels continued the siege through the winter but by spring the rebel commanders determined that it would be fruitless to continue and the rebel forces withdrew back to Fort Ticonderoga. In part they were persuaded to withdraw by the appearance in the St. Lawrence River of a Royal Navy squadron on April 12, 1776[27]. Canada would not be seriously threatened again for the duration of the American Revolutionary War.

On July 4, 1776, the British-Americans took the momentous step of sundering their political allegiance to the Crown and declared the thirteen colonies independent. Great Britain contested the unilateral declaration of independence and a large-scale war in the colonies ensued. In Canada, Carleton took over the ships on the lakes that were under a management contract to Blackburn on August 10, 1776, and Carleton also chartered eight private vessels for government use. An order was issued prohibiting private marine activities on any of the Great Lakes. The order was applied initially to those merchants who could not obtain a pass from the colonial government but later, in 1778, all private commercial traffic was totally banned by an order from the new Governor General, Frederick Haldimand[28]. The economic effect on merchants in Canada was considerable because only those providing services to the military were able to obtain transport for their goods. The small Canadian firms that had survived from the days of the French Bourbon regime were particularly hit hard by these regulations[29].

27. JR Hill, ed., *The Oxford Illustrated History of the Royal Navy*, (Oxford: University Press, 1995) 103.
28. Malcolmson, "Nature of the Provincial Marine", *Northern Mariner*, 29; MacLeod,*The Tap of the Garrison Drum: The Marine Service in British North America*, 107, 112.
29. MacLeod, *The Tap of the Garrison Drum: The Marine Service in British North America*, 140-41.

The Provincial Marine at this juncture consisted of the sixteen gun *General Gage* and the fourteen gun *Earl of Dunmore*, on the upper lakes which were augmented by Commodore Grant's own private transport service including the schooners *Hope* (taken into the Provincial Marine on August 25th), *Angelica* and *Faith*. Two other merchant-owned vessels, *Archange* and *Felicity* were also available. All of the private merchantmen were armed with swivel cannons. On Lake Ontario the Provincial Marine consisted only of the *Haldimand* which was augmented by two Grant-owned merchantmen, *Charity* and *Caldwell*[30].

Rene Hippolyte La Force was assigned to oversee the construction of the new schooner *Seneca* and was given command of that ship upon her commissioning. *Seneca* was the first vessel in the Provincial Marine in which the operational language was French[31]. La Force was also restored to his former position under the French regime as commander of the colonial government's naval forces on Lake Ontario[32]. However, in 1777, LaForce became ill and to ease the pressure of his duties he was appointed as superintendent of the shipyard at *Pointe au Baril*. Jean-Baptiste Bouchette was appointed as his successor as master of the *Seneca*, in which he served for the remainder of the war. LaForce was superseded as commanding officer on Lake Ontario in June 1778.[33].

Lake Champlain however, was the centre of naval operations on the lakes during the American Revolutionary War. Governor

30. Ibid, 105.
31. Ibid, 116.
32. Desloges, "LaForce, Rene Hippolyte", *Dictionary of Canadian Biography, vol 5*.
33. La Force eventually recovered his health and he continued to serve as Master and Commander of Naval Armament, superintending the dockyard at Navy Island and even resumed the naval command on Lake Ontario after the lake commander was lost when the shallow draft *Ontario* capsized and sank in a storm with the loss of all hands in November 1780 (MacLeod, The *Tap of the Garrison Drum: The Marine Service in British North America*, 149). La Force reached the rank of a commodore in the Provincial Marine before retiring on half pay in 1784 after the conclusion of the war (Desloges, "LaForce, Rene Hippolyte", *Dictionary of Canadian Biography, vol 5*).

General Carleton had to provide for the naval defence of the province along the Lake George-Lake Champlain invasion route and he turned to the commander of the Royal Navy's squadron at Quebec, Commodore Charles Douglas, for help. Douglas provided 400 sailors from his warships and requisitioned another 250 seamen from transport ships that had brought reinforcements to the province in 1776. After dismantling vessels at Chambly and Quebec for transport and portage to Fort St. Jean, they succeeded in establishing a squadron of warships consisting of an 18-gun ship supported by two armed schooners, a radeau, and more than 20 gunboats[34].

The Americans were entrenched at Fort Ticonderoga with newly promoted Brigadier General Arnold appointed to the command of the American naval force at Crown Point in August 1776. In October 1776, the two fleets clashed at the battle of Valcour Bay. Captain Pringle of the Royal Navy commanded the British squadron on Lake Champlain, which consisted of the 18 gun ship *Inflexible*, the 14 gun schooner-rigged flagship *Maria*, the 12 gun schooner *Carleton*, a radeau, *Thunderer*, with 12 guns and two howitzers, a gondola, *Loyal Convert*, which was armed with seven guns, and approximately twenty gunboats. Facing off against them was General Arnold's squadron consisting of the sloop *Enterprise* with 12 guns and 10 swivels, the schooner *Royal Savage*, similarly armed, the schooner *Revenge* with six guns and 10 swivels, and eight gunboats with 10 guns and eight swivels between them. In addition, there were four galleys including Arnold's flagship *Congress*, armed with various types of guns, and several gondolas[35]. The broadside weight of the two fleets clearly favoured the British, although much depended on Pringle's ability to effectively deploy the *Thunderer*, which was slow and ungainly.

---

34. Ibid.
35. Gardner W Allen, *A Naval History of the American Revolution*, 166-67. The galleys and gondolas had varied armaments.

On the 11th battle was joined and a heavy action ensued. The *Royal Savage* was run aground and abandoned. The British fired the ship during the night to prevent the Americans from retaking the ship[36]. Having been worsted during the battle Arnold slipped his fleet past the British fleet in the night and set sail back to Crown Point. Upon discerning the American escape on the morning of the 12th Captain Pringle gave a chase and the Americans were forced to sink two gondolas which were too badly damaged to continue. On the 13th the British managed to come up on the Americans and swift broadsides forced the *Washington* to surrender. Captain Pringle then turned his attention to the *Congress*, which he attacked and forced to seek shelter in the mouth of a small creek, together with four gondolas. Arnold abandoned his vessels and set them on fire before retreating overland to Fort Ticonderoga[37]. The Americans were left with only four small vessels on Lake Champlain following this defeat and those vessels were taken the following year by the British squadron when it supported the ill-fated southern offensive of General John Burgoyne[38].

At the important western post of Detroit Lieutenant Governor Henry Hamilton began the construction of Fort Lernoult to supersede the old French fortification of Fort Pontchartrain, which was vulnerable, and the British Indian Agents Matthew Elliot, Alexander McKee, and Simon Girty worked to maintain the loyalty of the western aboriginal tribes to the Crown[39].

With naval superiority over the Americans established on the Great Lakes and Lake Champlain Governor General Carleton turned his attention to the organization of the colonial naval forces. Unwilling to be dependent upon the Royal Navy, he

36. Ibid, 171.
37. Ibid, 175.
38. Malcolmson, "Nature of the Provincial Marine", *Northern Mariner*, 30.
39. Philip P. Mason, *Detroit, Fort Lernoult and the American Revolution*, (Detroit: Wayne State University Press, 1964) 11.

formally established the Provincial Marine in 1778 and obtained permission from the Admiralty for the secondment of a naval officer, Lieutenant John Schank, as Commissioner of His Majesty's Naval Yards and Docks upon the Lakes, reporting to Carleton. Beneath Schank Lieutenant William Chambers held the command of the squadron on Lake Champlain, Master and Commander James Andrews commanded on Lake Ontario where the colonial government's force now consisted of *Seneca, Haldimand, Caldwell* and the new row-galley *Mohawk*[40], and Captain Alexander Grant continued in command on the remainder of the Great Lakes[41]. In the absence of Commissioner Schank, orders for the Provincial Marine issued from the senior army officer on each station in the quartermaster-general's office. Carleton's successor, Governor General Haldimand, continued the efforts to place the marine service on a firm basis and he wrote several memoranda on the subject upon his return to metropolitan Britain in 1784. Haldimand was adamant that a return to the contract system was unwarranted, and that the marine service must remain under the control of local army commanders with its vocation focussed on marine transport on the lakes[42].

The American Revolutionary War dragged on into the 1780's becoming a European conflict as well as a North American conflict before a joint American-French operation in Virginia resulted in a decisive defeat for the British army at the Battle of Yorktown in 1781, the signal event which made the subsequent British acceptance of American independence inevitable. It has been said that when Lord Cornwallis's troops paraded in surrender to General Washington after that battle, the British army band played a tune entitled "The World Turned Upside Down." The world had indeed turned upside down in North America.

40. Ibid, 114.
41. Ibid 31
42. MacLeod, *The Tap of the Garrison Drum: The Marine Service in British North America*, 164.

Ironically, after the Treaty of Paris ended the war in 1783, Americans who had once feared the threat of an invasion from the north by the French, and who had joined in the imperial effort to oust France from North America, were now once again wary of a threat of an invasion from the north. However, now the threat came from the British, America's erstwhile protecting power, rather than France, with whom America was now in alliance. For Great Britain, Canada, and not America, would now be the centre of British imperial power in North America.

Great Britain and the United States agreed to a boundary between the United States and British North America that incorporated the St. Lawrence River and the Great Lakes. The two states decided that the water boundary would form a natural division between them and elected to place the border in the middle of the lakes and rivers generally following the equidistant principle, which was compatible with international law, and with the views of international legal scholars such as Grotius and Vattel[43]. However, Great Britain and the United States modified the equidistant rule in cases where an island would be bisected by the international border. In such circumstances the two states decided that the state which would obtain the greatest extent of the bisected island would be given the entire island. The application of this principle proved sound and only a few minor border issues involving islands in the Detroit River, and in the straits between Lake Huron and Lake Superior, were left for conclusion in a later negotiation[44]. By setting the international border using the equidistant principle Great Britain and the United States prevented any portion of the Great Lakes from

43. Piper, *The International Law of the Great Lakes*, 9.
44. Ibid, 13. In the Webster-Ashburton Treaty of 1842 the islands at the mouth of the Detroit River were divided, with Sugar and Stony Islands given to the United States and Bois Blanc Island to Canada, with American rights to use the navigable channel between Bois Blanc Island and the mainland. In the straits between Lake Huron and Lake Superior St. George Island was given to the United States. Only one other maritime border change subsequently occurred. In 1850 Great Britain ceded Horseshoe Reef to the United States so that the latter could construct a lighthouse for the port of Buffalo, New York.

becoming international waters and the whole of the lakes are today within the sovereignty of Canada and the United States of America[45].

On the lakes, although the end of the American Revolutionary War led to reductions in the strength of the Provincial Marine the force was now firmly established as an arm of the colonial government, and it continued to exercise maritime supremacy throughout the Great Lakes in the years after the American Revolution.

45. Piper, *The International Law of the Great Lakes*, 18.

1783-1812 THE PROVINCIAL MARINE SECURES THE MARITIME BORDER

The Treaty of Paris in 1783 ended the war between Great Britain and the newly independent United States of America. Canada and the adjacent colonies of Nova Scotia, St. John's Island, and Newfoundland emerged relatively unscathed from the war but social change was in the offing, as loyalists from the United States emigrated to the remaining British territories in North America. A substantial influx of English-speaking loyalists into the province of Quebec resulted in constitutional changes, with Parliament in 1791 splitting the province into two new colonies, Lower Canada (Quebec) and Upper Canada (now Ontario) which lay west of the Ottawa River.

Although the Treaty of Paris required Great Britain to surrender its fortified posts on the southern and western shores of the Great Lakes system, colonial government officials felt that for internal security, as well as for maintaining the standing of the Crown with the aboriginal first nations, the border posts should be retained. They declined to transfer the posts to the United States ostensibly because the individual states had refused to pay legitimate debts owed to British subjects. Thus, important settlements such as Oswego, Niagara, Detroit, and Michlimackinac remained under British rule[1].

---

1. Philip P Mason, *Detroit, Fort Lernoult and the American Revolution* 20.

The Provincial Marine was now fully established as an arm of the colonial government but was considerably reduced by the peace, which negated the need for a substantial number of armed vessels on the Great Lakes. This hybrid army-navy service returned to its prewar vocation as an auxiliary transport service. However, with the influx of new immigrants commerce began to operate at a much larger scale than before, and the Provincial Marine was inadequate to meet all of the needs of the growing business community in Canada. Consequently, there was also a return of private marine services which had been banned by the order of Governor General Carleton for security reasons in 1776. By 1787, the formal ban was lifted after several private vessels had previously appeared on the lakes. In addition, the colonial government's Indian Department maintained one or two vessels of its own to attend to departmental business in the belief that the Provincial Marine could not meet all of that department's needs on a timely basis. However, the Indian Department often had to rely on the Provincial Marine to supply crews for its small vessels[2].

The Provincial Marine maintained two vessels on Lake Ontario and three on Lake Erie and Lake Huron, as well as one schooner on Lake Champlain. The colonial government gave permission to a mining concern to construct a sloop and several barges to mine copper deposits on the shores of Lake Superior but that venture soon failed, and the ships were laid up[3]. The North west Company, a Montreal-based fur trading competitor of the Hudson's Bay Company, built one ship for service on Lake Superior, the seventy-five ton sloop-rigged *Otter*, in 1785[4].

Royal Navy personnel did not retain a connection with the Provincial Marine which became an exclusively Canadian manned and operated service. As a colonial institution, the

2. MacLeod, *The Tap of the Garrison Drum: The Marine Service in British North America*, 199.
3. Leacock, *Canada and the Sea*, 33.
4. Ibid, 33.

Provincial Marine attracted a fair number of Francophone seamen. The Lake Ontario complement was 40% Francophone in 1787, and the working language of the *Seneca*, under the command of Captain Jean-Baptiste Bouchette, was French. Although the percentage of Francophones among the Lake Ontario seamen in the Provincial Marine had dropped to 20% by 1792, the statistics for the upper lakes showed a significant increase. The Francophone complement on the upper lakes was 17% in 1787 but rose to 24% five years later. Many more Francophones worked in the dockyards, where the pay was better[5].

In fact, pay was a point of continuing grievances in the Provincial Marine. Seamen in the Provincial Marine were paid a salary fixed at 40 shillings per month over the course of decades[6] which sometimes necessitated the payment of a bonus to spur recruitment and retention. Competition for seamen between the private merchant service and the Provincial Marine was stiff, and the lure of the American east coast ports which always sought out experienced seamen was very real. At a time when economic expansion put a premium on skilled seamen, many were motivated to desert the Provincial Marine for better economic opportunities. Desertion was less evident amongst the Francophone seamen employed in the Provincial Marine but was more prevalent amongst Scottish-born immigrants and, to a lesser extent, Irish-born immigrants[7]. Few deserters were ever apprehended[8].

For those who did remain with the service many chose not to renew their contracts as they expired, moving on into more lucrative positions with the private merchant marine on the lakes and that put pressure on the Provincial Marine to find

5. MacLeod, *The Tap of the Garrison Drum: The Marine Service in British North America*, 173.
6. Ibid, 211.
7. Ibid, 210.
8. Ibid, 172.

replacements for them[9]. As a result, there were public concerns about the quality of the crews, with public observations made of their ill-discipline and poor training[10]. For their part, the seamen resented the assignment to them of additional duties above and beyond those that were customarily considered to be the duties of seamen, including cutting wood, undertaking dockyard services, or personal services for the officers, fetching firewood, and providing garrison duty at Point Frederick[11]. In such circumstances retention of skilled seamen remained a problem and at times it became difficult to man the ships for the want of seamen, making it necessary to assign soldiers to crew the ships[12].

Part of the decline in efficiency may have been due to the fact that a commissioner for the service was not appointed after the departure of Schank in 1784, and the two local commanders on Lake Ontario and Lakes Erie and Huron, who restyled themselves as commodores, took their orders from the local officers of the army's Quartermasters Corps. It goes without saying that the army had little experience in running a marine service.

From a command perspective, Commodore Grant continued as the senior officer on the upper lakes throughout this period until shortly after the outbreak of the War of 1812, when Major General Isaac Brock retired him after a 53-year career on the Great Lakes that began under General Amherst and Captain Loring on Lake Champlain during the Seven Years War. In his later years Grant rarely went to sea preferring to live on his substantial property at Grosse Point Farms, Michigan, where he had continued to reside even after Detroit was transferred to the United States in 1796 and his headquarters was transferred to

9. Ibid, 201.
10. Malcolmson, "Nature of the Provincial Marine", *Northern Mariner*, 31.
11. MacLeod, *The Tap of the Garrison Drum: The Marine Service in British North America*, 202.
12. Malcolmson, "Nature of the Provincial Marine", *Northern Mariner*, 32.

Amherstburg. Maintaining a foreign residence was certainly an unusual circumstance given Grant's position as commander of the Provincial Marine forces that would be called upon to defend Upper Canada in the event of a war between Great Britain and the United States, but it probably reflected the familiarity of the populations on both sides of the border[13]. Grant was succeeded on the upper lakes by Commodore George Hall[14]. On Lake Ontario, Commodore Betton was succeeded in 1794 by Jean-Baptiste Bouchette. Betton had often been ill, and Bouchette had frequently taken his place as master of the Lake Ontario flagship, Onondaga. Bouchette in turn was superseded by John Steel in 1803, retiring from the service after running afoul of Lieutenant Governor Peter Hunter[15]. Finally, Huge Earle succeeded to the command on Lake Ontario in January 1812[16].

During the Upper Canada governorship of Lieutenant Governor John Graves Simcoe (1791-1796) a regular shuttle service was established on Lake Ontario to ensure that one government vessel was always in port in Niagara and Kingston. On their regular runs the vessels would carry military and colonial government supplies, private cargoes for merchants, and passengers, including aboriginal leaders attending conferences with the colonial government[17]. At times the lack of manpower for the Provincial Marine became a critically limiting factor in the provision of its services and the colonial government was compelled to contract for the services of private vessels, particularly at Detroit[18]. Although the Provincial Marine continued to carry private cargoes, the total number of such cargoes declined during the period following 1788, when commercial marine transport services became more widely

13. MacLeod, *The Tap of the Garrison Drum: The Marine Service in British North America*, 211.
14. Malcolmson, *Warships of the Great Lakes*, 85.
15. MacLeod, *The Tap of the Garrison Drum: The Marine Service in British North America*, 214-15.
16. Malcolmson, *Warships of the Great Lakes*, 85.
17. MacLeod, *The Tap of the Garrison Drum: The Marine Service in British North America*, 183.
18. Ibid, 189.

available. However, it remained the essential marine transportation service for both the army and the colonial government until the War of 1812[19].

The Provincial Marine maintained shipyard bases at Kingston and Niagara. At Kingston, the main dockyard was relocated to a site at Point Frederick near the former Fort Frontenac from Carleton Island to provide for better security. In the west, the most important facility was at Detroit, where the British had retained Fort Lernoult notwithstanding the terms of the Treaty of Paris. A shipyard had been constructed at Detroit and was used by the Provincial Marine both for repair of its ships, and for new construction.

The failure of the British to evacuate the forts in the west remained a recurring difficulty in relations between colonial Canada and the United States. The terms of the Treaty of Paris fixed the international border through the middle of the lakes and rivers, and with all but the northern tip of Lake Champlain becoming American territory. While retention of the border forts supported Great Britain's attempt to sustain the loyalty of the aboriginal First Nations to the Crown, the legal fact remained that Britain had conceded these posts to the United States in the treaty that ended the revolutionary war.

In the meantime, President Washington had ordered the American army to conduct operations along the western frontier to subdue the aboriginal population who were contesting the influx of American settlers into the newly opened territories beyond the Appalachian mountains[20]. A campaign led by Major General Arthur St. Clair ended in disaster with the overwhelming defeat of the US army by the aboriginal first nations at the Battle of the Wabash on November 4, 1791. However, President Washington reconstituted US forces for a

19. Ibid, 324.
20. Mason, *Detroit, Fort Lernoult and the American Revolution,* 22.

follow-up campaign and that effort, conducted by Major General Anthony Wayne, led to the defeat of the aboriginal forces at the Battle of Fallen Timbers. This defeat of the aboriginal first nations raised significant concerns for the colonial government. Initially, there was concern that the over-holding British settlements could be attacked by General Wayne, but Wayne had received no instructions from President Washington to take action against the British. However, the natives had provided the British with General St. Clair's papers captured following their earlier victory at the Wabash and the British were able to read Secretary of War Henry Knox's advice to St. Clair that " . . . the delicate state of affairs render[ed] it improper at present to make any naval arrangements on Lake Erie.[21]" While the United States had not created any naval forces on the Great Lakes, the subject was obviously present in the minds of the officials overseeing the nation's military affairs.

To deal with the problem of the over-holding British in the territories assigned to the United States by the peace treaty, President Washington asked Chief Justice John Jay to undertake a diplomatic mission to Great Britain to settle the border issue and other irritants left over from the revolutionary war. The growing American presence along the frontier, together with the increasing priority of the struggle against revolutionary and Napoleonic France put the British in a receptive mood to negotiate. Those negotiations proved to be successful and the two nations entered into a treaty known informally as the Jay Treaty, which provided for the final evacuation of the British western posts that lay on the wrong side of the border fixed by the Treaty of Paris no later than July 1, 1796. As it turned out, the British left Detroit on July 11, 1796, and Michlimackinac only on September 1st. To replace those important border posts new forts were constructed by the colonial government in 1796 on

---

21. Quoted in A L Burt, *The United States, Great Britain and British North America*, (New York: Russell & Russell, 1940, 1961) 117.

the Detroit River at Amherstburg, and on St. Joseph's Island in Lake Huron[22]. The Amherstburg Navy Yard was built adjacent to the fort and included two blockhouses, a guardhouse, a storehouse, a lime and mortar house, and a ropewalk, as well as space for building stocks.

Fort Amherstburg, or Fort Malden as it came to be known[23], was an army garrison, naval dockyard, British Indian Department headquarters, and an important meeting place. Built on the east side of the Detroit River between 1797 and 1799 by Captain Hector McLean of the Royal Canadian Volunteers on a portion of the townsite lands reserved for military use[24], it served as the British Army headquarters in southwestern Upper Canada during this period. Additionally, at Niagara-on-the-Lake, Fort George was built between 1796 and 1799 to protect Navy Hall, an important administrative post for the Provincial Marine. Fort George allowed the colonial government to command the Niagara River following the transfer of Fort Niagara to the United States as a result of the Jay Treaty[25].

By 1796 the crucial Lake Ontario squadron of the Provincial Marine consisted of *Onondaga*, *Mississauga* and *Mohawk* with two small gunboats, *Buffalo* and *Bear* (which were later renamed the *Catherine* and *Sophia*, after Lieutenant Governor Simcoe's daughters). The sloops *Francis* and *Maria* were built at Amherstburg for service on the upper lakes[26]. During this period the Provincial Marine did not commonly call at the provincial

22. Mason, *Detroit, Fort Lernoult and the American Revolution*, 23.
23. The name of the fort was originally Fort Amherstburg and it is referred to as such by some writers (see, for example, Pierre Berton, *The Invasion of Canada, 1812-1813* (Toronto: McClelland and Stewart, 1980). The Americans who occupied the post in the War of 1812 named it Fort Malden and that name is how it subsequently became known, and is still known today. In this book the more common name of Fort Malden is used.
24. Minister of Indian Affairs and Northern Development, *Fort Malden National Historic Park*, (Ottawa: Queen's Printer and Controller of Stationary, 1966) 3.
25. Parks Canada, *Fort George National Historic Site of Canada*: Walking Tour, (Gatineau (Que.) 2002).
26. MacLeod, *The Tap of the Garrison Drum: The Marine Service in British North America*, 192, 193.

capital at York, which led to complaints by Peter Russell who was the Administrator of the colonial government in Upper Canada about the quality of the services provided by the Provincial Marine. Those complaints were only partially alleviated by the construction of the yacht *Toronto* for the exclusive use of the civil authorities, which helped to maintain communications across the far-flung colony[27].

Amherstburg became an important centre for shipbuilding and repair. Under the direction of John Norman the yard began by constructing small boats[28] but soon progressed to more substantial projects. To replace the transports *Francis* and *Maria*, a new 90-ton ship was ordered at Amherstburg that could accommodate both the occasional requirements to transport troops as well as the more routine transportation of cargo. The Amherstburg shipyard encountered cost pressures in the construction of that ship due to the poor condition of the local roads over which it was necessary to haul cut timber, together with the fact that the oak knees[29] required for the construction of the ship necessitated pulling up oak trees by their roots[30]. The shipyard contracted for planking, lumber, and knees but attempted to reduce its costs by using its own carpenters in the winter to cut the lumber needed for framing. Oak and pine were the preferred woods in Great Lakes shipbuilding, although cedar was also used. Local blacksmiths often refashioned iron fittings that were salvaged from vessels that were broken up to use in newly constructed vessels (at least until a local ironworks industry developed) and blocks and other necessities were purchased from ship chandlers at Quebec[31]. Using such methods, new ships such as the *General Hunter* and the *Queen Charlotte*

27. Ibid, 198. The *Toronto* was wrecked at York in 1811 (MacLeod, 221).
28. Parks Canada, *Shipbuilding at Fort Amherstburg 1796-1813*, (Ottawa: Minister of Indian and Northern Affairs, 1978) 5.
29. Knees are the curved wood for attaching the ship's deck beams to the hull frame.
30. Parks Canada, *Shipbuilding at Fort Amherstburg 1796-1813*, 7.
31. MacLeod, *The Tap of the Garrison Drum: The Marine Service in British North America*, 205.

were constructed and launched at Amherstburg in 1805 and 1810[32]. The harsh winters with their snow and ice promoted decay on the ships and in an attempt to forestall decay the ships were normally hauled out of the water for the winter months. Nevertheless, decay was an ever present problem for lake shipyards and few ships lasted more than eight years in service[33].

Substantial efforts were made in the 1790's and early 1800's to renew the Provincial Marine fleet, as several of its vessels had been in service since the American Revolutionary War, and were worn out. When Lieutenant Governor Simcoe arrived in Upper Canada in 1792 he found in commission the newer *Onondaga* and *Mississauga* together with the older *Caldwell* and *Mohawk*, in addition to two gunboats, the *Buffalo* and the *Bear* on Lake Ontario. On the upper lakes the newer *Ottawa* and *Chippewa* and the older *Dunmore* and *Felicity* were based along with two gunboats[34]. In the same year a decision was taken to replace the old *Maria* on Lake Champlain with a new schooner, the *Royal Edward*[35]. By 1798 *Ottawa*, *Maria* and *Francis* were in service on the upper lakes while *Onondaga*, *Catherine* and *Sophia* were all condemned[36]. As for naval bases, Simcoe recognized their need and identified harbours at York (Toronto) and Grand River as possible future bases for gunboats[37].

During the years leading up to the War of 1812 the senior administrators of the colonial government and the military commanders in Upper Canada continued to express serious reservations about the efficiency of the Provincial Marine service. An early attempt by Lieutenant Governor Simcoe to reform the service foundered in the mid-1790's after relations with the United States improved following the Jay Treaty[38], and

32. Parks Canada, *Shipbuilding at Fort Amherstburg 1796-1813*, Ottawa, 1978, 8, 12.
33. Malcolmson, *Warships of the Great Lakes*, 50.
34. MacLeod, *The Tap of the Garrison Drum: The Marine Service in British North America*, 177.
35. Ibid, 178.
36. Ibid, 200.
37. Ibid, 181.

in 1806 the newly-appointed military commander in Upper Canada, Colonel Isaac Brock, sought to remedy the deficiencies in the Provincial Marine. He appointed Lieutenant Colonel Pye to the command of the Provincial Marine and gave him a mandate to improve the service[39]. As a result, the 20-gun *Royal George* was built at Kingston in 1809[40], and the 17 gun *Queen Charlotte* at Amherstburg in 1810, both square-rigged ships with shallow drafts[41].

While the Provincial Marine maintained the colonial government's naval supremacy on the Great Lakes, the United States was not wholly unresponsive. Initially, the United States had not been concerned with developing a substantial navy. Nevertheless, President Washington asked Congress to authorize the construction of a small fleet of large oceangoing frigates and Congress duly authorized six large frigates. The utility of the frigates became apparent with the signing of the Jay Treaty which angered France and led to a naval quasi-war between the United States and France from 1797-99, during the presidency of John Adams[42].

After coming to power in France, Napoleon Bonaparte dreamed of reestablishing the French empire in the New World, and he arranged for the transfer back to France from Spain of the huge Louisiana Territory which Spain had secured at the end of the Seven Years War. Napoleon also sent a French expeditionary force with orders to retake the former French colony of Haiti from its post-revolutionary government as a prelude to reinforcing the Louisiana Territory. However, the French expedition to Haiti ended in disease and disaster, and Napoleon reconsidered his imperial dreams in North America. As a result,

38. Malcolmson, "Nature of the Provincial Marine", *Northern Mariner*, 32.
39. Parks Canada, *Shipbuilding at Fort Amherstburg 1796-1813*, Ottawa, 1978, 8.
40. Malcolmson, "Nature of the Provincial Marine", *Northern Mariner*, 33.
41. Parks Canada, *Shipbuilding at Fort Amherstburg 1796-1813*, Ottawa, 1978, 12-13.
42. George C Douglas, *1812: The Navy's War* (New York: Basic Books, 2011) 7.

Napoleon agreed to sell the newly reacquired Louisiana Territory to the United States, which the administration of President Thomas Jefferson was quick to accept. At a stroke, the size of the United States doubled, and it became a great continental power no longer confined to the eastern seaboard of North America.

Meanwhile, Great Britain was locked in a titanic struggle with Napoleonic France, although the British North American colonies were little touched by the war. Britain consolidated its control of the world's oceans by victories over the French, Spanish, Dutch and Danish fleets at the battles of The Glorious First of June, Cape St. Vincent, Camperdown, the Nile and Copenhagen. The final maritime triumph of the Royal Navy over the navies of the European continent came with Vice-Admiral Horatio Nelson's great naval victory over the combined fleets of France and Spain at the Battle of Trafalgar[43]. Afterwards, Great Britain used its power at sea to enforce a blockade of France and to impress seaman from foreign ships to satisfy the insatiable demand for crews by the Royal Navy, actions which caused serious difficulties in Britain's relations with the United States. The United States objected strenuously to the presumed right of Great Britain to stop American flagged vessels on the oceans and to remove seamen who were born British subjects but who had become naturalized US citizens. While Britain recognized dual citizenship it did not recognize or provide for the renunciation of the status of a British subject, and that was the source of the difficulty between America and Britain. Further, as a practical matter, mistakes sometimes occurred and natural born Americans were occasionally impressed into the Royal Navy against their will[44].

President Jefferson dispatched William Pinkney to Britain as an

43. Ibid, 11.
44. Donald R. Hickey, *Don't Give Up the Ship: Myths of the War of 1812*, (Champaign (Illinois): University of Illinois Press, 2006) 20.

envoy to help Ambassador James Monroe develop a new friendship treaty between the two countries. However, when Pinkney returned with a treaty that would not limit the British claimed right of impressment, Jefferson repudiated the draft treaty negotiated by his diplomats. Jefferson probably miscalculated in rejecting the proposed treaty. It has been suggested that he thought France would probably prevail in the struggle between the two great European empires, and that either greater concessions could be wrung from a defeated Britain or the threat of American trade sanctions would force greater British concessions, should Britain prevail in its struggle against France[45].

Meanwhile, the British Privy Council issued Orders-in-Council to restrict neutral trade with French-dominated Europe. The first of those orders was issued in June 1807 and it barred neutral vessels from engaging in the European coasting trade between enemy ports. The second, issued on November 11, 1807, required neutral merchantmen to stop at British ports and obtain licenses for trading with Europeans. Essentially, that required neutral ships to trade with Europe through Britain. The final Order-in-Council issued in April 1809 established a blockade of all French occupied ports between the Ems River in northwestern Germany and the ports of Pesaro and Orbitella in Italy[46]. This restrictive trade action inflamed the American government as well as public opinion in the United States. President Jefferson responded with non intercourse legislation that restricted the freedom of Americans to trade with Europe, but the economic effects were much more severe on the United States than on the European states.

In the *Chesapeake – Leopard* Incident the USS Chesapeake was fired on by *HMS Leopard* and boarded on the high seas. Four

45. Ibid, 17-18.
46. Ibid, 23.

crewmen were taken off the US warship as possible deserters from the Royal Navy, increasing the poison between the two countries. The British saw themselves in a life and death struggle with Napoleon whom they viewed as a threat to the entire world, including the USA, and it was therefore essential to ensure that the Royal Navy was adequately manned[47]. The American presidents Jefferson and Madison however, were pro-French and deeply antagonistic towards Great Britain. Both saw Great Britain as a continuing threat to the United States because of its possession of Canada and Britain's willingness to support the aboriginal first nations in the west as they contested American encroachment on their traditional lands. Both Jefferson and Madison wished to oust the British from Canada and to incorporate the Canadian provinces into the United States[48] On the western frontier many American settlers thought they would never be safe from the threat of attack by aboriginals while the British remained in Canada. The war hawks in congress, who sought conflict with Britain in order to force Britain out of Canada (and who also sought to force the Spanish out of Florida) included Henry Clay of Kentucky, John C. Calhoun of South Carolina, and Felix Grundy of Tennessee. These tensions continued to escalate during the early years of the nineteenth century.

On the Great Lakes, the United States army purchased the sloop *Detroit* in 1796 and operated it as an US army vessel on Lake Erie and Lake Huron. Later the brig *Adams* was built at Detroit and operated from there by the army in much the same manner as the ships of the Provincial Marine. The Adams was commanded by a lieutenant from the 2nd US Infantry Regiment and served as a public means of transport on the Great Lakes[49]. Two gunboats

47. Ibid, 21.
48. Ibid, 36-39.
49. Malcolmson, *Warships of the Great Lakes*, 54.

were also constructed on Lake Champlain and the brig *Oneida* was built at Oswego in 1809 for the US Navy[50].

As war clouds began to gather, efforts were made to enhance the superiority of the Provincial Marine on the lakes. The 13 gun *Lady Prevost* was launched at Amherstburg in 1810. The Provincial Marine was organized into two divisions. The first division, under Commodore John Steel, patrolled Lake Ontario from Kingston and consisted of the 20 gun *Royal George*, a 150-ton square-rigged corvette, and the older (and rather decrepit) *Earl of Moira*[51], (with the 10 gun *Prince Regent* added in June 1812[52]. The second division, under Commodore Alexander Grant, was based at Amherstburg and patrolled Lake Erie, and the smaller Lake St. Clair, and occasionally patrolling into Lake Huron. It consisted of the 17 gun square-rigged corvette *Queen Charlotte*, launched in 1810, the *Lady Prevost*, which was completed in July 1812, and the *General Hunter*[53]. Both Steel and Grant were in their seventies and overdue for retirement. The decaying *Royal Edward* mouldered at Fort St. Jean at the north end of Lake Champlain with only a single caretaker aboard[54].

Major General Brock, now serving in a dual capacity as the military commander in Upper Canada and the Administrator of the colonial government in Upper Canada (the governorship being temporarily vacant) saw the danger clearly and did what could be done to enhance the Provincial Marine as tensions rose between Great Britain and the United States. He replaced both Steel and Grant, appointing George Hall on the upper lakes and

50. Ibid, 56.
51. Malcolmson, "Nature of the Provincial Marine", *Northern Mariner*, 33.
52. MacLeod, *The Tap of the Garrison Drum: The Marine Service in British North America*, 331.)
53. Parks Canada, *Shipbuilding at Fort Amherstburg 1796-1813*, Ottawa, 1978, 14. Both of the corvettes were designed as shallow draft vessels and the square rigs were intended to make them less vulnerable to a loss of propulsion during battle, as it was believed that the smaller and more numerous square sails perpendicular to enemy broadsides rendered the sails less likely to be shot away than the fore and aft rigged sails of schooners.
54. Malcolmson, *Warships of the Great Lakes*, 58.

Hugh Earl on Lake Ontario in their places[55]. He also moved the headquarters of the service from Kingston to York on the assumption that more distance would render the headquarters less vulnerable to an American attack. Experienced seamen were obtained for the Provincial Marine in Quebec, and companies of the Royal Newfoundland Fencible Regiment were assigned to the ships, to act as marines, but those efforts were insufficient to transform an auxiliary transport service into an efficient naval fighting force. The blunt fact was that the colonial government had not made the investments in professionalism and training over a sufficient number of years that would have ensured an effective naval force on the Great Lakes at the outbreak of the war.

On the American side of the lakes the commander of the brig *Oneida* on Lake Ontario had moved the base of his ship from Oswego to Sackett's Harbour, considering that to be a better location than Oswego. The US army continued to maintain the brig *Adams* at Detroit.

Britain and the United States now drifted towards war. Distracted by its life and death struggle with Napoleonic France, Great Britain did not fully perceive how its policies on trade and impressment of seamen had damaged its relations with the United States. Important public officials, such as Presidents Jefferson and Madison, still harboured antipathy towards Britain as a consequence of the American Revolutionary War, fuelled by their fear of British power, and their antagonism to monarchical government. Many American political leaders sought a war of aggrandizement to increase the territory of the United States through the conquest of Canada, which was a tempting possibility, since Great Britain was too engaged in the Napoleonic War to offer substantial resistance to a determined American assault on Canada. Several prominent US politicians

55. Ibid 62.

argued that the conquest of Canada would be easy, requiring only the marching of troops into the country. Indeed, the initial influx of loyalists into Canada following the American revolution had been followed by the immigration of many others who were lured only by the prospect of obtaining title to good land. There was no strong sense of national consciousness in Canada and, in fact, the only people in the country who were described as Canadians were the French-speaking inhabitants. The English-speaking people considered themselves to be Americans. Even the British government had recognized this peculiar feature of their colony, as shown by the text of the Jay Treaty which had referred to "His Majesty's Government in America" and to the Governor General, the oldest (and most senior) political office in Canada, as "His Majesty's Governor General in America." Many American political leaders thought that the American inhabitants of Upper Canada would flock to the US flag once it was raised north of the border. Of approximately 11,000 militiamen enrolled in Canada, the Governor of New York thought that half of them would join the Americans if the United States invaded Canada[56].

There was yet another important driver for war on the part of the United States. The last and greatest of the aboriginal political leaders allied with European powers in North America had emerged on the world stage in the years preceding the war, in the form of the great Chief Tecumseh, who, together with his brother, known as the Prophet, led the aboriginal opposition to American encroachment on the traditional lands of the aboriginal people in the west. Tecumseh organized a "vast confederacy" of the aboriginal peoples in the west and south and began a struggle against the Americans that would shortly merge into the Canadian struggle for survival in the War of 1812[57]. The Americans feared the threat posed to their expansion on

56. Patrick A Wilder, *The Battle of Sackett's Harbour: 1813*, (Baltimore: Nautical and Aviation Publishing Co.) 1993, 10.
57. Minister of Indian Affairs and Northern Development, *Fort Malden National Historic Park*, 3.

the western frontier by Tecumseh and his adherents, and they knew that the British Crown maintained its traditional alliances with the western tribes. Many Americans with frontier interests blamed Great Britain for aboriginal attacks, and avidly sought to detach the western aboriginal first nations from their traditional alliances with Britain[58].

The first shots of the conflict occurred on Lake Ontario even before a formal state of war was declared. In April 1812, President Madison declared a ninety-day trade embargo and the following month Lieutenant Woolsey, in command of the *USS Oneida* at Sackett's Harbour sortied into Lake Ontario to enforce the embargo. On June 5, 1812, he stopped and seized the Canadian merchantman *Lord Nelson*, which was engaged in an innocent passage between Canadian ports. Woolsey took the Lord Nelson as a prize but that action was wrong, and the United States subsequently admitted liability, and paid compensation for the seizure, although not until 1927, which was more than a century after the seizure took place[59]. On June 18, 1812, the United States declared war on Britain, automatically including Canada and other British North American colonies in that declaration.

---

58. Donald R. Hickey, *Don't Give Up the Ship: Myths of the War of 1812*, 30-31.
59. Ibid, 105; Malcolmson, *Warships of the Great Lakes*, 62. The *Lord Nelson* was renamed the *Scourge* and served with the US Navy on Lake Ontario until it was lost in a storm (Bamford, *Freshwater Heritage*, 58, 61).

1812-1814 THE UNITED STATES OF AMERICA ATTEMPTS TO CONQUER CANADA

The War of 1812 spanned all of British North America but was primarily centred in Canada, and especially Upper Canada (now the province of Ontario) along its maritime boundary with the United States. There was little military activity in the Atlantic provinces owing in large part to the refusal by the New England states to actively prosecute the war. Nevertheless, some eastern forces, notably the Newfoundland Fencibles Regiment, served in Upper Canada. Essentially, there were five active fronts in the war: the traditional Lake Champlain invasion corridor, the St. Lawrence River frontier between Cornwall and Kingston, the Niagara Peninsula frontier, the Sandwich-Amherstburg frontier along the Detroit River, and, in the far west, Michlimackinac and the Upper Mississippi region. Naval control of the Great Lakes soon proved to be key to the success or failure of the land campaigns undertaken by both sides.

At the outset of the war the Provincial Marine could deploy in its first division on Lake Ontario the 20 gun *Royal George*, the 12 gun *Duke of Gloucester*, and the 10 gun *Earl of Moira*. In July, the squadron was augmented by the new 12 gun *Prince Regent*, launched at York[1]. The second division, based at Amherstburg on the Detroit River, consisted of the 20 gun *Queen Charlotte*, the 10 gun *General Hunter*, and the 13 gun *Lady Prevost*[2]. Additionally,

---

1. Mark Lardas, *Great Lakes Warships 1812-1815* (Oxford: Osprey Publishing, 2012) 31.

the colonial government had a fleet of 263 bateaux for use in resupply missions on the St. Lawrence River and the Great Lakes between Quebec and the fort at St. Joseph Island.

Lieutenant Woolsey, the American naval commander on Lake Ontario, sortied from Sackett's Harbour once or twice immediately after the outbreak of the war to harry Canadian merchantmen. However, the naval strategy devised by the Governor General and Commander-in-Chief in Canada, Lieutenant General George Prevost, and implemented by the Administrator and military commander in the province of Upper Canada, Major General Isaac Brock, remained defensive in its orientation. Knowing the internal deficiencies in the Provincial Marine likely dissuaded them from ordering offensive operations despite the Provincial Marine's ostensible naval superiority on all of the lakes at the outset of the war. Furthermore, at least initially, efforts continued to be made by Great Britain to stop the war through diplomatic initiatives before it became a hot war[3].

Nevertheless, Commodore Earle did sail from Kingston to bombard Sackett's Harbour on July 19, 1812. The USS Oneida was quickly laid up under the protection of the American fort and some of its guns were landed to fire at the Canadian squadron. A rather desultory bombardment by Commodore Earle ensued without any real damage being done to the American ship or to the fort. Eventually, the Provincial Marine ceased its bombardment and departed. All in all, it was not a very auspicious beginning to offensive naval operations by the Provincial Marine and it underscored the lack of a true naval capability by the Provincial Marine[4].

General Brock had been increasingly concerned about the state

2. Ibid, 39.
3. George C Douglas, *1812: The Navy's War*, 51.
4. Theodore Roosevelt, *The Naval War of 1812* (Reprint New York: Modern Library, 1999), 85.

of the Provincial Marine as the threat of war neared, and even stated at one point that tremendous efforts would be required to improve the capabilities of the force[5]. Nevertheless, he took full advantage of the existing naval supremacy provided by the Provincial Marine on Lake Erie to rush troops to southwestern Upper Canada along the Detroit River frontier[6]. Brock considered the post at Amherstburg to be of prime importance and he planned to safeguard it by an attack on Detroit, Michigan[7]. The commander of the US North-Western Army on the Detroit frontier in Michigan, Brigadier General William Hull, crossed the Detroit River in force on July 12, 1812, and occupied Sandwich, Upper Canada. On July 16th Hull's forces engaged pickets that had been deployed from Amherstburg's Fort Malden to protect the bridge over the Canard River, in the first wartime engagement on Canadian soil.

The American war plan called for a three-pronged offensive against Canada. Attacks would be made east from the Detroit and Niagara frontiers while a strong force moved up the traditional Lake Champlain invasion route to take Montreal. If successful, the attacks would cut off Upper Canada from Lower Canada and allow its conquest by the United States. The conquest of Lower Canada was more problematic, as British naval superiority on the Atlantic meant that it could reinforce the fortress city of Quebec which was the key to controlling Lower Canada. General Hull had struggled to bring his forces to the border before undertaking a limited incursion into Canada but he retreated back to Michigan on August 7-8, 1812, as the colonial forces opposing him were built up[8].

General Brock, having taken advantage of the Provincial Marine's naval superiority on Lake Erie to rush three hundred

---

5. W Kaye Lamb, *The Hero of Upper Canada* (Toronto: Rous & Mann Press), 16.
6. George C Douglas, *1812: The Navy's War*, 98.
7. W Kaye Lamb, *The Hero of Upper Canada*, 15.
8. Hull left a small rearguard force at Sandwich until August 11th.

troops to Fort Malden, took personal command at the front. Perceiving General Hull to be vacillating, and the opposing American army to be suffering from low morale, Brock embarked on a bold strategy of attack in conjunction with Chief Tecumseh, the colonial government's great aboriginal wartime ally. Key elements of Brock's offensive operations included efforts to deceive the Americans as to the overall strength of the forces Brock had under his control, the psychological threat of a massacre of the Fort Lernoult garrison by the aboriginal warriors under Chief Tecumseh, and the bombardment of the fort by the *Queen Charlotte* and the *General Hunter*. As a result, General Hull surrendered his army to General Brock who took possession of Detroit and annexed all of the Michigan territory to the Crown – the largest loss of United States territory until the conquest of the Philippines by Japan in 1942.

Detroit was a very significant victory for the colonial government and it consolidated both public morale and public support for the war effort when it was most needed in the early days of the war[9]. As a result, and contrary to their expectations, the Americans did not gain support from the local population in Canada. The Upper Canada militia responded loyally to the call to arms and performed decently in the field. The Francophone population in Lower Canada also remained loyal, guided to a large extent by the attitude of the Roman Catholic Church which supported Britain in its larger military efforts to reverse the French revolution and which calculated that the interests of the church in Lower Canada were much better served by a British administration than by an American one[10].

The victory at Detroit was therefore facilitated by the Provincial Marine, a fact that Governor General Prevost reported to the Secretary of War in London[11]. American reaction to the absence

9. W Kaye Lamb, *The Hero of Upper Canada*, 19.
10. George C Douglas, *1812: The Navy's War*, 170.
11. Ibid, 92.

of an effective American naval presence on the Great Lakes, and to the defeat at Detroit, was swift. Secretary of the Navy Paul Hamilton ordered Captain Isaac Chauncey, the commandant of the naval base at New York, to travel to Lake Ontario and assume command of the inland naval forces with orders to purchase or build whatever ships he required[12]. Chauncey assumed command on September 1, 1812[13] and called upon shipbuilder Henry Eckford to build a new shipyard at Sacketts Harbour and sent him one-hundred artificers, six-hundred navy personnel from New York, and one-hundred US marines to assist with the work[14]. Eckford had been born in Scotland and had emigrated to Canada and worked as an apprentice to his uncle, John Black, a shipbuilder at Quebec. At the age of 21 he emigrated to New York City where he had become one of the leading American shipbuilders[15]. Chauncey also hired Noah and Adam Brown, and Daniel Dobbins, to start new yards at Presque Isle and Erie, Pennsylvania[16]. Later, the Brown Brothers would also start a yard at Vergennes, Vermont, to support the US Navy's needs on Lake Champlain[17].

In Canada, the colonial government was not idle. The imperial government granted Governor General Prevost authority to commence an emergency shipbuilding program. A master shipbuilder together with 128 carpenters and shipwrights arrived at Kingston on December 28, 1812 and all but 50 were immediately sent onto the shipyards at York and Amherstburg. At the latter shipyard a new corvette was built, the 490-ton *HMS Detroit*[18], armed with 19 guns (one long 18-pounder, two long

12. Malcolmson, *Warships of the Great Lakes*, 64.
13. Roosevelt, *The Naval War of 1812*, 86.
14. Malcolmson, Warships of the Great Lakes, 65.
15. Patrick A Wilder, *The Battle of Sackett's Harbour*, 8.
16. Lardas, *Great Lakes Warships*, 11.
17. Ibid, 12.
18. During the capture of Fort Lernoult and the settlement at Detroit General Brock's forces were also able to seize the US army ship *Adams* which the colonial government renamed *Detroit*. However, that ship was later cut out in a daring attack by the US Navy at Fort Erie but it grounded before making good its escape. The *Detroit* was fought over and pounded by

24 pounders, six long 12 pounders, eight long nine pounders, a twenty-four-pounder carronade and one 18-pounder carronade[19]). Amherstburg also built two gunboats, *Eliza* and *Myers*[20]. Governor General Prevost bypassed the Provincial Marine's traditional builder, John Dennis, by bringing in new shipbuilders from Lower Canada, which led to administrative delays and disputes, eventually impacting the colonial government's shipbuilding efficiency[21].

For both sides the process of building new ships meant establishing a basic footprint for the proposed ship and extracting what woods were locally available for shipbuilding. Under wartime conditions the builders were forced to use unseasoned green lumber in the construction process. The woods used included ash, spruce, elm, pine, chestnut and maple, in addition to oak and cedar. The skilled work was done by experienced shipwrights and carpenters but local labourers provided the general capacity each yard required. Iron fittings had to be transported to the lake yards from afar and, in wartime haste, clamps and wooden blocks were employed to join deck beams to the ship's hulls in lieu of knees. The new ships were built fast and without a great deal of concern for their potential longevity. They were only required to win one major battle in order to take control of one or more of the lakes and both governments realized that all of the ships would wear out after a few years of naval service[22].

The Americans had an advantage in that iron fittings for their ships could be obtained from a foundry in Philadelphia. The colonial government, on the other hand, had to obtain its iron fittings from Lower Canada, which was the site of the closest

both British and American artillery before the Americans set the ship on fire and destroyed it.
19. Parks Canada, *Shipbuilding at Fort Amherstburg 1796-1813*, Ottawa, 1978, 15.
20. Ibid, 14.
21. Malcolmson, *Warships of the Great Lakes*, 70.
22. Lardas, *Great Lakes Warships*, 12.

iron foundry. Additionally, all of the naval guns for the colonial squadrons had to be brought in from Great Britain[23].

The Royal Navy continued to favour traditional methods of ship construction and traditional woods; for example, the British did not adopt the use of hanging knees but the British did opt to use iron nails instead of treenails, which was an innovation[24]. Essential materials such as sail canvas, cordage, tackle, and anchors and chains and even paint could not be produced locally and had to be sent to Canada for use in the shipyard which added to the overall costs of construction. Under the pressure of war the ships were often rushed to completion which added considerably to their cost.

Commodore Chauncey adopted an aggressive strategy on Lake Ontario as the strength of his forces waxed. He harried Commodore Earl's Provincial Marine squadron continually through the autumn of 1812. His forces chased the *Royal George*, which made a fortunate escape into Kingston harbour on November 9, 1812[25]. Chauncey also chased the *Governor Simcoe* which hit a shoal on its way into Kingston harbour and sank at its pier. The sloop *Elizabeth* was taken by the Americans even though it was under an escort by the *Earl of Moira*[26]. Against these American successes the Provincial Marine's *Royal George* only managed to destroy an American storehouse at the mouth of the Genesee River, and to take two small schooners[27]. By the end of 1812 the demoralized first division of the Provincial Marine languished in the harbour at Kingston, and Commodore Chauncey had undisputed control of Lake Ontario although the Provincial Marine still maintained control on the upper lakes.

23. Robert Malcolmson, *Lords of the Lake: The Naval War on Lake Ontario 1812-1814* (Toronto: Robin Bass Studio, 1998) 68.
24. Lardas, *Great Lakes Warships*, 15.
25. Ibid, 49.
26. Ibid, 53.
27. MacLeod, *The Tap of the Garrison Drum: The Marine Service in British North America 1755-1813*, 224.

The colonial government realized that loss of naval control on Lake Ontario would undermine the safety of Upper Canada[28] and that the Provincial Marine was entirely unsuited to the role of an active naval force. The Acting Deputy Quartermaster General, Captain Alexander Gray, reported to Governor General Prevost that the officers of the Provincial Marine had lost their public reputations and the service would face defeat if it had to meet a superior American force on the lakes when the campaign resumed in the spring of 1813[29]. Alarmed by this report, Governor General Prevost wrote to the Royal Navy's station commander in North America, Admiral Sir John Borlase Warren, who was based at Bermuda, seeking his assistance. Warren responded favourably to Prevost's request for assistance and agreed to dispatch a group of Royal Navy officers to take command on the Great Lakes and on Lake Champlain. Meanwhile, the imperial government also took action to enhance the defensive capacity of Upper Canada on the Great Lakes. On March 8, 1813, it authorized the Admiralty to take over the control and direction of the lake forces and the Admiralty responded by appointing Captain Sir James Yeo as commodore of the lake forces the very next day. Yeo received his formal instructions on March 19th and he departed for Canada two days later[30].

On April 22, 1813, the colonial government issued a general order transferring the Crown's property in the Provincial Marine, including the ships, dockyards and stores, to the Royal Navy[31] and directed that the officers of the Royal Navy would supersede Provincial Marine officers on the lakes. However, the general order went on to state that there would be no reduction

28. Malcolmson, *Lords of the Lake*, 58.
29. Wilder, *The Battle of Sackett's Harbour*, 33.
30. MacLeod, *The Tap of the Garrison Drum: The Marine Service in British North America 1755-1813* 229.
31. Rear Admiral HF Pullen, *The March of the Seaman, Occasional Paper No. 8 of the Maritime Museum of Canada* (Halifax: Maritime Museum of Canada, 1961) 6.

in Provincial Marine officer's salaries. Despite the extension of an olive branch concerning their salaries most of the Provincial Marine officers were upset at this turn of events and correctly perceived that this decision marked the end of the Provincial Marine as an institution. Many of the Provincial Marine officers refused to serve under the new arrangements and preferred to leave the service[32]. Others accepted shore positions and those that remained were absorbed by the Royal Navy along with the ships of the Provincial Marine[33].

The Provincial Marine was much maligned in history for its inadequacies, which became all too apparent after the outbreak of the War of 1812. The reality, however, was that the Provincial Marine was never intended to be an offensive naval force. Rather, it was a coastal transport service and revenue enforcement instrument which had the additional function of preventing piracy and upholding the colonial government's authority on the Great Lakes. Essentially, it afforded the colonial government an efficient means of communication with its far-flung outposts in the province of Upper Canada. While the Provincial Marine did suffer from inefficiency and lacked both naval discipline and naval training its deficiencies often reflected the fact that the administration of the Provincial Marine was assigned to the army, as an adjunct to the Quartermaster-General's office. The army lacked any great depth of knowledge or skill in the management of an armed fleet of vessels and it is not surprising that the Provincial Marine never approached the operating standards of the Royal Navy.

Although the naval defence of Canada was within the scope of duties of the Provincial Marine, it was only in moments of tension between Great Britain and the United States that any real attention was paid to the deficiencies of the Provincial Marine as a fighting service. Only then were haphazard efforts made to

32. Malcolmson, *Lords of the Lake*, 113.
33. Malcolmson, *Warships of the Great Lakes*, 77.

reform the service to give it into a more warlike aspect. Soon, however, the tensions would subside and the Provincial Marine then lapsed back into its old ways of operating. As a transport service it did meet the needs of the colonial government at a critical juncture in Canada's history and it deserves to be well-remembered for its success in its primary vocation as a transport service, and for its crucial control of the Great Lakes (particularly the upper lakes) during the early months of the war, which made possible the victory at Detroit.

Even with all of its acknowledged deficiencies the Provincial Marine was able to provide effective support to the army during the early stages of the War of 1812. Although Commodore Chauncey harried Commodore Earle in the autumn of 1812, forcing Earle to shelter his ships under the guns of the fort at Kingston, Chauncey was never able to compel Earle to battle. By avoiding a decisive battle in the early stages of hostilities, Commodore Earle preserved his fleet-in-being on Lake Ontario, and deprived the United States of an unrestricted naval supremacy on the most important of the Great Lakes. When Royal Navy officers arrived on the lake in 1813 to assume responsibility for the naval defence of the province, they were impressed to find a substantial squadron of ships at Kingston ready for transfer to the navy.

On the upper lakes the Provincial Marine retained naval supremacy throughout the first year of the war. The Provincial Marine provided Major General Brock with the means of transporting essential reinforcements to the garrison at Fort Malden which made possible his successful assault on Detroit. In its main vocation the Provincial Marine must be accounted a success over the course of its formal life from 1783 to 1813, although as a naval force it was never more than a water militia. That the Provincial Marine fell below the expectations of a professional naval service should not detract from its success as an auxiliary service, nor from the important and largely successful role it played in the initial stages of the war.

Meanwhile, on land, the American war strategy of a three-pronged offensive had been upended by Brock's victory at the Battle of Detroit. To compensate, the Americans sought to advance across the Niagara Peninsula separating Lake Ontario and Lake Erie, by crossing the Niagara River which formed the border between Upper Canada and New York. The colonial government had fortified the border by building Fort Erie adjacent to the town of Buffalo, New York, and Fort George at the outlet of the Niagara River into Lake Ontario, where the new fort vied for dominance with Fort Niagara on the US side of the border. On October 13, 1812, an American invasion force collided with British regular and colonial troops at the Battle of Queenston Heights which ended with a significant victory as the Americans were forced back across the border. However, the victory came at the cost of the life of the talented and energetic General Brock, whose absence in future campaigns would be telling. As a testament to the respect that Brock engendered even amongst his enemies, the batteries at Fort Niagara on the American frontier fired a salute during his funeral held at Fort George a few days after the battle[34]. As the armies of both sides entered into their winter quarters in the winter of 1812-13, the colonial government in Canada found itself in an advantageous position following the campaigns of 1812.

When winter lifted, and preparations began for the 1813 campaign season, the colonial government's naval strategy was transformed. Admiral Warren had sent Lieutenant Barclay and several other officers to take command of the lake forces from the Provincial Marine. Barclay assumed temporary command of the ships on Lake Ontario but on May 15th he was superseded by

34. W Kaye Lamb, *The Hero of Upper Canada*, 27.

Commodore Sir James Yeo and Barclay was sent to Amherstburg as commander of the forces on the upper lakes[35].

The naval officers took steps to improve the situation on the lakes. Improvements were made at Point Frederick in Kingston including the construction of stone buildings, a floating battery, and a hospital, the whole being placed under naval administration[36], and by establishing separate administrative structures for naval activities, including separate establishments for individual ships and dockyards[37].

Along the St. Lawrence River frontier the land war was not actively prosecuted in the early part of the war, other than one or two raids by a South Carolinian officer, Captain Ben Forsythe, on Gananoque and Elizabethtown. Colonel Pearson, the British army commandant at Fort Wellington, actively promoted continued relations between Canadians and Americans in order to avoid open conflict on the vital St. Lawrence River.[38]. Nevertheless, although it was a much quieter front, the St. Lawrence River saw its share of naval skirmishes. In July 1813 two-small US schooner-rigged gunboats, the *Neptune* and the *Fox*, successfully ambushed a convoy of fifteen bateaux that was being escorted by the Royal Navy's gunboat *Spitfire* with the loss of most of the convoy. In November 1813, US gunboats engaged their Royal Navy counterparts during the amphibious operation that resulted in the Battle of Crysler's Farm, and in the final year of the war, US Navy gunboats were successful in seizing and scuttling the British gunboat *Black Snake* in June 1814.

Throughout 1813, the opposing commodores on Lake Ontario, Yeo and Chauncey, maneuvered for position and attempted to lure the other into a decisive battle. The British mounted a joint

---

35. Malcolmson, *Warships of the Great Lakes*, 77.
36. Malcolmson, *Lords of the Lake*, 230.
37. Ibid, 242.
38. Pearson and his subordinates even continued to attend social gatherings on the US side of the border

army-navy attack on Sackett's Harbour on May 29, 1813, but the British attack was repulsed although the British were almost able to burn the American warship *General Pike*, which was being constructed there. The attack on Sackett's Harbour resulted in bad relations between Commodore Yeo and Governor General Prevost because the latter felt the navy had not supported the attack adequately but the attack worried Commodore Chauncey as he now realized that his shipyard was inadequately defended[39].

The opposing fleets again maneuvered against each other between August 7 – 10, 1813, but those actions were largely inconclusive although the American schooners *Hamilton* and *Scourge* were lost in a gale on August 8th, and the gunboats *Julia* and *Growler* were taken by the British on the 10th[40]. The effect of these engagements was to promote caution on the part of both commanders with the result that a decisive engagement on Lake Ontario became less and less likely. When the opposing naval squadrons on Lake Ontario approached one another the leeward squadron generally moved away since it had the unfavourable wind[41]. In the absence of decisive superiority, both Yeo and Chauncey began a naval arms race, with each seeking to outbuild the other in an attempt to achieve overwhelming naval supremacy on Lake Ontario.

On Lake Erie it was a different matter. While the Provincial Marine had maintained naval control throughout the first year of the war, the United States had commenced construction of two brigs at Erie, Pennsylvania. The *USS Lawrence* and the *USS Niagara* were constructed by the Brown Brothers' shipyard and were of similar tonnage to *HMS Detroit*. The Dobbins shipyard also contributed two new schooners, *Porcupine* and *Tigris*, and by the early summer of 1813 the US Navy was in a position to seize naval supremacy on the upper lakes. A young Master

39. Malcolmson, *Warships of the Great Lakes*, 79.
40. Ibid, 83-84.
41. Roosevelt, *The Naval War of 1812*, 135.

Commandant in the navy, Oliver Hazard Perry, was appointed as the commodore of the US Navy's upper lakes squadron, consisting of *Lawrence, Niagara, Caledonia, Scorpion, Porcupine* and *Tigris*. Although they were deficient in long guns, Perry's ships were amply armed with carronades and they could deliver heavy blows to an enemy ship at short ranges. Furthermore, he had well-trained crews for his ships. Seventy per cent of Perry's crews consisted of US navy personnel or merchant seamen, and the remaining 30% of his crew complement consisted of a combination of US marines, US army soldiers, and volunteers[42].

At Amherstburg, Captain Barclay commanded a Royal Navy squadron consisting of ex-Provincial Marine vessels *Detroit, Queen Charlotte, General Hunter, Lady Prevost* and the three gun *Little Belt*, a prize taken from the Americans in July 1812. Barclay's ships were deficient in carronades and lacked the overall throw-weight of the American squadron, although they did have the advantage in long guns. However, Barclay's flagship, *Detroit*, possessed six different calibers of guns which impeded its efficiency as a fighting machine[43]. Upon assuming command Barclay had complained about the resources that were available to him including a lack of stores, interference from the army (which at one point took away his carpenters fitting out *Detroit* and insisted that they work on gunboats) and the poor quality of his crews. It does appear that Barclay had difficulty adapting to a Canadian command since one of his complaints concerned the fact that some of his Francophone crews could not comprehend English[44]. When Barclay put out into Lake Erie for battle, his crews consisted of 60 Royal Navy personnel, 110 ex-Provincial Marine seamen, and 230 British army infantrymen[45].

42. Malcolmson, *Warships of the Great Lakes*, 95.
43. Robert Malcolmson and Thomas Malcolmson, *HMS Detroit: The Battle for Lake Erie* (St. Catherines: Vanwell Publishing, 1990), 88. Due to the loss of essential stores at York, the *Detroit's* heavy armament had been stripped from the defences of Fort Malden (Minister of Indian and Northern Affairs, *Fort Malden National Historic Park*, 4).
44. Parks Canada, *Shipbuilding at Fort Amherstburg 1796-1813*, Ottawa, 1978, 15.
45. Malcolmson, *Warships of the Great Lakes*, 95.

Commodore Perry was a young, aggressive officer of 27 years who came from a family of naval officers, and was therefore anxious to make a name for himself in the US Navy. Bringing the Royal Navy's Lake Erie squadron to battle and defeating it was his overriding objective. Barclay, on the other hand, had several considerations to bear in mind. His squadron suffered from deficiencies in armament and skill in comparison to the American squadron. Furthermore, the loss of naval control on Lake Erie would undermine the position of the army along the frontier, requiring its probable withdrawal from Michigan and from southwestern Upper Canada. Barclay's best strategy was to blockade the American squadron at Erie, Pennsylvania, during its construction and to attack it if an attempt was made by Perry to bring the *Lawrence* and the *Niagara* across the sandbar that blocked the ships from the lake. That indeed was the strategy that Barclay initially employed but he subsequently removed the guard ships for a brief period to replenish them and Perry rushed to move his brigs safely across the sandbar.

Barclay might also have considered a more defensive strategy by lying close to Fort Malden and, in effect, adopting the preservation of a fleet-in-being strategy although doubtless Perry would have attempted to challenge Barclay to accept battle. However, languishing in port was not a naval practice that was likely to win the fame and renown in the Royal Navy that Barclay sought. In the end, Barclay determined to give battle to the American squadron. On September 10, 1813, the two squadrons met in the decisive battle of the naval war on the Great Lakes during the War of 1812. The action took place near West Sister Island on the American side of Lake Erie[46] and it resulted in the complete defeat of the Royal Navy squadron.

Although Barclay had the advantage in long guns, and the wind was also in his favour, he allowed his squadron to be engaged at

46. Minister of Indian and Northern Affairs, *Fort Malden National Historic Park*, 4.

a short range where the American carronades on Perry's ships could fire a greater broadside throw-weight than Barclay's squadron could match. Even so, Barclay almost won the battle because Perry's flagship, the *Lawrence*, came in for concentrated fire from the British side while its sister ship, the *Niagara*, remained aloof from the main action. Displaying great daring, Perry abandoned his wrecked flagship[47] in a small boat and boarded the undamaged *Niagara*. Sending the Niagara's master off to bring up his smaller warships, Perry then pierced the British line with the *Niagara*, and subsequently with his smaller vessels, engaging the British at short range with terrible effect and causing the *Detroit* and *Queen Charlotte* to become entangled, and ultimately forcing Barclay to surrender. In tribute to the sacrifices of his men on the *Lawrence* Perry returned his pennant to that ship and it was from the *Lawrence* that he formally received the British surrender around 4:00 P.M. on the day of the battle[48].

In scale and scope, the Battle of Lake Erie had no previous parallel in the various naval struggles to control the Great Lakes. Perry received the surrender of all of Captain Barclay's vessels, marking the first time in history that an entire squadron of the Royal Navy was surrendered to an enemy following a battle. As Commodore Perry famously stated to his superiors, "we have me the enemy and they are ours.". The victory secured Perry's reputation in the pantheon of American military heroes and his battle flag hangs today in the US Naval Academy in Annapolis, Maryland.

Barclay's superior, Commodore Yeo, considered Barclay to have been reckless in engaging an enemy with a superior throw-weight of armaments at short range but Barclay was not

---

47. Although it is famously recorded that Perry's battle flag stated "Don't Give Up the Ship" the *Lawrence* struck her colours after Perry left the ship but the Royal Navy was unable to take possession of the *Lawrence* before the battle ended. (Roosevelt, *The Naval War of 1812*, 148).
48. Malcolmson and Malcolmson, *HMS Detroit: The Battle for Lake Erie*, 111.

censured. In fact, after his release from prisoner-of-war status on parole Barclay was feted by the colonial government and the Canadian commercial establishment. In Montreal on April 20, 1814, he received a gift of inscribed silverplate from the grateful citizenry acknowledging that while Captain Barclay did not meet with victory he deserved to have won the battle[49]! Wishful thinking indeed! One can hardly imagine Americans expressing a like sentiment if Perry and Barclay's roles had been reversed.

In the meantime the colonial government had to face the consequential realities of the defeat. On the American side an army under Major General William Henry Harrison had been reconstituted in the northwest with fresh recruits. With the loss of the Royal Navy squadron on Lake Erie the Americans now exercised naval supremacy on the upper lakes and it was obvious to Major General Proctor, commanding the right division of the Army of Upper Canada along the Amherstburg-Sandwich frontier, that it would be impossible to hold onto the conquered Michigan Territory, and without the ability to resupply his forces by lake vessels even the western frontier could not be held. The supply lines to the east by land were simply too long and inefficient. Realizing the gravity of his situation, Proctor abandoned Michigan, which was retaken by the Americans on September 27, 1813. On that same day Proctor abandoned and burned Fort Malden and its shipyard and retreated east with his division.

For Chief Tecumseh and the aboriginal confederacy allied to the Crown the defeat of the Royal Navy in Lake Erie was a catastrophe, as it forced the British out of the American Old Northwest permanently, and allowed the American army to destroy both the aboriginal war capacities as well as Tecumseh's aboriginal confederacy. So severe was the impact of the defeat on aboriginal aspirations that for several days after the naval

49. Barry Gough, *Fighting Sail on Lake Huron and Georgian Bay: The War of 1812 and its Aftermath* (St. Catherines: Vanwell Publishing, 2002), 49.

battle the British would not impart any information about their defeat to Tecumseh because they understood that news would be a heavy blow to the War Chief's ambitions.

Tecumseh railed against Proctor's decision to retreat but as naval supremacy was lost, and the fort at Amherstburg had been stripped of its guns to arm the now defeated naval squadron, Proctor and Tecumseh had no choice but to retreat eastwards. Seizing his opportunity, General Harrison invaded Upper Canada in pursuit of the retreating British army taking both of the towns of Sandwich and Amherstburg without resistance. Harrison pursued the retreating forces of the colonial government and he caught up with them near Moraviantown, on the Thames River. In the Battle of Moraviantown (which Americans call the Battle of the Thames River) on October 5, 1813, the American attack broke the line of the dispirited British troops most of whom surrendered. Proctor and some of his troops managed to escape eastwards from the battlefield but Chief Tecumseh and his warriors refused to give up and fought on until Tecumseh was killed, which finally broke the resistance by the aboriginal force. Tecumseh's body was desecrated on the battlefield by the victorious American troops, underscoring the race-hatred aspect of the war between US troops and the North American aboriginal population. Only the expiration of the US troops enlistments prevented Harrison from taking further Canadian territory. Having destroyed the British, colonial, and aboriginal forces, the Americans retreated back to the Sandwich – Amherstburg frontier in Essex County.

The loss of naval control on Lake Erie also impacted the colonial government's position on Lake Huron and on Lake Superior. At the outset of the war the colonial government had seized the American fort at Michlimackinac before the American garrison was warned about the US declaration of war, thus giving the colonial government an important strategic advantage. The armed transport schooner *Nancy* did not participate in the Battle of Lake Erie and had escaped from the Americans into Lake Huron following the Royal Navy's defeat where it engaged in resupply missions to Michlimackinac from a new naval base at the mouth of the Nottawasaga River[50]. After the Detroit River was closed to navigation by American naval supremacy, the colonial government established a new resupply route from York along Yonge Street to Holland Landing, on the Holland River. From there the new route traversed Lake Simcoe to Kempenfeldt Bay where it returned to land and covered a nine-mile portage to Willow Creek. Through Willow Creek the route reached the Nottawasaga River which led into Lake Huron. Fort Willow was constructed at the junction of the nine-mile portage with Willow Creek and storehouses were built in conjunction with the fort. About thirty bateaux were constructed to move supplies along the maritime portion of the supply route from the Nottawasaga River to Fort Michlimackinac. This route was far from US forces and therefore well protected although it was less efficient than the former all-lake route since it required portages. Nevertheless, it afforded the colonial government the means to continue to resupply the British garrison at Fort Michlimackinac. Royal Navy Lieutenant Miller Worsley was assigned to command the naval forces on Lake Huron, and he assumed command of *Nancy*, in the summer of 1814.

The US Navy had also established a separate command for the upper lakes and the Madison Administration appointed Commodore Arthur Sinclair as commander of its naval forces on the upper lakes. In July 1814, he sortied into Lake Huron to support the US Army attempt to retake Fort Michlimackinac. He found the colonial government's fort at St. Joseph's Island abandoned and he burned it, also taking the Northwest Company's trading vessel *Mink* as a prize[51]. Reorganization also occurred on the Canadian side of the border with the final

50. Ibid, 62, 64.
51. Ibid, 90.

transfer of the naval forces operating on the Great Lakes from army control to the British Admiralty in May 1814. As a consequence, existing ships were reclassified into the Royal Navy's ship classification structure and some of the existing warships were renamed. A detachment of Royal Marines was posted to the naval ships on the Great Lakes replacing militia troops, and a dockyard commissioner was appointed at the Point Frederick naval base in Kingston[52].

The colonial government did not maintain armed ships on Lake Superior. Rather, it relied on the Northwest Company to provide security which the company did provide through an armed schooner, the *Perseverance* which travelled between Sault Ste. Marie and Fort William. Learning that the Northwest Company schooner was lying at Sault Ste. Marie, St. Clair sent an officer and boat crew to seize it in a daring raid. The Americans took the vessel but subsequently wrecked the ship on the rocks in an attempt to bring their prize from Lake Superior into Lake Huron[53]. Although the Americans obtained naval control of Lake Superior by this action, Sinclair did not follow up by actively asserting control of Lake Superior because his orders required him to focus on the retaking of Fort Michlimackinac. A joint US Navy-US Army attack on Fort Michlimackinac on July 26, 1814, failed however, and Sinclair then sailed for the mouth of the Nottawasaga River where he destroyed the concealed *Nancy* in August[54]. Sinclair left the *Scorpion* and the *Tigris* to patrol Lake Huron while taking the remainder of his squadron back to Lake Erie. Lieutenant Turner, in command of the small Lake Huron squadron sailed back to St. Joseph's Island with *Scorpion* and *Tigris*.

52. John R. Grodzinski, "April 1813: Naval Base, Point Frederick" in *Veritas*, Kingston, Summer 2012, 22 at 24.
53. Gough, *Fighting Sail on Lake Huron and Georgian Bay*, 94.
54. After the war the North-West Company, which still owned the *Nancy*, was provided with an award of 2200 pounds sterling as compensation for the loss of the ship. The owners were also compensated for the transport services that the *Nancy* actually performed during the war.

Meanwhile, Royal Navy Lieutenant Miller Worsley whose command, *Nancy*, Sinclair had so recently destroyed, embarked on a small boat voyage in a canoe and a bateau with a daring plan to seize the American vessels. Finding the American warships at St. Joseph's Island, Worsley attacked *Tigris* and took her as a prize on the night of September 3rd without arousing suspicions on the *Scorpion*. Maintaining the American colours as a *ruse-de-guerre* Worsley then mounted an attack on the *Scorpion* and seized it as well. The Royal Navy had now wrested temporary control of Lake Huron (and by inference both Lake Superior, and Lake Michigan) from the US Navy[55] which it then retained for the duration of the war. Worsley built winter quarters at Schooner Town on the Nottawasaga River, which was about four miles from the mouth of the river.

On the crucial Lake Ontario naval front the two opposing commanders, Commodore Yeo and Commodore Chauncey, had fallen into a defensive mind set which led them inevitably into a shipbuilding war. The British experimented with the use of prefabricated shipbuilding kits to expedite fleet replenishment, which allowed Britain to make use of the skilled labour in British yards that were increasingly being rendered redundant by the lapsing of the Napoleonic wars. Kits were built in Britain, disassembled, and then transported to Canada where less-skilled Canadian tradesmen could fit the ships together again[56]. However, only the frigate *Psyche* was completed in this manner before hostilities ceased.

The Americans had shipyards at Vergennes, Vermont, Sackett's Harbour, New York, Erie and Presque Isle, Pennsylvania, and Detroit, Michigan, that could satisfy their naval needs on the lakes. With a large-enough workforce now available, and proximity to industrial foundries at Pittsburgh for the necessary

55. Gough, *Fighting Sail on Lake Huron and Georgian Bay*, 110-11.
56. Ibid, 16.

iron fittings, the US Navy was able to construct a substantial naval fleet on the Great Lakes. Commodore Chauncey expended all of his efforts on building a superior fleet on Lake Ontario and as the war progressed he increasingly resisted calls from the US army for the navy to support land actions, claiming that the US warships must be preserved for a "higher destiny" of attacking the Royal Navy's fleet in a hoped-for decisive action[57].

As both commanders calculated their chances with mathematical exactitude, their conduct of the naval war became driven by statistics as first one, then the other, sheltered in port, when the calculations of relative strength factored against him[58]. It must be considered however, that at least in the case of Commodore Yeo, his aversion to attempting a decisive battle on Lake Ontario was the correct strategy. Much like Sir John Jellicoe in the First World War, who was said to be the only man who could have lost that war in a single afternoon, Yeo had to consider what the defeat of his squadron could mean for the strategic conduct of the war. Without control of Lake Ontario the army in the field could easily be cut off from its main supply line through Lower Canada to Great Britain, thus leading to the loss of Upper Canada which, in turn, would have permitted the Americans to advance on Montreal from the west, just as the British had accomplished in the Seven Years War. Thus, a defeat on Lake Ontario could have been devastating to the colonial government in Canada and it might have allowed the Americans to accomplish one of their chief war aims, the conquest of Canada. Yeo himself admitted as much, reportedly stating to one of his officers: "If we were on the high seas, I would risk an action at all hazards; because, if I were beaten, I could only lose the squadron; but to lose it on this lake, would involve the loss of the country[59]."

57. Alan Taylor, *The Civil War of 1812: American Citizens, British Subjects, Irish Rebels & Indian Allies* (New York: Vintage Books, 2011) 392.
58. Roosevelt, *The Naval War of 1812*, 203.
59. Reminiscences of Lieutenant James Richardson quoted in William F. Coffin, *1812: The War*

The naval arms race therefore continued, reaching its apex in the construction of a first-rate ship at Point Frederick, the ship of the line *HMS St. Lawrence*, in 1814. The *St. Lawrence* was the only capital ship of either navy to sail on the Great Lakes. It was the equal in size of any other ship of the line in the Royal Navy then serving on any of the oceans of the world. Designed by the naval architect F. Strickland, the *St. Lawrence's* dimensions were huge. The ship was 221 feet long (191 feet long on the upper deck) and 52 feet, 6 inches in breadth. Its height from the bottom of its keel to the upper rail on the deck was 45 feet and it displaced 2305 tons burden[60]. The *St. Lawrence* was fitted with 122 gunports, although it was only known to have carried 102 guns[61] and this massive warship accommodated a crew of approximately one thousand men[62]. Built of oak and cedar at a cost of one-million pounds sterling, with three tall square-rigged masts carrying 20 sails[63], it was a marvel to behold and gave Yeo instant control of Lake Ontario from the time he hoisted his pennant aboard it in October 1814. Although the American navy never challenged the *St. Lawrence*, nature did. The ship was almost destroyed by a lightening strike on the main mast on October 19, 1814. Fortunately, the bolt of electricity failed to reach the magazine and the prepared charges that were stored there, which would have detonated and destroyed the ship[64].

Seeking not to be outdone by the Royal Navy, the US Navy embarked on the construction of its own ships of the line on Lake Ontario, the *New Orleans*, which was partially completed, and the *Chippewa*, both of which would have carried 90 guns[65] but the

and its Moral (Montreal: 1864) and cited in Ronald L Way, *The Day of Crysler's Farm*, (Repr. Toronto: The Ontario-St Lawrence Development Commission, 1961), 189.

60. Robert B. Townsend, *The Story of HMS St. Lawrence* (Carrying Place: Odyssey Publishing, 1998) 13-14.

61. Ibid, 27.

62. Ibid, 14.

63. Ibid.

64. Malcolmson, *Lords of the Lake*, 308.

65. Lardas, *Great Lakes Warships*, 12.

end of the war forestalled their completion. The *New Orleans* was placed under a protective cover and was allowed to stand on the building stocks until 1883[66].

Both sides made extraordinary efforts to ensure that their respective squadrons were manned and ready for action. When Commodore Yeo ran short of experienced sailors in 1814, a draught of 217 men was sent from the maritime provinces to the Great Lakes. They travelled by land in the harshness of winter from St. John, New Brunswick, travelling initially by sleighs but for the most part marching overland to arrive at Kingston before the spring break up[67]. Equally extraordinary efforts were made on the American side. When it proved impossible to arrange land transport for a 300-foot hemp cable more than 20 inches in circumference, and weighing 9600 pounds, which was required for the rigging of Commodore Chauncey's new heavy frigate *USS Superior* under construction at Sackett's Harbour, the 55th Regiment of New York militia volunteered to carry the approximately five-ton cable from Sandy Creek near Oswego, to Sackett's Harbour between June 9-10, 1814[68].

On Lake Champlain, the naval front had been quiescent at the beginning of the war with the United States exercising apparent supremacy. However, in 1813, two American sloops chased British gunboats into the Richelieu River where the sloops were subsequently becalmed and then taken as prizes. Master Commandant Thomas Macdonough, in command of the US Navy forces on Lake Champlain, commenced a rebuilding program that prompted further shipbuilding by the Royal Navy commander on Lake Champlain, Commander Daniel Pring. A smaller version of the Lake Ontario naval arms race was the result of their efforts. When Governor General Prevost devised a plan to invade the United States along the Lake Champlain axis,

66. Ibid, 4.
67. H F Pullen (Rear Admiral) *The March of the Seamen*, 1961.
68. Donald R. Hickey, *Don't Give Up the Ship: Myths of the War of 1812*, 257.

a confrontation between the two opposing squadrons became inevitable. On September 11, 1814, they met in battle near Plattsburg, New York. Pring had been superseded in command by Captain George Downie who sailed up to the anchored American line and, after anchoring, commenced firing[69]. A heavy action resulted but the decisive manoeuver belonged to Macdonough who had anchored his ships so that they could be pivoted. He used kedge anchors to wind his ships around in order to deliver multiple broadsides killing Downie and forcing Downie's flagship and most of the remaining Royal Navy squadron to surrender[70]. Governor General Prevost decided that without naval superiority his planned invasion of the United States would be fruitless and he abandoned his offensive. The United States navy retained control of Lake Champlain for the duration of the war. Macdonough's skilful victory precluded a British invasion and underscored the importance of naval supremacy on the lakes. It was the last significant naval engagement of the War of 1812 on the lakes.

By the autumn of 1814 the United States had failed to gain a decisive victory over the colonial government in Canada, although it had regained the territory that Brock's victory had initially taken from it and it had defeated Proctor's division in the field at Moraviantown, forcing colonial forces to retreat in tatters towards the Niagara region. Yet the people of Upper Canada had not received the Americans as liberators as the Americans had expected at the outset of the war. Although there were sympathizers and even some who actively assisted the invading US forces by and large the civilian population had remained loyal to the colonial government. This meant that the taking of Upper Canada would require a substantial army of occupation – something that the US army, with its periodic expiration of enlistments, and its reliance on state militias that

69. Lardas, *Great Lakes Warships*, 27.
70. Donald R. Hickey, *Don't Give Up the Ship: Myths of the War of 1812*, 133.

sometimes refused to serve beyond US territory – was unable to provide. Lower Canada had hardly been touched by the war. Other than some skirmishes in the Lake Champlain border area the only significant engagement occurred at the Battle of Chateauguay where Colonel Charles de Salaberry turned back an American invasion force south of Montreal.

Of far greater significance to American war objectives was the destruction of Chief Tecumseh's aboriginal confederacy in the west, and the death of the great warrior chief himself. With his passing went the last chance for the aboriginal people to establish an aboriginal political entity that could preserve the rights of aboriginal people in the face of advancing settlement. The western frontier had been made secure for American settlement in the Old Northwest and the linkage between the Crown and the aboriginals beyond Canada's borders had been broken by the defeats inflicted on the British and its allied aboriginal forces. For the United States this was a significant achievement, and one that was made possible by Commodore Perry's great victory at the Battle of Lake Erie.

There was a larger picture to consider as well. Britain's life and death struggle to prevent Napoleon's domination of the European continent had ultimately been successful, even though much of the credit accrued to 'general winter' as Napoleon's great invasion army in Russia was utterly broken by the severity of the Russian winter. Emperor Napoleon's retreat from Russia ultimately forced his abdication from the French throne in 1814. Although he would return to power in France briefly in 1815, he could never again muster the resources and forces he needed to overcome his European opposition. Napoleon's last gamble at the Battle of Waterloo would prove to be his unmaking at the hands of Britain's great field marshal, the Duke of Wellington, and Napoleon was sent to live out his days on the island of St. Helena in the south Atlantic. With the end of the Napoleonic wars Britain had the capacity to reinforce Canada with massive numbers of troops and to redeploy major Royal Navy units from the European blockade to the American blockade. The British began active amphibious operations on the eastern seaboard of the United States and attacked Washington, D.C. through Virginia, causing the President to flee the capital and resulting in the burning of the White House (then called the Executive Mansion) in retaliation for the burning of the public buildings in York (Toronto) by an American raiding force in 1813. Towards the end of the year the British were planning a major attack on America's recently-acquired Louisiana Territory at New Orleans.

A general war-weariness now surfaced among the American people and was reflected in American public opinion. The War of 1812 was one of the least popular wars in American history and in the New England states there had been outright opposition to the war from its beginning. Although President Madison was eager to make one more attempt to conquer Canada the US Congress was not in favour of another attempt, nor was it in favour of the taxes which the President had sought from it to pay for a new invasion attempt.

The Canadian and British public were also weary of war or, at least in the case of the British public, the taxes required to finance wars, and the imperial government in Britain had never really been enthusiastic about the American War. From the outset it had wished that it might have been avoided. With all sides facing war weariness and revenue pressures, and with the threat that a substantial reinforcement of British forces in North America could prove disastrous to American interests in the long run, there was a growing impetus to seek peace. Accordingly, it was agreed that representatives of Great Britain and the United States would meet at the Dutch city of Ghent and negotiations commenced there in August 1814.

The British believed that they had the stronger position going into the negotiations and thus the British Foreign Minister, Viscount Castlereagh, articulated a strong position, calling for the preservation of Britain's maritime rights (i.e., impressment of British subjects on the high seas), the protection of aboriginals in North America, and the maintenance of Britain's alliance with them, border adjustments to minimize future border disputes between Canada and the United States, and a resolution of east coast fishery access for American-flagged fishing vessels[71].

Castlereagh was particularly concerned with ensuring the creation of an aboriginal buffer state between Canada and the United States and to obtain control of the Great Lakes. Fearing a naval arms race in the future between the imperial government and the United States on the Great Lakes Castlereagh wished to have all of the Great Lakes placed within Canadian territory but he recognized that the United States would never agree to that. Instead, he instructed his diplomats to seek the removal of all US naval vessels from the Great Lakes and a restriction limiting American marine activities on the Great Lakes to commercial activities only[72].

None of Castlereagh's demands were palatable to the American public however, and the Americans were heartened in September 1814 by a successful defence at Baltimore where a British amphibious operation was repulsed (and an American lawyer on a mercy mission penned the words that became the US national anthem, the Star-Spangled Banner). Faced with European instability, war, (tax) weariness at home, and the prospect of a protracted war in North America, the Prime Minister, Lord Liverpool, instructed Castlereagh to have done with it and settle with America. The resulting Treaty of Ghent restored the situation on the ground as it had existed in 1812 without territorial aggrandizement on either side. The United States

71. Mark Zuehlke, *For Honour's Sake: the War of 1812 and the Brokering of an Uneasy Peace* (Toronto: Alfred A Knopf Canada, 2006) 297.
72. Ibid, 310.

withdrew its troops from the Sandwich and Amherstburg frontier area in the extreme south-west of Upper Canada (including Fort Malden and the Amherstburg dockyard) which it had occupied after Barclay's defeat and Proctor's withdrawal. The colonial government had taken some US territory around Prairie du Chien near Lake Superior in what is now the state of Wisconsin and that territory, together with a part of Maine (which was then part of the State of Massachusetts) that had been taken by the British in a seaborne assault, was returned to the United States.

The United States did not gain any protection from impressment for those of its citizens that were dual citizens of both the United States and Great Britain but with the end of the Napoleonic War the Royal Navy was reduced in size and the British no longer found it necessary to stop ships on the high seas for impressment. Britain obtained no concessions regarding the aboriginal population in the Old Northwest of the United States and the west remained open to future American domination of the aboriginal population. The old alliance of the western aboriginal nations and the Crown of Great Britain could no longer be maintained.

The treaty was signed on Christmas Eve of 1814 but news of the peace did not reach North America before one last major engagement was fought at the Battle of New Orleans. There, a significant British regular army force under the command of General Edward Pakenham, the Duke of Wellington's brother-in-law, was defeated by an American force under Major General Andrew Jackson. That battle ultimately had no military significance for the outcome of the war since the peace treaty had already been signed (although it was not until February that the US Senate was able to ratify it) but the victory allowed Americans to end the war on an emotional high note and gave the country confidence.

What did the war accomplish? In the end it did not accomplish very much, in practical terms. The United States did not achieve its political and military objectives in relation to Great Britain or Canada. Neither the United States nor Great Britain, or Canada, acquired any additional territory as a result of war conquests. And yet the war is often viewed as a successful draw, at least from the American and Canadian viewpoints, although the war is often overlooked in Great Britain.

For the United States, the destruction of the aboriginal confederacy that Tecumseh had worked so hard to accomplish was of considerable benefit. Never again would the United States have to contend with a sophisticated aboriginal political opposition to its western expansion. The way was clear to expand into the west and although conflict with the aboriginals would be present they would be dealt with separately, as individual tribes, and either cowed into submission or suppressed with superior military force. The British were obliged to observe that process and could no longer foment discord towards the United States among the western tribes. The country as a whole was more cohesive coming out of the war as it had successfully fought off the superpower of the age, and the final victory at New Orleans gave psychological force to the public feeling of accomplishment. The US Navy had emerged from the war covered with glory as it had succeeded on the lakes and on the high seas. The renown won by American sailors in the war would form an important part of the narrative of the US Navy in the years to come. The US Army had not done as well but the United States would reform its army practices by ceasing to rely on state militias as the backbone of its forces and would develop a more professional army service.

For Canada, the War of 1812 was also significant. It too, developed a sense of cohesiveness as a result of the war and, in fact, it was the war that began to develop a national consciousness among the inhabitants of Canada. Before the war, it was common for the Anglophone inhabitants of Canada to refer to themselves as Americans. Only the Francophone inhabitants were referred to as Canadians. After the war, the population as a whole began to refer to themselves as Canadian, despite their linguistic differences. The common defence of Canadian territory by the Anglophone and Francophone militia had given the population (or at least the Anglophone component) a new perspective of themselves as a people that were different from Americans. And although it was not true, the myth of the militia as the prime defenders of Canada during the war contributed to the development of national feeling. That the colonies had been preserved at all was a major achievement in the eyes of many, and for the Canadian elites it gave impetus to their efforts to preserve a form of monarchical government linked to Great Britain in North America.

For Great Britain the war resulted in the maintenance of the status quo in its empire. The North American colonies had been retained, a result that was unexpected to some. The Duke of Wellington had actually expressed surprise that his colleagues in the British military had successfully defended Canada from the United States. However, its alliance with the aboriginal tribes along the western frontier adjacent to American territory was broken and could not be mended again, which diminished British political influence in the interior of the continent. Although the military had performed well enough, its victories had also been matched by defeats foreshadowing the growing power of the United States in the New World, a disquieting thought. The defeats suffered by the Royal Navy were particularly worrisome as Britain prided itself on the efficacy of its navy. A mixed bag then, but at the end of the day the lustre of the world's leading power had not been crucially dimmed by the outcome of the war. Yet there was a lingering concern about managing future relationships in North America.

For the aboriginal population adjacent to the territories of the

United States there were only defeats, and the loss of their great champion, Chief Tecumseh. Never again would great aboriginal nations such as the once-dominant Iroquois confederacy contend with the settler political entities after the dissipation of the aboriginal confederacy that Tecumseh sought to entrench. Within the territory of the colonial government relations remained well enough and violence between the colonial authorities and the aboriginal first nations did not occur. South of the border in the United States it would be a different story, and relations would worsen as Americans continually pushed back the western frontier throughout the nineteenth century.

On the lakes, as the war ended, the various officials in each country would turn their minds to the naval question and seek to determine the best solution for maintaining peace on the lakes into the future.

1815-1818 THE RUSH-BAGOT AGREEMENT: THE NEGOTIATION

As the spring of 1815 came to North America Canadians could look with a grim relief at the narrow escape of the country from the American invasion. Despite odds favouring the success of American arms the colonial government (with the sustained support of the imperial government) and its military commanders in the field had maintained a successful defence of the colonial realm. Unlike the American Revolutionary War, or the Seven Years War, the American strategists in the War of 1812 never effectively capitalized on the weaknesses of Canada's position by seeking to cut the Quebec – Montreal – Kingston supply line through a successful invasion of the country along the Lake Champlain – Richelieu River invasion route, or by taking Kingston during one of the periods in which Commodore Chauncey could exert naval supremacy on Lake Ontario[1]. Instead, much of the American effort was expended farther to the west, along the Detroit River frontier. Faced with two competing strategic objectives, the conquest of Canada or the conquest of the western first nations, the US government vacillated. The result of American hesitancy over competing strategic objectives

---

1. American historian Alan Taylor suggests that the Madison Administration was being unduly sensitive to the private interests of a wealthy American financier by avoiding a contest along the St. Lawrence River frontier that might have cut the essential supply line from Lower Canada to the front line forces in Upper Canada. (Taylor, *The Civil War of 1812: American Citizens, British Subjects, Irish Rebels & Indian Allies*, 269, 274).

was a narrow escape from conquest for the Canadian colonial government.

Sixty years of intermittent warfare had now confirmed to Canadians that the maritime defence of the Great Lakes and of Lake Champlain was vital to the overall defence of the country. In three great conflicts during this period the country had been successfully invaded twice (in 1759 and 1775), after the country's naval defences had crumbled, and one invasion had resulted in the conquest of the country. In the third and final conflict multiple invasions of the country were ultimately unsuccessful because the naval defences on Lake Ontario and Lake Champlain had held, allowing only the extreme south-west of Upper Canada to fall into American hands after the army was forced to retreat by the loss of naval supremacy on Lake Erie. These lessons were likewise not lost on the imperial authorities in London who were ultimately responsible for the country's defences.

The naval arms race which had occurred on Lake Ontario (and which was beginning on Lake Champlain in the latter stages of the war) was worrisome to both London and Washington. In 1812 the Provincial Marine consisted of four ships fitted out with 20 guns and manned by 205 seamen but by 1815 the naval force protecting Canada on the Great Lakes had expanded to nine warships fitted out with 518 guns and manned by 1600 Royal Navy officers and seamen, with two additional 100-gun warships building on the stocks[2]. A similar and equally significant expansion of the US naval forces on the Great Lakes had also occurred as a result of the war. If the war had continued into another year, there would have been more than one ship of the line in operation on Lake Ontario, and the naval shipbuilding escalation would have continued at great expense to both countries. The incongruity of maintaining fleets of ships of the line on the Great Lakes at a time when national governments

2. John R. Grodzinski, "April 1813: Naval Base, Point Frederick", *Veritas*, Kingston, Summer 2012, 22 at 24.

lacked many of the tools for revenue collection, and enhancement, and faced fiscal pressures, loomed large in the minds of the political actors in both countries. Secretary of State James Monroe worried about the policy of naval augmentation on the Great Lakes, which he regarded as dangerous and likely to promote a collision between Britain and Canada on the one hand, and the United States on the other, a view which he expressed to the new British minister in Washington, Charles Bagot[3].

In Washington, the politicians in Congress were particularly anxious to see a reduction in national government expenditures on armaments with the conclusion of the war. On February 17, 1815 (which was the same day that the Senate voted on ratification of the Treaty of Ghent) a resolution calling for the reduction of the US Navy's freshwater forces was passed and only ten days later formal legislation to permit President Madison to demobilize and dispose of the freshwater squadrons was enacted[4]. The view in Washington was that naval armaments on the lakes would only be required if the British insisted upon maintaining a large naval force. If expenditures were not required public funds for defence would be best allocated to other requirements, such as the nation's seagoing navy and coastal fortifications. Worked was stopped on the ships which were under construction and Master Commandant Woolsey, now restored to the command he held at the outbreak of the war, began to roof over his major vessels[5].

The unilateral winding down of American naval forces on the lakes was not an adequate policy for President Madison however. For America, it was essential that the threat of aboriginal uprisings on the western frontier be eliminated. The United

3. Terence Fay, *Rush-Bagot Agreement: A Reflection of the Anglo-American Detente, 1815-1818* (Washington: Georgetown University, 1975), 224.
4. AL Burt, *The United States, Great Britain and British North America*, 388.
5. Malcolmson, *Warships of the Great Lakes*, 135.

States viewed the Royal Navy's squadrons on the Great Lakes as an instrument of British control over the aboriginal population, and the United States simply could not accept the prospect of Great Britain continuing to exercise some measure of political control over the American aboriginal population through the instrument of the Royal Navy[6]. Secretary Monroe, writing to John Quincy Adams, the American minister in London acknowledged the supremacy of the Royal Navy on Lake Ontario and the necessity for that in order for the British to protect Canada but he also held that the preservation of the existing American naval supremacy on the upper lakes was essential in order for the United States to control the aboriginal first nations within its own borders[7]. Adams, however, believed that a larger navy was essential for the United States to maintain a deterrent against Great Britain[8].

On the other side of the border Commodore Yeo departed and work stopped on the two new first-rate warships[9]. A brief resumption of the Royal Navy's prewar practice of stopping US ships to search for deserters along the Detroit River frontier resulted in American protests, particularly from Governor Cass of Michigan. The wrangling over this practice came to a head after the armed schooner *Tecumseth* stopped an American merchantman, the *Union* in the summer of 1816 and was resolved when the imperial government instructed its officers on the lakes to desist in the practice of stopping American ships on the Detroit River to search for deserters. These new instructions became standard throughout the Great Lakes and eventually on the high seas. A major cause of the War of 1812 was quietly resolved on the Detroit River[10]. The authorities now recognized that the vulnerability of Amherstburg precluded its prewar role

6. Fay, *Rush-Bagot Agreement*, 221.
7. Ibid, 225.
8. Ibid, 227.
9. Malcolmson, *Warships of the Great Lakes*, 136.
10. Alan Taylor, *The Civil War of 1812, 435.*

as a major dockyard and work began on the construction of a new main dockyard for the Royal Navy at Penetanguishene, on Lake Huron, with another new naval depot planned for the mouth of the Grand River near what is now Port Maitland[11]. Yet the growing power of the United States certainly gave the British pause to consider the prospects of future success against the United States. In 1816, the Royal Navy's commander on the North American station noted that Canada was too distant from Great Britain to be successfully defended[12]. The Royal Navy could not access the Great Lakes from the ocean and the lake defence could only be maintained by a dedicated lake fleet. Since the United States was now possessed of a growing demographic and industrial power, it would, in the future, have a natural advantage in any naval arms race on the lakes. It was clear that the imperial government would be forced into an expensive and interminable shipbuilding competition to maintain a Canadian defence. That would be a strain on imperial government finances at a time when Great Britain faced growing worldwide imperial commitments. The Duke of Wellington counselled the imperial government not to look to Canada in the future as a base of offensive operations against the United States because the country could no longer be successfully defended by imperial arms. The imperial government also had to consider that Britain had suffered economically during the long wars against France and was much in need of a peace dividend through a major reduction in military expenditures.

Thus, both Great Britain and the United States were disposed to find ways to avoid future expenditures on landlocked fleets, a motivation that was welcome in Canada where large parts of western Upper Canada still showed the scars of war. Several times in the past United States diplomats had suggested the demilitarization of fortifications and naval forces along the

11. Barry Gough, Fighting Sail on Lake Huron and Georgian Bay, 140.
12. Ibid, 145.

border between the United States and Canada. John Adams had made the initial suggestion during the negotiations that led to the Treaty of Paris in 1783, and it was raised again by John Jay in the negotiations that led to the Jay Treaty in 1794[13]. On both occasions the British government had demurred, and for good reason. A demilitarized border would inevitably have favoured the United States since the lack of lake squadrons and fortified land bases would have allowed the United States to easily invade and conquer Canada in the event of another conflict between the United States and Great Britain[14]. When peace negotiations took place at Ghent in 1814, one of the American diplomats, Albert Gallatin, once again raised the prospect of disarmament on the Great Lakes but although informal discussion of the subject occurred between the negotiating teams nothing came of it[15].

Despite revenue pressures, the imperial government had forged ahead with its plans to maintain a sufficient naval establishment on the Great Lakes to deter American aggression, or to meet it head-on if it materialized. The imperial government planned to maintain ten warships in readiness on the Great Lakes and on Lake Champlain[16]. Officials in Washington feared that Great Britain would not only keep a strong naval force on the Great Lakes but would also attempt to add to the number of its existing warships on the lakes[17]. The United States now decided to try to forestall the need for large naval armaments on the lakes. This time, the United States decided not to seek a demilitarization of the border region, perceiving that Great Britain would not be receptive to such an entreaty. Rather, the United States decided

13. A L Burt, *The United States, Great Britain and British North America*, 33; Don Courtney Piper, *The International Law of the Great Lakes*, 105.
14. C P Stacey, *The Undefended Border: The Myth and the Reality* (Ottawa: Canadian Historical Association, 1953 (1996)), 4.
15. Fay, *Rush-Bagot Agreement*, 28.
16. Barry Gough, *Fighting Sail on Lake Huron and Georgian Bay*, 147.
17. James Morton Callahan, *The Neutrality of the American Lakes and Anglo-American Relations* (Baltimore; John Hopkins Press, 1898) 66.

to advance the concept of a bilateral naval arms limitation agreement with respect to the lakes.

John Quincy Adams, the US Ambassador to the Court of St. James in London, reported in August that the British still intended to maintain freshwater naval forces in North America. On November 16, 1815, Secretary of State James Monroe wrote to Adams and instructed him to propose a limitation of naval armaments on the Great Lakes[18]. In his instructions to Ambassador Adams Monroe assessed the dangers of a naval arms race on the lakes stating to Adams that a naval arms race would require huge expenditures by both sides and would increase the risk that through some misadventure hostilities might erupt again on the lakes. To forestall that, Monroe advised that the President was open to limiting the naval forces of each state on the Great Lakes and Lake Champlain to a moderate, and preferably small number of vessels, or even to dispense with any armed vessels on the lakes except those required for revenue enforcement[19].

Adams carried out his instructions during a meeting he subsequently held with the British Foreign Minister, Viscount Castlereagh, on January 25, 1816. Castlereagh was taken aback by the US initiative and he was inclined to be suspicious of it[20]. Castlereagh was concerned with how disarmament could prejudice the military position of the imperial government because its supply train to Canada was much farther than anything the Americans would have to contend with. However, he eventually saw the merit in avoiding a system of escalating armaments production on the Great Lakes[21]. Nevertheless, the discussions between Minister Adams and Viscount Castlereagh

18. A L Burt, *The United States, Great Britain and British North America*, 388.
19. Rt. Hon. Sir Charles Fitzpatrick (Chief Justice) *An Address Delivered by the Rt. Hon. Sir Charles Fitzpatrick Before the Lawyers Club, New York City, March 17, 1917* (private publication, 1917) 5.
20. Ibid.
21. A L Burt, *The United States, Great Britain and British North America*, 389.

ended with Castlereagh expressing only lukewarm support on the subject and promising to consult with his cabinet colleagues further about it. Adams reported back to Secretary Monroe on January 31, 1816, and gave the opinion that he did not expect the proposal to be accepted since it was obvious that the United States would have the advantage in any renewed conflict between the two states. The United States could build a new lake fleet much more quickly than the British could[22]. Adams opinion prompted a further response from Secretary Monroe who told him:

"The increase of naval armaments on one side upon the lakes during peace, will necessitate the like increase on the other, and besides causing an aggravation of useless expense to both parties, must operate as a continual stimulus of suspicion and of ill-will upon the inhabitants and local authorities of the borders against those of their neighbours. The moral and political tendency of such a system must be to war and not to peace[23]."

Adams wrote to Castlereagh to emphasize that a naval arms limitation agreement on the Great Lakes would still preserve great advantages to Great Britain. The British army in Canada and the maritime provinces exceeded the size of the US army, and the Royal Navy would remain dominant on the oceans and seas. Furthermore, Canada could not be the subject of a surprise attack by the United States since Congress would have to debate war and to formally declare it, giving both the colonial governments in Canada as well as the imperial government time to prepare for war[24]. Still believing that any prospects of an agreement with Great Britain were dismal, Ambassador Adams advised Secretary Monroe on March 30, 1816, that the American proposals were unlikely to be accepted[25].

22. Fitzpatrick, *An Address Delivered by the Rt. Hon. Sir Charles Fitzpatrick*, 6.
23. Quoted in Fitzpatrick, *An Address Delivered by the Rt. Hon. Sir Charles Fitzpatrick*, 6.
24. Fay, *Rush-Bagot Agreement*, 217.
25. Fitzpatrick, *An Address Delivered by the Rt. Hon. Sir Charles Fitzpatrick*, 8.

But by April, the British government had come around to the American way of thinking about the naval question on the North American lakes. Although technically the entry into an agreement was a matter for the whole cabinet to decide upon and to recommend to the Prince Regent, in reality this was a question that mainly concerned the Foreign Minister. Castlereagh had to weigh a number of competing factors. Another war with the United States was certainly possible and as the experience of the past wars had shown command of the lakes was essential for the defence of Canada. While the proposed agreement would not preclude a naval defence of the country, it would be much easier for the United States to ramp up its naval force on the lakes in both numbers of ships and the number of seaman than it would be for the colonial government in Canada, or for Britain, to do likewise. Canada might be lost as a consequence of a misjudgement by the imperial government on this issue. Furthermore, British naval opinion was averse to an agreement[26].

On the other hand, Castlereagh was conscious of the enormous expense that might be required in order to match the United States in a naval arms race on the Great Lakes, and he felt a political urgency to reduce military expenditures now that Britain's Napoleonic wars were in the past[27]. The incongruity of a massive battleship such as the *St. Lawrence*, constructed at great expense and now condemned to sail perpetually around Lake Ontario, may have influenced Castlereagh's thinking on this subject. HMS *St. Lawrence* was the dominant warship in the Americas but it would never leave Lake Ontario. Huge naval ships on the landlocked Great Lakes would have no enemy other than the opposite country's vessels. The opposing commanders and crews would heighten international tensions by a super-vigilant watchfulness of the other side, compounded by professional speculations on who would come out victorious in

26. C P Stacey, *The Undefended Border*, 5.
27. Fay, *Rush-Bagot Agreement*, 9.

any contest between them[28]. Both sides would live in perpetual fear of the other power's fleet descending upon its shores in a swift and bold attack. Taking a larger view of the question Castlereagh opted to accept the risks of an arms limitation agreement with the United States.

Minister Adams was summoned to meet with Castlereagh on April 9, 1816, and, as Adams reported to Monroe, Castlereagh gave his endorsement, in principle, to the American suggestion, and asked if Adams had authority to enter into a formal agreement on the subject. Adams did not have formal authority and he was forthright enough with Castlereagh to express uncertainty about whether he would soon obtain such instructions. Castlereagh then suggested that it might be best for him to place the matter in the hands of the British Minister in Washington, Charles Bagot, a suggestion to which Adams readily acceded[29].

Meanwhile, in Washington, Secretary Monroe had become impatient and he broached the subject directly to Minister Bagot on May 2, 1816. Bagot knew nothing about the subject however, not yet having been acquainted of the American initiative by Castlereagh. Lacking instructions, Bagot could only report on the subject back to London. In doing so, Bagot represented that by agreeing to Monroe's proposal Great Britain would inevitably put Canada in a compromised military position, a prospect that Castlereagh was certainly alive to. However, even if that were true (and it was true) the only alternative for Great Britain was to engage in an expensive naval shipbuilding competition with America in peacetime that would be expensive and might ultimately be proved futile given the growing economic strength of the United States[30].

28. Fitzpatrick, *An Address Delivered by the Rt. Hon. Sir Charles Fitzpatrick*, 8.
29. A L Burt, *The United States, Great Britain and British North America*, 389.
30. Ibid, 390.

Castlereagh wrote to Bagot in Washington, advising in a dispatch dated April 23rd of the discussions that had taken place in London and instructing him to negotiate with Monroe with a view to accepting any precise formulation of a naval arms limitation *ad referendum*. Bagot was further instructed to consult with the colonial government in Canada on the subject as part of his approach to the United States[31].

Charles Bagot came from the English aristocracy and he had gained exposure to foreign affairs by his association with George Canning, who had served as British Foreign Minister before the War of 1812. However, Bagot had held no office for a considerable period of time before and during the war, and he had little direct diplomatic experience before he took up the post of minister plenipotentiary and envoy extraordinary to the United States of America on July 31, 1815, at the age of 34. Consequently, the negotiations for the naval arms limitation agreement became one of his first major diplomatic tests[32]. His mentor, Canning, had counselled Bagot on the virtue of equanimity in embarking upon such a sensitive assignment so soon after the conclusion of hostilities, particularly as the Americans were aware that Britain, despite its great strength, had obtained only divided success against the United States[33]. To add lustre to Bagot in what was appreciated to be a difficult assignment Bagot was made a member of the Privy Council before departing from Britain with his young wife Mary, the niece of the Duke of Wellington[34]. The Bagots quickly ingratiated themselves into Washington society.

Bagot commenced negotiations with Monroe in July 1816. Monroe emphasized to Bagot that President Madison wanted a

31. Ibid, 391.
32. Jacques Monet, "Bagot, Sir Charles," *Dictionary of Canadian Biography*, Vol VII, University of Toronto/Universite Laval, 1983.
33. Fitzpatrick, *An Address Delivered by the Rt. Hon. Sir Charles Fitzpatrick*, 10.
34. Fay, *Rush-Bagot Agreement*, 212.

naval agreement to be given priority with respect to all of the extant diplomatic issues between the two countries, and that a precise formulation of any limitation agreement was seen as necessary from the American perspective[35]. The result of the face to face negotiations between Monroe and Bagot invited the exchange of letters and memoranda to further the objects of the negotiations[36].

Following Castlereagh's instructions, Bagot wrote formally to Secretary Monroe on July 26, 1816, inquiring about the American proposals for limiting naval armaments on the Great Lakes. Monroe responded promptly by replying one week later stating that the United States proposed that both countries limit their naval armaments on the Great Lakes to one vessel not exceeding one hundred-tons burden and armed with a single eighteen-pound cannon on Lake Ontario, and, on the upper lakes to two vessels also of one hundred tons burden, each to be armed with a single eighteen-pound cannon, and on the waters of Lake Champlain to one vessel not exceeding the like burden of one hundred tons and similarly armed with a single eighteen-pound cannon. All other armed vessels on the Great Lakes and Lake Champlain would be dismantled forthwith, and the two countries would neither build nor arm any other vessel on the Great Lakes. The naval forces of each party maintained on the Great Lakes and Lake Champlain would thereafter be restricted in its duty, to the protection of the country's revenue laws, the transportation of troops and goods, and such other services that would not interfere with the armed vessels of the other party

35. Ibid.
36. The full text of the correspondence exchanged between Minister Bagot and Secretary Monroe on the subject of limiting naval armaments on the Great Lakes can be accessed at the following location: Avalon Project, (http://avalon.law.yale.edu/) Lillian Goldman Law Library, Yale University, New Haven, Conn., Ambassador Charles Bagot, and Secretary of State James Monroe. The source for the documents archived in the Yale University Avalon Project are: Hunter Miller, ed., *Treaties and Other International Acts of the United States of America, Vol 2*, Documents 1-40: 1776-1818, (Washington: Government Printing Office, 1931).

to the agreement. Finally if either of the parties subsequently formed an opinion that the arrangement did not accomplish the objectives that were intended by the agreement, and desired to withdraw from it, that party could give a formal notice to the other party of its intent to withdraw from the agreement and after the expiration of the notice period prescribed by the agreement it would be void and of no further effect. Monroe suggested that if Bagot had authority to enter into an agreement on these terms Monroe had instructions from the President to immediately enter into an agreement for this purpose and that such agreement could be embodied in a formal convention between the two states, or, in an exchange of notes, or in any other form that suited Great Britain. If Bagot did not have authority to enter into a formal permanent agreement but did have sufficient authority to enter into an interim agreement for the same purpose Monroe would be happy to enter into such an interim arrangement. If Bagot did not feel that his authority extended so far as an interim arrangement Monroe still inquired whether Great Britain and the United States might agree to at least suspend all further naval construction on the Great Lakes or the equipping of naval vessels. The exchange was revealing as it showed that Monroe was under great pressure from the President to achieve an agreement that would remove the offensive force of the Royal Navy from the Great Lakes, and to dispense with the need for the United States to continue to invest in naval armaments along its northern shoreline[37].

Bagot replied promptly, and in an agreeable manner, carefully noting that the views of both the colonial government in Canada and the admiralty were required before he could express any commitments, which compelled him to refer the matter to the imperial government in London. However, Bagot was open to entering into an interim commitment on his own authority to suspend the construction and fitting out of any British armed

37. Ibid, Secretary of State James Monroe to Ambassador Charles Bagot.

vessels on the lakes while awaiting the views of his home government. On August 6th he wrote back to Secretary Monroe expressing his intention to refer the matter to London but in the meantime expressing his agreement to the suspension of any further construction or equipping of war vessels on the Great Lakes and Lake Champlain[38].

Secretary Monroe was somewhat disappointed with this result, as he hoped to implement an agreement between the United States and Great Britain on this subject immediately. Both Madison and Monroe were anxious to conclude an agreement with Britain as soon as possible. Monroe therefore wrote back to Ambassador Bagot and pressed him to at least enter into an interim agreement to restrict new naval armaments on the lakes pending the receipt of instructions for Bagot from the imperial government in London. Failing that, Monroe remained open to Bagot's proposal that further construction and equipping of war vessels on the lakes should be suspended but he insisted that the United States would require up to date information concerning all existing deployments of ships of the Royal Navy on the Great Lakes. He wrote to Bagot in those terms on August 12, 1816[39].

Bagot however, would not enter into any arrangements that went beyond his authority in the absence of instructions from London incorporating the views of the navy and the colonial government. He immediately wrote a letter back to Monroe on August 13th explaining this limitation in the plainest terms. However, he did accept the American Secretary's point about the need for intelligence on the current strength and deployment of Royal Navy units on the lakes and promised to obtain that information for the Americans. As a further concession to Monroe, Bagot unilaterally pledged that all "further augmentation" of the British lake forces would be immediately halted[40].

38. Ibid, Ambassador Charles Bagot to Secretary of State James Monroe.
39. Ibid, Secretary of State James Monroe to Ambassador Charles Bagot.

There the matter rested for the time being. In the interim however, the British government continued to take steps to reinforce Canada with war materiel, raising American anxieties. James Monroe wrote to Ambassador Adams in London complaining that "The limited powers that were given to Mr. Bagot had much appearance that the object was to amuse us rather than to adopt any effectual measure. The supply in the interim of Canada with a vast amount of cannons and munitions is a circumstance which has not escaped attention[41]."

Despite American concerns, Bagot had written to Commodore Owen, the Royal Navy's commander on the lakes on August 14th, apprising him of the negotiations and requesting that he refrain from any further augmentation of the lake forces pending an agreement with the United States. Bagot also requested an up to date statement of the status of the Royal Navy establishment on the lakes[42].

Monroe's anxieties were assuaged, as Ambassador Bagot was true to his word and on November 4, 1816, he sent to Secretary Monroe the following statement concerning the existing naval forces belonging to the Crown on the Great Lakes and Lake Champlain:

"Statement of His Majesty's Naval Force on the Lakes of Canada 1st September 1816.

Lake Ontario.

St Lawrence can carry 110 guns-laid up in ordinary.
Psyche [in service] 50 guns.
Princess Charlotte [in service] 40 guns.
Niagara 20 [guns]. Condemned as unfit for service.
Charwell 14 [guns] Hauled up in the mud condemned likewise

40. Ibid, Ambassador Charles Bagot to Secretary of State James Monroe.
41. Quoted in Fitzpatrick, *An Address Delivered by the Rt. Hon. Sir Charles Fitzpatrick*, 10.
42. Fay, *Rush-Bagot Agreement*, 235.

Prince Regent 60 [guns]. In Commission but unequipped being merely used as a Barrack or receiving Ship and the Commander in Chief's Head Quarters

Montreal, in Commission carrying 6 guns used merely as a Transport for the service of His Majesty.

Star. Carrying 4 guns used for current duties only, and unfit for actual service. *Netley* Schooner. Carrying no guns attached for the most part to the Surveyors, and conveying His Majesty's servants from Port to Port.

There are besides the above some Row Boats capable of carrying long guns- 2 seventy four gun Ships on the Stocks, and one Transport of 400 Tons, used for conveying His Majesty's Stores from Port to Port.

On Lake Erie.

Tecumseth and *Newash* carrying 4 guns each, and *Huron* and *Sauk* which can carry 1 gun each. these Vessels are used principally to convey His Majesty's Servants and Stores from Port to Port.

On Lake Huron.

The *Confiance* and *Surprize* Schooners which may carry one gun each, and are used for purposes of Transport only.

On Lake Champlain.

12 gun Boats, 10 of which are laid up in ordinary, and the other two (one of which mounts 4 guns and the other 3 guns) used as guard boats, besides the above there are some small row Boats which are laid up as unfit for service.

Keel, Stem, and Stern Port of a Frigate laid down at the Isle Aux Noix.

(signed) J BEAUMGARDT
Captn of H. M. Ship *Prince Regent* and Senior Officer[43]."

Despite the fact that Monroe was seeking election to the presidency in the autumn of 1816, and was presumably occupied with that task, he responded only three days later with a memorandum explaining the disposition of the US naval forces on the lakes:

"On Lake Ontario

Brig *Jones* (18 guns). Retained for occasional service.
Schooner *Lady of the Lake* (1 gun). Employed in aid of the revenue laws.
Ship *New Orleans* (74 guns). On the stocks, building suspended.
Ship *Chippewa* (74 guns). On the stocks, building suspended
Ships *Superior* (44 guns), *Mohawk* (32 guns), *General Pike* (24 guns), *Madison* (18 guns); and the brigs *Jefferson* (18 guns), *Sylph* (16 guns), and *Oneida* (18 guns).

Dismantled.
Schooner *Raven*. Receiving vessel.
15 barges (each, 1 gun). Laid up for preservation.

On Lake Erie

Schooners *Porcupine* and *Chent*[44] (each, 1 gun). Employed in transporting stores. Ship *Detroit* (18 guns), and brigs *Lawrence* (20 guns), and *Queen Charlotte* (14 guns). Sunk at Erie.
Brig *Niagara* (18 guns). Dismantled at Erie.

On Lake Champlain

Ships *Confiance* (32 guns), and *Saratoga* (22 guns); brigs *Eagle* (12 guns), and *Sinnet* (16 guns); the schooner *Ticonderoga* (14 guns); and 6 galleys (each, 1 gun). All laid up at White Hall[45]."

43. Yale University, Avalon Project, Ambassador Charles Bagot to Secretary of State James Monroe.
44. A misspelling of "Ghent".
45. Yale University, Avalon Project, Secretary of State James Monroe to Ambassador Charles Bagot.

The very next day, November 8, 1816, Monroe wrote again to Bagot to confirm that orders had now been given to the US Navy not to augment its existing lake forces "beyond the limit of the British naval force[46]."

Monroe's letter of November 8th to Bagot crossed a letter from Bagot to Monroe of the same date in which Ambassador Bagot sought clarification from Monroe concerning the disposition of American forces on the upper Great Lakes[47]. Bagot was concerned that the American statement did not disclose the presence of any American naval forces on the upper lakes[48]. Monroe replied immediately to Bagot, reassuring him that US naval forces on Lake Erie also represented the American naval capacity on the upper lakes.

And there the matter rested while the imperial government in London considered final approval of the proposed agreement. In due course, after first obtaining the consent of the Prince Regent[49], following the receipt of the formal advice of the cabinet, Castlereagh instructed Ambassador Charles Bagot to enter into the proposed agreement with the United States. A final issue concerned the time for notice to be given to the other party in the case of a withdrawal from the agreement. Given the delays attendant in communications across the Atlantic ocean, Bagot pressed for a six-month notice instead of three months, which was acceptable to the United States[50].

It was now the spring of 1817 and Secretary of State James Monroe, having been elected President of the United States the previous autumn, succeeded Madison as President on March 4, 1817. Monroe chose as his new Secretary of State the American

---

46. Ibid.
47. Ibid, Ambassador Charles Bagot to Secretary of State James Monroe.
48. Ibid, Secretary of State James Monroe to Ambassador Charles Bagot.
49. A regency had been established in Great Britain under the Prince of Wales owing to the mental incompetency of King George III.
50. A L Burt, *The United States, Great Britain and British North America*, 394.

Ambassador to the Court of St. James in London, John Quincy Adams. However, it was not possible for Adams to immediately assume the post so veteran diplomat Richard Rush was appointed Acting Secretary of State. Although he had very little to do with the negotiation of the agreement, it would be Rush's name that would forever be associated with it instead of Monroe, who was primarily responsible for negotiating the agreement with British Ambassador Bagot. Indeed, a strong case can be made that the agreement ought to have been called the Monroe-Castlereagh Agreement because the two foreign ministers exercised the guiding hand in the diplomacy conducted over this issue by their respective countries. Nevertheless, history has recorded this agreement by the names of the principal actors who were present in Washington when the agreement between the United States and Great Britain was formalized.

The letters which formalized the agreement between the two nations (with Canada naturally considered part of Great Britain for the purposes of the agreement at this point in Canadian history) stated:

"April 28, 1817

The Undersigned, His Britannick Majesty's Envoy Extraordinary and Minister Plenipotentiary, has the honour to acquaint Mr Rush, that having laid before His Majesty's Government the correspondence which passed last year between the Secretary of the Department of State and the Undersigned upon the subject of a proposal to reduce the Naval Force of the respective Countries upon the American Lakes, he has received the Commands of His Royal Highness The Prince Regent to acquaint the Government of the United States, that His Royal Highness is willing to accede to the proposition made to the Undersigned by the Secretary of the Department of State in his note of the 2d of August last.

His Royal Highness, acting in the name and on the behalf of

His Majesty, agrees, that the Naval Force to be maintained upon the American Lakes by His Majesty and the Government of the United States shall henceforth be confined to the following Vessels on each side-that is

On Lake Ontario to one Vessel not exceeding one hundred Tons burthen and armed with one eighteen pound cannon.
On the Upper Lakes to two Vessels not exceeding like burthen each and armed with like force.
On the Waters of Lake Champlain to one Vessel not exceeding like burthen and armed with like force.

And His Royal Highness agrees, that all other armed Vessels on these Lakes shall be forthwith dismantled, and that no other Vessels of War shall be there built or armed

His Royal Highness further agrees, that if either Party should hereafter be desirous of annulling this Stipulation, and should give notice to that effect to the other Party, it shall cease to be binding after the expiration of six months from the date of such notice.

The Undersigned has it in command from His Royal Highness the Prince Regent to acquaint the American Government, that His Royal Highness has issued Orders to His Majestys Officers on the Lakes directing, that the Naval Force so to be limited shall be restricted to such Services as will in no respect interfere with the proper duties of the armed Vessels of the other Party.

The Undersigned has the honour to renew to Mr Rush the assurances of his highest consideration.

CHARLES BAGOT"[51]

51. Yale Avalon Project [Source: *Treaties and Other International Acts of the United States of America, Volume 2*, Documents 1-40 : 1776-1818, Edited by Hunter Miller, Washington, Government Printing Office, 1931]

"DEPARTMENT OF STATE,

April 29. 1817.

The Undersigned, Acting Secretary of State, has the honor to acknowledge the receipt of Mr Bagot's note of the 28th of this month, informing him that, having laid before the Government of His Britannick Majesty, the correspondence which passed last year between the Secretary of State and himself upon the subject of a proposal to reduce the naval force of the two countries upon the American Lakes, he had received the commands of His Royal Highness The Prince Regent to inform this Government that His Royal Highness was willing to accede to the proposition made by the Secretary of State in his note of the second of August last.

The Undersigned has the honor to express to Mr Bagot the satisfaction which The President feels at His Royal Highness The Prince Regent's having acceded to the proposition of this government as contained in the note alluded to. And in further answer to Mr Bagot's note, the Undersigned, by direction of The President, has the honor to state, that this Government, cherishing the same sentiments expressed in the note of the second of August, agrees, that the naval force to be maintained upon the Lakes by the United-States and Great Britain shall, henceforth, be confined to the following vessels on each side,- that is:

On Lake Ontario to one vessel not exceeding One Hundred Tons burden, and armed with one eighteen-pound cannon. On the Upper Lakes to two vessels not exceeding the like burden each, and armed with like force, and on the waters of Lake Champlain to one vessel not exceeding like burden and armed with like force.

And it agrees, that all other armed vessels on these Lakes shall be forthwith dismantled, and that no other vessels of war shall be there built or armed. And it further agrees, that if either party should hereafter be desirous of annulling this stipulation and should give notice to that effect to the other party, it shall cease to be binding after the expiration of six months from the date of such notice.

The Undersigned is also directed by The President to state, that proper orders will be forthwith issued by this Government to restrict the naval force thus limited to such services as will in no respect interfere with the proper duties of the armed vessels of the other party.

The Undersigned eagerly avails himself of this opportunity to tender to Mr Bagot the assurances of his distinguished consideration and respect.

RICHARD RUSH"[52]

The Rush-Bagot Agreement was now an accomplished fact. But what had it accomplished? Firstly, it prevented the construction and fitting out of new, incremental additions to the naval vessels of each state on the Great Lakes and Lake Champlain by limiting the number of naval vessels each side could maintain on the lakes. Naval ships were restricted to four on each side. One ship each was permitted to both nations on Lake Ontario and Lake Champlain but the ships were not to exceed one hundred-tons burden[53], and two ships were permitted to each nation on the upper lakes (i.e., Lakes Erie, Huron, Michigan and Superior). The warships on any of the lakes could only be armed with one eighteen-pounder long range cannon. At the time, the 18-pounder was the standard intermediate cannon armament on frigates and could fire a cannonball that would penetrate a foot of oak side-planking at one thousand yards. The number, size, and armament of these ships were judged sufficient for enforcement

---

52. Ibid.
53. An estimate of the tonnage of a ship during the age of sail that was based on the length and the maximum beam, or width of the ship expressed in a mathematical formula.

of the sovereignty and laws of each state on their respective sides of the border but the size of the gun would not pose a threat of significant offensive action against either state. The agreement permitted new construction of war vessels on the Great Lakes only for the purpose of replacing vessels that were worn out. With those restrictions the naval arms race on Lake Ontario, or on any of the other lakes, was consigned to history.

Secondly, to the extent that the existing squadrons on the lakes exceeded the permissible limits, either with respect to the number of ships, or the armament of existing ships, the agreement called upon the parties to lay up, dismantle, or divest, the surplus ships or armaments. The Rush-Bagot treaty was not a true disarmament agreement because there was no positive obligation on either party to remove all of the surplus ships and armaments from the lakes. In fact both sides laid-up ships that were no longer required under the terms of the agreement but which might be required in the future if hostilities once again developed between the two powers. Thus both sides maintained ships on the Great Lakes and Lake Champlain for some time after the agreement, as part of a reserve fleet. Those ships, described as laid-up in ordinary in the phraseology of the Royal Navy had all of their upper rigging and guns removed, together with the stores and other accoutrements of a ship of war and placed in the hands of a ship keeper with all other crew demobilized. The artifacts removed from the vessels were placed in storage and could be quickly obtained if relations between the two countries deteriorated once again in the future. Often, roofs were built over the decks of the ships that were laid-up to protect them from the elements, and the ships held in reserve slowly decayed over the ensuing years as they rested at anchors in port, or on the stocks.

Thirdly, the agreement stipulated that the permissible warships on the lakes were enjoined from interfering with the warships of the other nation that were engaged in their lawful pursuits.

This covenant was intended to minimize the frictions that could result if and when the armed ships of each nation found themselves in close proximity to each other on the lakes.

Finally, the agreement provided that either party could terminate the agreement but only upon giving a six-month notice to the other party. The notice period provided time for the recipient party to provide for its own naval defence on the lakes, as any notice to quit the agreement could only be interpreted by the other side as an anticipatory declaration of war.

Some matters that would later prove to be irritants were not addressed. For example, the use of special purpose vessels to enforce custom and revenue laws was not addressed in the agreement. Such vessels would require armaments in order to force a fleeing vessel to lay-up and be boarded but might not necessarily be considered naval vessels if, as was case, they were not under the control of the naval authorities in either country. Additionally, no mention was made of the possibility that a temporary augmentation of naval forces on the lakes might be required during periods of rebellion or insurgency. Finally, although it was not contemplated at the time, nothing in the agreement addressed the possibility of the construction of vessels on the Great Lakes for use on saltwater seas.

The major omission of the Agreement however, was the lack of anything in it with respect to the construction and maintenance of static fortifications, including naval bases. Although the Rush-Bagot Agreement has often been credited with demilitarizing the international border between the two countries that was not the case. The Rush-Bagot Agreement addressed naval forces on the Great Lakes but it did not impose any limitations concerning the maintenance of naval bases in the Great Lakes, or the creation of land-based fortifications. In the years following the agreement both sides, Great Britain in particular, would spend large sums of money on the construction of static fortifications in the Great Lakes region as a defence against a possible attack.

Despite its flaws and omissions however, the agreement was a good one. It drew out the fang of the Royal Navy which lay like a shadow across the Great Lakes and the Old Northwest of the United States, and it removed the risk of a sudden descent by warships of either country on any Great Lakes community. The six-month denouncement period prescribed by the Agreement gave Canada some assurance that it would be able to obtain help from Great Britain if the United States once again embarked on a warlike path.

In the aftermath of the signing of the Rush-Bagot Agreement both sides took the necessary steps to implement it. In British legal practice the agreement took effect immediately because the executive branch of the government had complete authority to enter into treaties and agreements with other states. From the British perspective it was unnecessary to enact any laws to implement the agreement. The required orders to the Royal Navy to conform to the agreement were well within the royal prerogative powers of the Prince Regent acting on the advice of his ministers.

In the United States however, the constitutional situation was less clear. Under the US constitution a treaty with a foreign power that was entered into by the President or another executive officer of the government required that the treaty be ratified by the US Senate in order to become binding upon the republic. Was the new agreement a treaty that was subject to the ratification of the Senate before it became effective[54]? Although President Madison did refer to the completion of the Rush-Bagot Agreement in his opening message to Congress in December

---

54. Terence Fay states that it remained an executive agreement until it was submitted to the Senate and ratified; Fay, *Rush-Bagot Agreement*, 249.

1817, he did not submit the agreement to the Senate for ratification.

Charles Bagot took advantage of a meeting with Secretary of State John Quincy Adams to inquire of Adams whether it was the intention of the President to submit the Rush-Bagot Agreement to the Senate for ratification. Adams subsequently discussed the matter with President Monroe who took the view that submission of the Agreement to the Senate was unnecessary. However, Adams noted that like documents were normally submitted at the opening of a session of Congress for the information of congressman and that had not been done in the case of the Rush-Bagot Agreement[55].

The concern lingered. President Monroe ultimately decided to send the Agreement to the Senate and ask it to consider whether its constitutional functions applied to an agreement of the kind represented by the Rush-Bagot Agreement. On April 6, 1818, President Monroe sent the Rush-Bagot Agreement to the Senate but was still unreconciled to the need for the Senate to "advise and consent," to the agreement. Monroe merely asked the Senate for its preliminary advice as to whether its agreement was actually required[56].

In the eternal struggle to define the boundaries between the separate legislative and executive branches of the United States government, the Senate chose not to answer the question posed by the President. Rather, it considered whether the agreement should receive the positive advice and consent of the Senate. Finding itself satisfied with the results of the diplomatic negotiations the Senate responded agreeably to the initiative and approved it ten days later by a resolution[57].

55. Yale Avalon Project, Hunter Miller's Notes on the Exchange of Notes 1817.
56. Ibid.
57. Ibid, Resolution of the Senate, dated April 16, 1818.

The final step in American constitutional practice was to proclaim the treaty in force through a presidential proclamation. A proclamation of the Rush-Bagot Agreement was issued on April 28, 1818, and printed in the leading newspapers of the day, and in the government's compilations of statutes and other important documents. With that, the Rush-Bagot Agreement came fully into force between the two North American states.

1818-1836 THE RUSH-BAGOT AGREEMENT: THE AFTERMATH

The Rush-Bagot Agreement marked a new departure in relations between Great Britain and the United States. Although in immediate terms it can be considered an American diplomatic victory because it removed the strongest branch of the British military from the interior of North America, where it could have continued to influence relations with aboriginal first nations during a time when the United States was seeking to consolidate its territory in the Old Northwest, it actually marks the start of a long detente and reconciliation between Great Britain and the United States that would ultimately lead to a close alliance between the two countries. For Great Britain, in particular, better relations with the United States would ease the access of British manufactured goods into the important American market. For Canada the agreement gave it relief from the prospect of a naval arms race along its southern border that could have led to a future war and it provided a basis for Canada to build its own security relationship with the United States in the future.

With the conclusion of the agreement both parties moved quickly to implement it. The US Secretary of the Navy, Benjamin Crowninshield, issued orders on May 2, 1817, for the reduction and maintenance of US naval forces on the lakes in compliance with the agreement, including the deployment of the schooners *Lady of the Lake* to Lake Ontario, and *Porcupine* and *Ghent* to the upper lakes, while a galley, *Allen*, was assigned to Lake Champlain[1].

On the Canadian side of the international boundary the Royal Navy also took steps to implement the agreement. In the midsummer of 1817 Captain Robert Hall commander of the lake force of the Royal Navy was ordered to pay off the ships and put them into reserve, with masts, guns, and stores removed[2]. As tensions eased, both sides gradually reduced their military investments in naval armaments along the lakes achieving a much sought-after peace dividend[3]. In its immediate aftermath, the Rush-Bagot Agreement resulted in the removal of 27 men-of-war from the Great Lakes and 1009 canons, carronades, and howitzers[4]. Of the 77 warships in service or on the stocks only eight small vessels remained after the agreement, and those were only armed with medium-sized naval weaponry. The Rush-Bagot Agreement removed 95% of the gross weight tonnage of the lake squadrons and 99% of their armaments[5]. It was a unique and significant diplomatic achievement in the post-Napoleonic world. Formal interstate warfare never again occurred on the Great Lakes, Lake Champlain, or on the St. Lawrence river west of Montreal[6].

The Agreement was well-received by the populations of the three countries. American newspapers commented favourably on it as a measure that would promote peace and goodwill. The Quaker publication, *Friend of Peace*, even called for the revocation notice period to be extended from six months to sixty years[7]! Leading

1. James Morton Callahan, *The Neutrality of the American Lakes*, 83.
2. Fay, *Rush-Bagot Agreement*, 47.
3. Jeremy Black, *Fighting for America*, 166.
4. Fay, *Rush-Bagot Agreement*, 250.
5. Ibid, 251.
6. As will be seen later, isolated acts of war and the suppression of rebellion and insurgency would bedevil this region in the middle of the nineteenth century leading to tensions between Great Britain, Canada, and the United States but formal war would be avoided. In the twentieth century, Canada would engage in naval warfare with Germany in the eastern St. Lawrence River.

American politicians maintained their ambivalent feelings towards Great Britain while Castlereagh promoted good relations with the United States in order to encourage British access to American markets[8].

The Royal Naval dockyard at Point Frederick in Kingston was maintained in operation as the chief naval depot in Upper Canada but it operated at a reduced capacity after the signing of the Rush-Bagot Agreement[9]. Among the last warships built at the Point Frederick naval dockyard was *HMS Radcliff*, possibly the same gunboat that was later sunk for preservation at Brown's Bay on the St. Lawrence River but subsequently raised and preserved as a historical artifact[10]. The former Provincial Marine dockyard at Amherstburg was closed due to its proximity to the United States and its consequential vulnerability to attack although Fort Malden was repaired and retained as a border fortification[11]. The proposed Grand River naval depot intended to replace the Amherstburg naval base was never completed. Although once intended to be a major naval station with up to one-thousand seamen and several warships it was abandoned and the work that had been done to prepare the site fell into ruin. The Royal Navy did build a new base at Penetanguishene on Lake Huron as a replacement for Amherstburg but it closed the base at Schooner Town on the Nottawasaga River, considering that site to be inadequate due to its lack of suitable shelter for ships and the danger of its shifting sand bar.

Holland Landing Naval Depot remained open for some years but

7. Fay, *Rush-Bagot Agreement*, 255.
8. Ibid, 258.
9. www.romc.ca/cam/mus/history-histoire-eng.asp (accessed 2011-07-15).
10. The vessel can be seen today preserved at Fort Wellington, in Prescott, Ontario.
11. After the creation of the Canadian Coast Guard in 1962, a coast guard base was reestablished at Amherstburg in 1965, carrying on the local tradition of a Crown marine base that had been established by the Provincial Marine in the eighteenth and nineteenth centuries. A provincial re-enactment society dedicated to preserving the historical memory of the Provincial Marine is also based at Amherstburg in the former Commissariat Building on the site of the King's Navy Yard.

operations gradually migrated from that place to the new naval base at Penetanguishene and the depot at Holland Landing began to languish. It was finally closed in the 1830's, when all of its remaining functions were transferred to Penetanguishene.

Both the Royal Navy and the United States Navy took steps to preserve their existing warships on the lakes in reserve. The ships were demobilized and the spars and rigging as well as all armaments were removed. The ships were then roofed over to protect them from the elements and preserved thus they remained a curiosity for many years afterwards[12]. Some of the ships were sunk in their harbours to preserve them, or kept as barrack-ships, while the smaller vessels were sold into the merchant trade[13].

The United States Navy closed its naval stations on Lake Champlain (Whitehall), Lake Ontario (Sackett's Harbour) and on Lake Erie (Presque Isle) in 1825[14]. However, the partially built ship of the line *New Orleans*, which had been building at the end of the war was preserved on the building stocks. A boathouse was built over the uncompleted first rate warship and there it remained for many decades. A winter storm destroyed the boathouse in 1880, which prompted the navy to sell the ship for its value as scrap in 1883[15]. The *Chippewa*, also a first rate that was on the stocks at the war's end, was sold for scrap in 1833[16]. Detroit's Fort Lernoult was renamed Fort Shelby after Detroit was retaken during the war and the US Army maintained a post there until 1826, after which the abandoned fort was given over to the municipality[17].

In 1831, the Admiralty decided that the political situation in

12. Costain, *Path of Destiny*, 332.
13. Lardas, *Great Lakes Warships 1812-1815*, 27-28.
14. Ibid, 30.
15. Malcolmson, *Warships of the Great Lakes*, 144.
16. Ibid, 142.
17. Mason, *Detroit, Fort Lernoult and the American Revolution*, 21.

Canada no longer required it to maintain a naval presence on the lakes. Consequently, Commodore Barrie, then commanding the lake forces, received orders to dispose of all of his ships, whether afloat, or on shore, and by sale if possible. Accordingly, Barrie put all of the Royal Navy vessels up for public tenders. Only one warship, the great battleship *HMS St. Lawrence*, which was used as a barracks after the war, and then roofed over, evinced any interest among buyers. It sold for 25 pounds to merchant Robert Drummond of Kingston who put the hulk to use as a cordwood dock for lake steamers. Subsequently, the hulk of the *St. Lawrence* was sunk in the lake[18]. Receiving no other offers for his ships, Commodore Barrie sunk them in Dead Man Bay, in Lake Ontario[19]. In March 1834 Barrie was ordered to close all Royal Navy bases on the lakes and Barrie himself was recalled to Great Britain, thus ending the active deployment of the Royal Navy on the Great Lakes[20]. Subsequent to 1838 the Royal Navy no longer maintained any record of ships in the service of the navy on the North American lakes[21].

While the navies on the lakes declined in strength, the opposite was occurring with respect to marine transportation. Throughout the postwar years merchant traffic on the Great Lakes continued to grow. Canadians had always used canoes and bateaux to move goods across the country and during the sovereignty of France schooners and sloops had plied the St. Lawrence River. Under British sovereignty, civilian merchantmen had been built to operate private transport services in addition to the officially sanctioned Provincial Marine on the Great Lakes and Durham boats, a type of flat-bottomed scow, became prevalent on the St. Lawrence River[22].

18. Townsend, *The Story of HMS St. Lawrence*, 24.
19. Costain, *The Path of Destiny*, 332.
20. Malcolmson, *Warships of the Great Lakes*, 143.
21. Ibid, 144.
22. Donald Creighton, *The Empire of the St. Lawrence*,(Toronto: MacMillan and Company, 1956) 144.

As war approached civilian merchantmen had plied all of the Great Lakes and did so once again after peace was restored. In the postwar era both the number and size of merchant sailing vessels on the Great Lakes increased, and there was a consequent decline in the number of bateaux.

Steam propulsion made an appearance on the St. Lawrence River before the war. In 1809 a steam vessel owned by the prominent Molson family of Montreal entered marine service[23]. Steamships appeared in regular service on Lake Ontario by 1816, Lake Erie by 1818, and on Lake Huron by 1822[24]. Steam tugboats appeared on the St. Lawrence River and were particularly useful in towing large timber rafts to Quebec[25]. In the United States marine service to Chicago from ports on Lake Ontario was opened in 1834, and grain was being shipped east by ship from Chicago from about 1836[26]. As the decade of the 1830's marched onwards, both steamship and sailing ship services were widely available on the Great Lakes for the carriage of both passengers and goods.

Although the naval arms race had been put aside by the Rush-Bagot Agreement no treaty governed the construction of fortifications or lines of communication to support army operations, and both the imperial government and the colonial government remained acutely aware of Canada's growing vulnerabilities as the United States developed industrial muscle and demographic depth south of the border. The postwar Governor General, the Duke of Richmond, had recommended fortifying Quebec City and building a canal system along the Rideau River as an inward line of communication which would be less vulnerable to American attack than the St. Lawrence River. The canal recommendation was also promoted by a military assessment commission that was sent to Canada by the

23. Creighton, *The Empire of the St. Lawrence,* 145; Stephen Leacock, *Canada and the Sea,* 37.
24. Costain, *The Path of Destiny,* 451; Callahan, *The Neutrality of the American Lakes,* 90.
25. Leacock, *Canada and the Sea,* 38.
26. Callahan, *The Neutrality of the American Lakes,* 90.

imperial government in 1825, which also recommended that fortresses be built at Halifax, Nova Scotia, and at Kingston, in Upper Canada[27]. Those recommendations were followed and the completed Rideau Canal system afforded the colonial government a secure line of communication between Kingston, where the fortress of Fort Henry was constructed on the promontory opposite Point Frederick, and Montreal thus bypassing the St. Lawrence River route[28]. South of Montreal, the British also fortified *Isle aux Noix*, the main naval station on the Richelieu River[29]. Navigation of the St. Lawrence River itself was not neglected. Commencing in 1821, the construction of the Lachine Canal was undertaken to surmount the rapids in the St. Lawrence River near Montreal. However, when the Lachine Canal was completed in 1826 it was only dredged to a depth of five feet which was sufficient for small craft but not for larger vessels. Continual efforts were made to deepen the canal to allow for the passage of larger vessels[30]. Eventually, Montreal, and not Quebec City, became Canada's primary eastern seaport.

The United States also undertook the construction of new fortifications, restoring Fort Niagara and commencing the construction of a new fort at Rouse's Point where the Richelieu river flows into Lake Champlain. Unfortunately, the border had been improperly surveyed at this point and when an official survey required by the Treaty of Ghent was completed in 1818 it was discovered that the American fortress was being constructed on Canadian soil. Work stopped immediately and the fort was abandoned until after 1842, when the Webster-Ashburton Treaty of that year obligingly transferred the title to the lands upon which the construction of the fort had started to the United

27. Stacey, *The Undefended Border*, 8.
28. Ibid. The Rideau Canal system is still operational in the twenty-first century and has been designated as a world heritage site by UNESCO. The imperial government also constructed the citadel at Halifax to protect the Royal Navy's main naval base in North America.
29. Fay, *Rush-Bagot Agreement*, 37.
30. Leacock, *Canada and the Sea*, 38. The Lachine canal as since been replaced by the St. Lawrence Seaway as a marine transportation corridor.

States. Afterwards, the United States completed the construction at Rouse's Point of Fort Montgomery, which remained the major US fortification along the Canadian border until it was eventually abandoned[31].

In the postwar period, the Americans consolidated their control and settlement of the Old Northwest, as well as the Southwest. As part of the postwar settlement the colonial government in Canada ceased to be a supporter of aboriginal first nations located in United States territory, and severed relations that had existed, in some cases, since the earliest days of British exploration and settlement in North America. As a result, the aboriginal first nations now had to deal with the United States on its terms and they were ultimately deprived of their ancestral lands and forced further west, or placed on reservations. The American frontier moved west as new states were admitted to the union from the Old Northwest, and the aboriginal first nations ceased to be an important military factor in the Great Lakes region. The United States expanded with the acquisition of the Republic of Texas, and the territory of Mexico above the Rio Grande River but there was no great expansion in the size of the US Army to exercise control of the new territories. Rather, the army stationed in the eastern United States was transferred to the west in order to quell the aboriginal first nations through a long series of Indian Wars. That westward movement of the army denuded the border with Canada of troops, giving rise to the concept of a demilitarized border in the popular imagination.

In Canada, the imperial government took steps to limit immigration from the United States and the conveyance of land to Americans. At the same time, the imperial government boosted immigration from Great Britain to Canada, especially Upper Canada, hoping to draw Canada more closely to metropolitan Britain[32]. That policy also went hand-in-hand with

31. Stacey, *The Undefended Border*, 9-10.
32. Fay, *Rush-Bagot Agreement*, 192-93.

new restrictive tariff barriers, and the implementation of trade regulations, both designed to reduce the influx of American goods, and American influence, into Canada. However, when New York responded by building the Erie Canal to bypass the St. Lawrence route, trade restrictions in Canada were lifted to compete with the new all-American canal route[33].

Over the course of the ensuing decades British manufactured products found markets in the United States and the United States found important markets in Britain for commodities, particularly cotton. Most of the transatlantic trade was carried in American-flagged vessels thus creating a mutually beneficial commercial relationship between the two powers. A burgeoning commercial relationship served to inhibit resort to war even when particular issues erupted which caused tension between the two states. Meanwhile, in Canada, tariffs on US products lessened and freer trade encouraged peaceful relations between Canadians and Americans[34].

As interchanges that were commercial as well as personal occurred in the postwar years the people of Canada and the United States began to think that peaceful relations between them were normative and that any differences arising between them should be resolved through peaceful dispute resolution by resort to diplomacy. By removing any threat of the sudden deployment of naval fleets to communities along the Great Lakes the Rush-Bagot Agreement was a first concrete step in building a peaceful relationship between Canada and the United States. Without the Rush-Bagot Agreement it is difficult to envisage how the modern peaceful relationship that has developed between Canada and the United States could have been successfully fostered. Nevertheless, national security issues would remain prominent for some decades afterwards, and, as we will see in the next section, the borderlands would attract

33. Ibid, 202.
34. Ibid, 207-08.

insurgencies and raise additional tensions in North American relations for some time to come.

PART TWO: REBELLIONS AND INSURGENCIES, 1837-1890

1837-1843 THE CANADIAN REBELLIONS, THE CAROLINE INCIDENT, AND THE PATRIOT WAR

The middle years of the nineteenth century would prove to be challenging years for efforts to maintain the Rush-Bagot Agreement. Rebellion would occur in both Canada and the United States, and in the latter country it would lead to a civil war. Insurgency would also be a critical factor for both countries, and the borderlands remained unsecured.

Trouble had been brewing in Canada for some time as the 1830's progressed. The outbreak of the 1837-38 Rebellions have been attributed to several causes by historians, including struggles for liberty and democracy, sovereignty, ethnic conflict between the country's Anglophone and Francophone elements, and tension between an oligarchic commercial class and a burgeoning agrarian class. Ultimately, however, the root cause was the failure of the political system in Canada to evolve since the close of the eighteenth century. Canada was still governed under a political model that did not provide an adequate degree of democracy for the population.

While the Crown had granted Canadians representative government in the form of a provincial assembly elected on the basis of a restricted franchise in both Lower Canada and Upper Canada, the assemblies could not perfect their control over the executive. The legislatures consisted of an elected assembly and an appointed upper house, the Legislative Council. Although the assemblies were popularly elected in both Lower Canada and Upper Canada, the enfranchised public (who were limited to free males, and who were subject to a property qualification) could not influence the appointment of members of the Legislative Council. Nor did they have any control over who the Governor chose to appoint as his formal constitutional advisors in the Executive Council for each province. Thus, notwithstanding that the electors had control over the appropriation of funds for the use of the government, through a requirement that the assembly approve government funding, they were unable to exercise political control over the colonial executive.

Over time, the governors became associated with an oligarchic merchant and elitist class in both provinces. In Lower Canada this group was known as the Chateau Clique and consisted of a mixture of the Scottish commercial class, and the French-Canadian seigneury class. In Upper Canada the influential group was known as the Family Compact and consisted of merchants and upper-class loyalists who had emigrated from the thirteen American colonies following the conclusion of the American Revolutionary War. These groups used imperial patriotism, their own personal and commercial connections, and (in Upper Canada) the established Anglican Church to advance their interests. Pressure for political change mounted but was unmet. Resentment began to build in both colonies due to the limited control by the electorate over the colonial government.

When the political explosion occurred, serious outbreaks of violence occurred in Lower Canada and to a lesser but still significant extent in Upper Canada. The main actors agitating for political change were Louis-Joseph Papineau in Lower Canada who was a well-known lawyer and politician and a long-serving Speaker of the Assembly, and William Lyon MacKenzie in Upper Canada, the proprietor of a radical newspaper. Reform politicians coalesced around Papineau and Mackenzie in opposition to the conservative Tories who sought to maintain their privileged socioeconomic position in the provinces. Mackenzie angered the Family Compact by the political attacks he mounted against them from his newspaper, *The Advocate*. In Lower Canada, Papineau had promoted the creation of the 92 resolutions in 1834, which encapsulated the grievances of French-Canadian and Irish radicals, and placed him at odds with the Chateau Clique. The situation was exacerbated by a financial and economic crisis that took place in early 1837, and which contributed to the political passions that gripped the country in the months preceding the outbreak of the rebellions. In that climate, political discourse fractured and an open rebellion against the colonial government broke out in both provinces. In Lower Canada Papineau wisely did not accept the leadership of those who sought a violent solution to the political problems of Lower Canada even though he had influenced the thinking of those who did. After the violent eruption occurred, he hastily departed for the United States.

The main military actions occurred in Lower Canada where Lieutenant General Sir John Colborne, the commander-in-chief of the military forces in British North America, defeated the rebels at the decisive Battle of Saint Eustache in December 1837. Meanwhile, in Upper Canada, MacKenzie led a rather comic-opera uprising that was swiftly dispersed by the militia. By the beginning of 1838 the rebellions were largely over, with the key agitators fleeing to the United States. There, however, they made common cause with Americans who were sympathetic to the rebel goals of political reform, and the potential independence of the Canadian provinces from Great Britain. American sympathizers and Canadian political refugees joined together and formed secret societies known as Hunter Lodges with the object of invading Canada and promoting violent political change by removing British influence from North America. The resulting Patriot War presented the colonial government with a difficult domestic and international challenge.

The opposition to the colonial government reflected a diversity of interests. Some, such as the emigres Mackenzie, Papineau, Nelson, and Duncombe, were Canadians who were active or sympathetic to the aims of the 1837 domestic rebellions in Upper and Lower Canada[1]. However, such Canadian political refugees were a minority in the insurgency. There were also some Canadians in Canada who continued to sympathize with the aims of the rebels but they also formed only a small minority of the population. By far the largest component of the Patriot insurgency were young American men, unconstrained by occupation or family responsibilities, who were attracted to the sense of adventure that the lodges represented. A rootless and shifting mass of young men eager to prove themselves is a familiar narrative in history. The true number of Hunter Lodge adherents is unknown but it was substantial – certainly thousands of American men participated in them together with a small number of Canadians. Typically, those young men were manipulated by others, often older, with more substantive reasons for seeking to oust the British from the northern half of North America. The British Minister in Washington, Henry Fox, lamented the fact that wealthy Americans resident in US border communities helped to foment the insurgency in the interests of land speculation for their private gain with relative impunity[2]. In fact, as in the case of the War of 1812, American expansionists looked with envy on the rich farmlands of southwestern Upper Canada north of the southern Great Lakes, and the combination of an anti monarchical and anti-British sentiment[3], together with an abiding hunger for land, drove many Americans to support the Hunter Lodges[4].

1. Only Papineau was born in Canada. Mackenzie was born in Scotland, Nelson was born in England and Duncombe was born in the United States. All were resident for many years in Canada at the time of the outbreak of the 1837 rebellions.
2. Donald E Graves, *Guns Across the River: The Battle of the Windmill, 1838* (Montreal: Robin Brass Studio Inc., 2001, 2013) 221.
3. A Commission for a Patriot Hunter officer displayed at Fort Malden in Amherstburg, Ontario, shows a large American eagle grasping a British lion in its talons and preparing to drop it into a large and deep hole.

In addition, many of the Americans who participated in the Patriot War were motivated by the example of Texas, where Americans who had flocked to Texas to aid American-born settlers in what was then a Mexican province in their struggle for independence were neither impeded nor punished by the United States for taking part in a rebellion against a neighbouring state with which Washington had maintained friendly diplomatic relations. Many young Americans hoped to do for Canada what their fellow countrymen had done for Texas. However, the administration of President Martin Van Buren which took office in 1837 had a different view of such filibustering by Americans, and it sought to stop the Patriot insurgency by the strict enforcement of American neutrality laws. Due to the large numbers of American Patriots, and their enthusiasm for the cause of Canadian liberation, that proved to be a harder task than one might imagine. Prodded by the imperial government however, the US army was deployed to the northern border by the Van Buren Administration to suppress the insurgents by enforcing US neutrality statutes, and the army's senior officers, particularly General Winfield Scott, acquitted themselves very favourably in a task that was doubtless contrary to the mood of American public sentiment[5].

The imperial government realized that it would have to shore-up the defensive posture of the empire in Canada in order to forestall the cross-border raids of the Patriots. Command of the seas by Great Britain allowed it to move regular army troops to Canada from Britain, Gibralter, and the West Indies, and to speedily move them from the littoral British North American colonies into Canada proper[6]. Considerable army reinforcements were sent to Canada to protect the country from both rebels and American insurgents.

4. Black, *Fighting for America*, 212.
5. Ibid,214-15.
6. Ibid, 211.

In December 1837, following the collapse of the domestic rebellion, Mackenzie and his cohorts decided to invade Canada from the United States and proclaim the creation of a Provisional Government, with himself as its temporary head, and Rensselaer Van Rensselaer, the son of an American general, as the commander of its military forces. On December 13, 1837, that object was accomplished when Mackenzie and Van Rensselaer together with 24 adherents occupied Navy Island in the Niagara River, and unfurled the Patriot banner, two stars on a blue field representing the two provinces of Canada, and a government Seal and began issuing scrip[7]. Owing to the force of the currents in the river, it was considered to be too difficult for the available loyalist forces ranged against Navy Island at Chippewa, Upper Canada, to mount a successful amphibious assault. Mackenzie and Van Rensselaer took advantage of the colonial government's inaction and began to reinforce their position on the island using an American steamship, the *Caroline*, to resupply the insurgent forces on Navy Island.

Colonel Allan McNab commander of the colonial government's troops facing Navy Island rather nonchalantly inquired of Captain Andrew Drew, a half-pay Royal Navy officer resident in Upper Canada, whether he could mount a successful cutting out expedition against the *Caroline*. When Drew affirmed that he could successfully mount such an operation, McNab gave him instructions to do so, and, calling together volunteers, Drew mounted a small boat expedition against the *Caroline* on the night of December 29, 1837, using seven small boats. Two of the boats were seen by insurgent pickets on Navy Island and were fired upon, causing them to turn back but the remaining five boats proceeded without being challenged and, after great exertions in the current, they came upon the *Caroline* anchored in American waters. The cutting out expedition was challenged on its final

7. Orrin Edward Tiffany, *The Canadian Rebellion of 1837-38*, (Buffalo: Buffalo Historical Society, 1905; repr. Toronto: Coles Publishing Co. Ltd., 1980) 30.

approach to the *Caroline* but nevertheless succeeded in boarding and seizing the vessel after a brief scuffle which caused the death of one American, Amos Durfee, and the wounding of several others before the vessel was secured by the Canadian force[8]. Captain Drew then set the *Caroline* on fire and attempted to send the ship over Niagara Falls but the blazing ship grounded on the river's east bank and was destroyed by fire[9]. Captain Drew and his men retired back to Canadian territory unharmed.

Instantly, the destruction of the *Caroline* was an international *cause célèbre*. Outrage was expressed by Americans from President Van Buren on down and many Americans thought that a war with Great Britain might be necessary to settle the matter. However, the Van Buren Administration sought to reduce the public tempers sparked by the incident and while claiming that the United States had been wronged it did not seek to enforce that claim by any overt act of retribution. A considerable diplomatic discourse over the incident ensued and eventually the circumstances of *Caroline's* destruction served to advance the principles of international law around the concept of the right to a pre-emptive attack by one state upon another state. The *Caroline* Test was subsequently formulated by United States Secretary of State Daniel Webster in 1842 at which time Webster stated that pre-emptive action by the colonial government in Canada would have been permissible if the "necessity of self-defence was instant, overwhelming, leaving no choice of means, and no moment of deliberation . . . and that the British force ... did nothing unreasonable or excessive; since the act, justified by the necessity of self-defence, must be limited by that necessity, and kept clearly within it[10]."

8. Graves, *Guns Across the River*, 31; Tiffany, *The Canadian Rebellion*, 35.
9. Graves, *Guns Across the River*, 32. Tiffany states that part of the ship went over the falls (Tiffany, *The Canadian Rebellion*, 35 fn 4.
10. Daniel Webster, 'Letter to Henry Stephen Fox" quoted in K E Shewmaker (ed.) *The Papers of Daniel Webster: Diplomatic Papers, vol. 1 1841-43* (Hanover, New Hampshire: Dartmouth College Press, 1983) 62.

Eventually, the *Caroline* Test would be based on the twin concepts of necessity and proportionality. The international actor relying on preemption must show that the action was made necessary by the particular circumstances and that a peaceful method of resolution was unavailable due to the immediacy of the threat. Secondly, the international actor making a pre-emptive strike must limit itself to the acts which are absolutely necessary for the purposes of a self-defence and may not go further than that. The United States took the position that no such necessity for immediate action had been warranted in the case of the *Caroline*, and therefore the actions of the colonial authorities in Canada had been impermissible.

The British government demurred and there the matter rested for some time. Eventually, one of the participants in the raid was captured in American territory and put on trial for the murder of Dufree but he was acquitted by a jury. In the 1840's during the negotiation of the Webster-Ashburton Treaty Lord Ashburton expressed regrets for the failure of the British government to make adequate explanations and apologies to the United States at the time of the incident and those regrets formed the basis of a reconciliation between the two states with respect to the incident[11]. The *Caroline* Test is now part of international law and forms the basis of the doctrine of a legal pre-emptive strike, which is possible where one country has allowed the use of its territory for the mounting of an unlawful (under international law) attack on another country[12].

Meanwhile Mackenzie and Van Rensselaer were unprepared to let the *Caroline* affair stand without a response. They appointed a notorious piratical smuggler, William Johnstone, a Canadian who had fled to the United States in the War of 1812 when his loyalty to the Crown was questioned, as the Commodore

---

11. Tiffany, *The Canadian Rebellion*, 41.
12. J L Granatstein and Dean F Oliver, *The Oxford Companion to Canadian Military History* (Don Mills (ON): Oxford University Press, 2011), 95.

of the Patriot Navy in the East. Johnstone and a number of his confederates (among whom was his 19-year-old daughter Kate, widely acknowledged as a local beauty along the St. Lawrence River) embarked on a series of attacks against the colonial government. In May 1838, Johnstone and his confederates dressed up as aboriginal warriors and seized the Canadian steamship *Sir Robert Peel* at Wells Island in US territory, shouting "Remember the *Caroline*" and forced the passengers ashore with their belongings. After robbing the passengers Johnstone burned the *Peel* down to the water line[13]. Later Johnstone raided Amherst Island, wounding one Canadian[14].

As the insurgency developed, the imperial government sought to shore up the security of Canada by dispatching troops to Lower and Upper Canada and resuscitating the moribund naval forces on the Great Lakes. To that end, the Admiralty sent Captain Williams Sandom to Kingston in April 1838, to revive the lapsed naval force. Sandom was an experienced and energetic officer who found the ex-Royal Navy squadron rotting underwater at Kingston but the armaments of the ships safely preserved in the 'stone frigate', a substantial stone building erected at Point Frederick to store the armaments taken off the squadron before its disposal.

Sandom was aware of the Rush-Bagot Agreement but he had to balance the legal and diplomatic obligations that the colonial government was compelled to labour under with the necessity of ensuring sufficient marine protection across the long maritime border between Canada and the United States. Ultimately he felt compelled to exceed the limitations of the Agreement in order to present an adequate naval force to quell the insurgency.

Moving quickly, Sandom was able to put together an effective squadron on Lake Ontario, which was, as always, the key lake

13. Graves, *Guns Across the River*, 53; Tiffany, *The Canadian Rebellion*, 54-55.
14. Graves, *Guns Across the River*, 55.

in the naval defence of Canada. Sandom purchased a 100-ton displacement, 30 HP one engine side wheel steamship for the colonial government and commissioned it as *HMS Experiment*. It was armed with one 18-pounder carronade and two 3-pounder brass guns. Sandom also chartered two privately owned steamers, *Cobourg*, a two-engine 12 HP vessel of 440 tons displacement which he armed with four 18-pounder carronades, and the *Queen Victoria* a single engine 60 HP steamer displacing 220 tons which he armed with one 12-pounder gun and two 12-pounder carronades[15]. Eventually, Sandom would add other ships to the squadron at Kingston, including one bomb vessel armed with a 5.5 inch mortar and two 18-pounder carronades, and three row galley gunboats, two of them armed with one 18-pounder gun, and the third with an 18-pounder carronade[16]. On the upper lakes the colonial government chartered the steamship *Thames*, and armed it with one 9-pounder gun, and the steamship *Cynthia*, which the government proposed to employ as an unarmed troop transport. Both ships were owned by merchant Duncan MacGregor[17].

Although the colonial government was adhering to the Rush-Bagot Agreement with respect to the naval forces on the upper lakes, the force on Lake Ontario (which also provided protection on the upper St. Lawrence River) clearly exceeded the limitations established by the agreement. Sandom tried to minimize the infractions by arming his vessels with short range carronades despite the fact that long guns were in storage at Point Frederick[18]. To American complaints that Great Britain had violated the Rush-Bagot Agreement, the imperial government took the view that any increase in the number of warships on the Great Lakes was only temporary, and was necessary for the

15. Ibid, App. B, 257.
16. Ibid.
17. Fred Coyne Hamil, *The Valley of the Lower Thames 1640-1850* (1951: repr., Toronto: University of Toronto Press, 1973) 235, 238.
18. Graves, *Guns Across the River*, 122.

suppression of the rebellion and its accompanying insurgency and therefore were for defensive purposes only[19]. This explanation appears to have been accepted by the United States as no further objections were made by it concerning the temporary increase in naval units beyond the limits specified in the Agreement[20].

The main naval action of the Patriot Insurgency took place near Prescott, Upper Canada, in November 1838. The insurgents planned to land and take Prescott in hopes of raising the surrounding countryside in the misinformed belief that the inhabitants of Upper Canada would rise in rebellion against the Crown and with the aid and assistance of the American insurgents the colony would be freed of British rule. Many of the insurgents were promised grants of land in Upper Canada once the colony had been liberated and the prospect of good land motivated more than a few.

By this time the Canadian rebels had mostly faded from the scene. Papineau had abandoned the cause and his successor, Robert Nelson, made one final attempt to invade and overthrow the colonial government in Lower Canada, which failed in November 1838. Mackenzie had quarrelled with Van Rensselaer and abandoned the cause by retreating to New York where he started a newspaper. Only the American-born Canadian Charles Duncombe remained active, serving as the banker and treasurer of the Hunter Lodges from his base at Cleveland, Ohio[21].

In pursuit of their objectives a substantial force of Patriot Hunters assembled in upstate New York, at Sackett's Harbour and Cape Vincent. The insurgents, numbering more than 200 men, took passage on the steam-passenger vessel *United States* for Ogdensburg, New York. During the passage the *United States*

19. Fitzpatrick *An Address Delivered by the Rt. Hon. Sir Charles Fitzpatrick,,* 13.
20. Callahan, *The Neutrality of the American Lakes*, 100.
21. *Graves, Guns Across the River*, 50.

encountered two small schooners, the Canadian *Charlotte* of Toronto and the American *Charlotte* of Oswego which were secretly chartered to the Patriots. Leaders of the insurgency persuaded the master of the *United States* to take the schooners in tow to Ogdensburg where some 200 insurgents boarded the schooners and sailed for Prescott[22].

Meanwhile, Sandom had received intelligence that the insurgents were on the move aboard the *United States* and he sent word to Colonel William Worth, the US army commander at Sackett's Harbour, warning him of the impending breach of the international peace by the Hunter Lodges. Worth sailed in the steamship *Telegraph* to intercept the insurgents before they could embark upon their attack and he actually passed the *United States* which was steaming in the opposite direction while it was carrying the insurgents. When Colonel Worth arrived at the suspected base of the insurgents at Cape Vincent and nearby Clayton all that he found was the lovely but piratical Kate Johnstone, surely a serendipitous discovery for Worth's young officers[23]!

At Ogdensburg the two *Charlotte* schooners departed for Prescott in the early morning on November 12, 1838, but their attempt to land failed because the pickets were aroused and they fired at the ships which, through misadventure, were unable to secure themselves to the wharfs at Prescott. By morning the patrol ship *HMS Experiment* under Lieutenant William Fowell had arrived and found the two *Charlottes* with their rigging entangled and aground in the middle of the St. Lawrence but in American waters. 'Commodore' William Johnstone also arrived in the morning from Ogdensburg and disentangled the two insurgent schooners and also managed to free one of them from the bank on which it had grounded. However, the other schooner was so

22. Ibid, 83.
23. Ibid, 102.

firmly stuck that Johnstone sent word back to Ogdensburg for assistance. The insurgent leaders who were on hand to witness the events of the invasion but who did not wish to participate in the battle stirred themselves sufficiently to seize control of the *United States* and take it into the river to tow off the grounded schooner.

Realizing what the insurgents were up to Fowell waited until the *United States* entered Canadian waters and then ran down and attacked it but without any real effect. The *United States* then fled upriver with the *Experiment* in pursuit. While the *Experiment* was engaged in pursuit of the *United States*, another small American steamer, *Paul Pry*, rushed out into the river to assist the grounded Oswego schooner *Charlotte,* which the *Pry* succeeded in pulling off the shoal on which it had grounded. Sensing that he ought to remain concerned about the schooner Fowell returned down the river in the *Experiment* to find the *Paul Pry* assisting *Charlotte* and the *Experiment* fired into them but they escaped back into American waters[24]. The *United States* meanwhile had returned to the fray and though unarmed sought to ram the *Experiment*. Fowell evaded the *United States* and then fired into it, at last getting results by killing its pilot and knocking out the steamer's starboard engine. The *United States* sought refuge in American waters and limped back into Ogdensburg[25].

The *Experiment* had driven off the American vessels but the Canadian *Charlotte* out of Toronto had succeeded in landing insurgents on Canadian territory at Newport, where there was a substantial mill. The insurgents were commanded by a Swedish fortune seeker masquerading as a Polish freedom-fighter named Nils von Schoultz. They took up a defensive position in the mill and its windmill tower which formed an effective military strong point. On November 13th twenty-five hundred British troops,

24. Ibid, 96-97.
25. Ibid, 99.

Canadian militia and aboriginal warriors from the Mohawk first nation surrounded the Patriot Hunters and participated in a siege, which led to the defeat and surrender of the insurgents on November 16th, though not without substantial losses being incurred by the loyalist forces[26]. During the struggle, Sandom concentrated his squadron at Prescott but found that his carronades were ineffective. He was forced to return to Kingston to extract long guns from the stone frigate and after doing so he was able to fashion floating batteries (manned in part by Mohawk warriors) that, together with the land-based Royal Artillery, were sufficient to reduce the insurgent strong points, and complete the army's success over the insurgents. After summary trials a number of the insurgents were hanged while many others (mostly Americans) were transported to Tasmania. Following the battle, President Van Buren issued a proclamation on November 21, 1838, stating that the United States did not support the insurgency and would not help the insurgents[27].

Patriot insurgents also attacked Upper Canada along the Detroit River frontier in 1838. In January, insurgents, including some 300 Canadian rebels, formed in Detroit and after raiding the local jail to obtain arms they seized the American schooner *Ann* and the sloop *George Strong* and moved them to Gibralter, Michigan, in order to mount an attack on Fort Malden at Amherstburg[28]. From there they moved a company of insurgents to Stony Island, an American-owned island in the Detroit River, and used it as a base to attack Bois Blanc Island on the Canadian side of the border, forcing off the British army pickets who were stationed there. The *Ann* commenced a bombardment of Fort Malden which no longer had heavy ordinance *in situ*[29], on January 8th, in company with *George Strong*. The army was

---

26. The final tally was 80 killed or wounded among the loyalist forces and 50 killed, 17 wounded and 166 taken prisoner among the Hunters (Graves, *Guns Across the River*, 181).
27. Graves, *Guns Across the River*, 199.
28. Hamil, *The Valley of the Lower Thames*, 229.
29. Minister of Indian and Northern Affairs, Fort Malden National Historic Park, 4.

unable to respond with countering artillery fire owing to the absence of guns at the fort. On the 9th the bombardment resumed but the garrison, which was armed only with rifles and small arms, was able to compel the surrender of the *George Strong*, and its American master and three American sailors were thrown into prison[30]. Later towards evening *Ann* returned and commenced a largely ineffectual bombardment with a 6-pounder, although some houses in Amherstburg were damaged. British forces kept up small arms fire on *Ann* and a marksman managed to kill *Ann's* helmsman which caused the *Ann* to ground near Elliott's Point, opposite the Essex and Kent militiamen. The militiamen waded out into the river and stormed the ship, killing and wounding several of the insurgents in the taking of the ship[31].

On February 25, 1838, there was an attack by the British garrison at Fort Malden on a substantial party of insurgents holding Fighting Island in the Detroit River, who were forced back and subsequently arrested by the American authorities. Another battle occurred on Pelee Island in Lake Erie on March 3, 1838, when insurgents from Ohio were routed by a force of soldiers from Fort Malden together with aboriginal scouts and militia.

Continuing or threatened incursions along the frontier prompted the colonial government to assign the chartered steamer *Thames*, armed with one 9-pounder gun, to keep watch along the Detroit River maritime frontier. For their part, the American authorities also kept watch on the ships that were berthed at Detroit. Late in the year the American authorities perceived that the threat had passed and eased up on the watch maintained over the ships berthed at Detroit. Sensing the relaxation of scrutiny by the authorities, the insurgents seized the steamer *Champlain* and used it to transport insurgents across

30. Hamil, *The Valley of the Lower Thames*, 230.
31. Hamil, *The Valley of the Lower Thames*, 230 d; Minister of Indian and Northern Affairs, *Fort Malden National Historic Park*, 4.

the Detroit River to raid Windsor, Upper Canada. The insurgents managed to commandeer the *Thames* and burned it at wharf-side. That was a significant blow to her owner, Duncan MacGregor, who also lost the *Cynthia* which the colonial government had used as a transport, in an accidental fire. MacGregor eventually received four thousand pounds in compensation for his losses[32]. A final, futile, raid was launched by the Patriot Hunters seeking to occupy Windsor on December 8, 1838, but the force of insurgents was routed by the Canadian militia and reinforcements sent from Fort Malden, although the insurgents did succeed in burning the local barracks at Windsor.

Eventually, the Patriot insurgency petered out and the so-called Patriot War came to an end. In 1841, President Tyler ordered the Hunter Lodges to be disbanded. Papineau and Mackenzie endured a period of exile before they were given amnesty and returned home where both resumed active political careers. Robert Nelson never returned to Canada. William Johnstone, the piratical 'Commodore' of the Patriot Navy in the East was arrested in New York state in November 1838 but released for lack of evidence. Re-arrested on new charges, he escaped from jail, was caught and eventually convicted of violating American laws by participating in the Prescott invasion and sentenced to one year in jail. His faithful daughter Kate went to jail with him to tend to his needs during his imprisonment. However, Johnstone escaped after six months incarceration and remained at large. Eventually he was pardoned and he settled down as a lighthouse and tavern keeper, still watched over by his loyal daughter Kate[33]. The colonial government continued to maintain a small marine force commanded by Royal Navy officers. Captain Sandom was retained in command for some years and was succeeded by Lieutenant Fowell, formerly of the *Experiment*, in 1843. After 1852 the colonies ceased to maintain any armed

32. Hamil, *The Valley of the Lower Thames*, 238.
33. Graves, *Guns Across the River*, 238.

vessels on the Great Lakes or the St. Lawrence River[34]. The steamer *United States* was repaired and it subsequently re-entered passenger service on Lake Ontario. However, the *United States* was no longer used in service on the St. Lawrence River because Canadians nursed hard feelings about the ship's role in the Battle of the Windmill, and they would no longer sail in it[35].

Canada was at peace but the underlying causes of the rebellions remained to be addressed by the imperial government in Great Britain. Lord Durham, an experienced diplomat, was sent to Canada as Governor General in the immediate aftermath of the violence that occurred in 1837 and he was given authority as a high commissioner to investigate the causes of the rebellion and to make recommendations for change. Subsequently, his famous Report on the Affairs of British North America recommended that a form of responsible government be granted to all of the North American colonies, and that unity amongst the colonies in British North America be promoted. Both of those recommendations were subsequently implemented, the first in new instructions sent to the Lieutenant Governor of Nova Scotia in 1846, and then two years later in Canada. The British North American colonies now emerged from the constitutional structure that had once prevailed in British America, and which had led the thirteen southern colonies to rebel against the Crown in 1775. The remaining British colonies now embarked on their own journeys towards autonomy in the British Empire. Unity among all of the colonies in British North America would take time, and would not take form until the 1860's. In the meantime, Lord Durham's recommendation for the creation of a unitary government for Canada by merging the two separate provinces of Lower Canada and Upper Canada into once province was accepted and implemented[36]. That recommendation ultimately

34. Stacey, *The Undefended Border*, 10.
35. Graves, *Guns Across the River*, 240.
36. As a result, Lower Canada was renamed Canada East and Upper Canada became Canada West.

proved unsuccessful but it did require the country's Anglophone and Francophone politicians to develop working relationships, and those associations and partnerships formed during the period of unitary government would provide the basis for political cooperation when the time eventually came to create a union of the provinces.

1843-1865 THE MIGHTY MICHIGAN AND THE AMERICAN CIVIL WAR

In the aftermath of the Patriot Insurgency the United States gave some new consideration to its northern border with Canada. The danger of a war with Great Britain and the ease with which colonial military forces were able to destroy the *Caroline* caused the federal government to bolster its northern defences. On land the United States commenced the construction of Fort Montgomery at the northern end of strategic Lake Champlain. Earlier, in 1816, the construction of an American fort had begun at Rouses Point and a substantial investment had actually been made before it was discovered by surveyors that the fort was being constructed on Canadian soil, following which the work was abandoned[1]. Under the Webster-Ashburton Treaty of 1842 the United States and Great Britain resolved several northeastern border issues including the cession of the land upon which the original fort had been constructed, thereby allowing the United States to recommence the construction of fortifications at that location. The new fort, named Fort Montgomery after the commander of the Continental Army's invasion force in 1775, was intended to be a massive fortification, the largest along the northern border, and a key strong point. Construction continued until approximately 1870 when the settlement of continental issues between Great Britain and the United States rendered the fortifications superfluous. In the

1. Stacey, *The Undefended Border*, 9.

1840's the US government also constructed Fort Wayne, named after Major General 'Mad' Anthony Wayne, a revolutionary hero, as a substantial strong point at Detroit, and a counterbalance to Fort Malden in Amherstburg, Upper Canada.

The 1840's were a time of rapid change in the United States, as the population continued to grow and move westward towards the Pacific. In the last days of his administration President Tyler (1841-45) offered terms of admission to the union to the Republic Texas, which had achieved independence from Mexico through a rebellion in 1835. The annexation of Texas was completed under Tyler's successor, James K. Polk, who embarked on a major expansion of US territory after consummating the acquisition of Texas. Polk launched a war against Mexico with the objective of seizing all of Mexico's territory north of the Rio Grande River. US invasion forces were successful and Mexico was forced to surrender approximately 40% of its territory to the United States, including large areas that subsequently encompassed the American south-west and mountain states together with California, the great Pacific coast prize that made the United States a transcontinental nation.

In the northwest there was a rising tide of migration of Americans into the Oregon Country, which Great Britain and the United States had jointly administered since 1818. The old governance structure was breaking down with the influx of Americans however, and many Americans demanded that the Oregon Country be incorporated into the United States. Great Britain asserted its own claim to the territory at least as far south as the mouth of the Columbia River but the United States remained intransigent and the possibility of another war between Great Britain and the United States suddenly began to appear more likely. However, in the end, cooler heads prevailed. Great Britain would have had great difficulty in fighting a war on the Pacific coast of North America and the United States could not feasibly conduct a two front war against Mexico and Great

Britain simultaneously. Both Great Britain and the United States were thus motivated to seek a peaceful resolution of the dispute and they eventually agreed to extend the previously demarcated border along the 49th parallel between the Great Lakes and the Rocky Mountains to the Pacific Coast, with Britain retaining all of Vancouver Island. A treaty to settle the international boundary was ratified on June 15, 1845.

The settlement of the Oregon boundary thus determined the international border between what would become Canada and the United States. Yet the massive expansion of the United States presented its own problems as the way was now open for the creation of more slave-owning states in the newly acquired southern territories, a prospect that appalled many Americans in the northern free states, who increasingly looked with disdain on the institution of slavery in America[2]. As time passed American politics became increasingly sectarian and the country began to edge towards a cataclysmic internal conflict.

The United States had now become a continental country stretching across North America but Canada remained a small eastern country. Consequently, the Great Lakes continued to loom large in both military and commercial calculations for the Canadian population. The abundance of water, the availability of water transportation, and the increasing concentration of population in the Great Lakes basin began to encourage significant industrial expansion on both sides of the border. A key aspect of growing commerce was the technological improvements to water-borne transportation through technological improvements to ship construction and propulsion, and the construction of networks of canals.

In both Canada and the United States governments began

---

2. Slavery in the British Empire, including British North America where it had never been prominent, was abolished in 1833. Earlier legislation to phase out slavery in Upper Canada was enacted in 1793.

investing in efforts to ensure navigational channels were dredged and to construct canals to allow vessels to navigate unimpeded by obstructions in the waterways. To maintain lines of communication in the event of a war with the United States the imperial government in Great Britain spent large sums of money in the 1820s and 1830s to construct the Rideau Canal, which allowed marine traffic to follow the Ottawa and Rideau Rivers between Montreal and Kingston, thus bypassing the upper St. Lawrence route which bordered the United States. By 1850 canals had also been built along the St. Lawrence River to enhance marine traffic, including the Lachine, Beauharnois, Farran's Point, Rapide Plat, and Galops canals. The Welland canal was constructed on the Niagara Peninsula and it allowed ship traffic to bypass the Niagara River and its impassable falls, thus becoming the most important canal on the Great Lakes[3]. The first Welland Canal was built by entrepreneur William Hamilton Merritt and was completed in 1829. Subsequently, the colonial government obtained title to the canal and rebuilt it in the 1840's. Eventually, a third and fourth canal would be opened, and finally, in 1965, the present bypass canal around the town of Welland was completed[4]. In the United States, the construction of the Erie Canal allowed water-borne traffic to reach the port of New York following a safer, all-American route from the Great Lakes, thus bypassing the upper St. Lawrence which bordered Canada.

For Canada a key element in its growing economic development was the entry into force of a Reciprocity Treaty between Great Britain (on behalf of Canada) and the United States which eliminated tariffs on the import of natural resource products from Canada into the United States. Although the economic impact of the treaty has since been questioned by economic historians in Canada, it appears to have had a stimulative effect

3. Creighton, *Empire of the St. Lawrence*, 420.
4. Berton, *The Great Lakes*, 149, 152.

on the Canadian economy. From a geopolitical perspective the Reciprocity Treaty was favourable to the United States by encouraging stronger economic ties between the United States and Canada.

After the disbandment of the Hunter Lodges the colonial government no longer feared border incursions from an American-based insurgency and the restoration of peace prompted authorities to allow their naval forces on the Great Lakes to decline[5]. In 1851 imperial troops were withdrawn from Fort Malden and pensioned soldiers were put in place there until the fort was finally given over to the local government and ceased to be maintained as a border fortification.

In the United States however, there was a continuing memory of the *Caroline* attack and the measures that the colonial government had taken during the emergency which had violated the Rush-Bagot Agreement, notwithstanding British explanations that the increases in the number of ships and their substantial armaments in excess of agreed limits were for defensive purposes only, and not directed against the United States. Furthermore, during the crisis in the 1840's involving the Oregon boundary issue, the colonial government subsidized the building of three steam-driven ships, including the *Mohawk*, the first naval vessel on the Great lakes with a hull that was constructed of iron[6]. Two of those steamships, *Minos* and *Toronto*[7] were subsequently fired upon in 1841 by unknown persons on Navy Island who had acquired a US field artillery gun[8]. To complaints that the new-builds were a violation of the Rush-Bagot Agreement the British Foreign Office provided assurances to the United States that the vessels were intended for

5. Tiffany, *The Canadian Rebellion*, 112.
6. Bradley A Rodgers, *Guardian of the Great Lakes: The US Paddle Frigate Michigan*, (Ann Arbor: University of Michigan Press, 1996) 15.
7. The other two vessels were the *Experiment* and the schooner *Montreal*.
8. Callahan, *The Neutrality of the American Lakes*, 117.

defensive measures in relation to the recent rebellions in Canada, and were not intended as a derogation from the existing legal obligations[9].

As a result of continuing concerns in the United States about the presence of armed ships on the Canadian side of the Great Lakes the Tyler Administration set out to build a substantial warship for service on the upper lakes, which led to the construction of the USS *Michigan*, the first steam-powered iron-hulled ship in the United States Navy. Built at Pittsburgh and completed in May 1842 the *Michigan* was disassembled and transported to Erie, Pennsylvania, where it was reassembled and launched on December 5, 1843. The *Michigan* was a side-wheel paddle steamer displacing 582 tons, and was 167 feet, 6 inches, in length, and 27 feet wide at the beam[10]. The *Michigan's* two inboard steam engines could develop approximately 330 h.p. and could drive the ship at more than 13 knots[11]. *Michigan's* original armament in 1844 consisted of one 18-pounder gun, although during the period of crisis in the American Civil War the ship carried an additional armament in excess of the armament permitted by the Rush-Bagot Agreement, and even after the Civil War the ship carried an additional secondary armament[12]. Although *Michigan* initially complied with the armaments restrictions imposed by the Rush-Bagot Agreement[13], the size of the ship clearly exceeded the maximum tonnage restriction of 100 tons. Nevertheless, Great Britain did not initially file any formal complaints over the size of the *Michigan* although there was, of course, great concern both in the colonial government and in the imperial government about the apparent breach of the Rush-Bagot limitations by the United States. The Foreign Minister, Lord Aberdeen, instructed the British Minister in Washington, Richard Pakenham, to warn

9. Fay, *Rush-Bagot Agreement*, 252.
10. Rodgers, *Guardian of the Great Lakes*, 19.
11. Ibid, 21.
12. Ibid, 147.
13. Ibid, 27.

the Tyler Administration that the imperial government would escalate its naval forces to ensure parity with America's lake warships, and would defend Canada[14]. Notwithstanding the British warnings, *Michigan* was commissioned on September 29, 1844, and from then until she was struck from the Navy list on May 6, 1912, *Michigan* dominated the Great Lakes.

Despite the fact that the imperial government knew of the *Michigan* from the time it was built it was not until 1857 that the government chose to complain formally to the United States that the *Michigan* exceeded the tonnage limitations set out in the Rush-Bagot Agreement. The United States conceded that the *Michigan* exceeded the tonnage limitations but noted that the ship did not exceed the treaty armaments limitations, which was the more important restriction in the US view[15]. Although the protest of the imperial government prompted the United States to consider removing the *Michigan* from the Great Lakes, American public opinion was decidedly opposed to a withdrawal, and Canadian merchants also supported the retention of the *Michigan* on the Great Lakes[16]. By 1857 neither the imperial nor colonial governments maintained any naval vessels on the Great Lakes and Canadian merchants probably viewed the Michigan as a useful instrument to maintain law and order on the lakes. The protests of the imperial government were lessened after *Michigan* assisted the colonial government by towing a caisson (a waterproof structure used for underwater construction) to facilitate the completion of a new lighthouse on Pelee Island in Lake Erie[17]. The colonial government offered its thanks to the United States Navy for that assistance[18].

In reality, the limitations set out in the Rush-Bagot Agreement

14. Black, *Fighting for America*, 234.
15. Fitzpatrick *An Address Delivered by the Rt. Hon. Sir Charles Fitzpatrick*, 14.
16. Rodgers, *Guardian of the Great Lakes*, 81.
17. Ibid, 82.
18. Ibid, 169, n. 17.

had already been overtaken by marine technological developments resulting from the Industrial Revolution. When the Agreement had been originally entered into large sailing ships had cruised the interior lakes but the invention of the steam engine, and the development of iron-hulled ships, caused a significant change to the design and construction of warships. To that argument the imperial government had no real answer and unless an effort was going to be made to change and update the Agreement itself it was better to accept the American position that the armament limitation was the key restriction rather than to press a claim about the size of the vessel in relation to the original limitations set out in the Agreement.

Similarly, the imperial government chose to give way to the United States on the question of revenue cutters. The United States had established a Revenue-Marine service as early as 1790 for the coastal enforcement of US revenue laws. The Revenue Marine was not, strictly speaking, a military service since the cutters employed in the Revenue Marine were all under the jurisdiction of the Secretary of the Treasury, rather than the Secretary of the Navy. However, the revenue cutters were armed, and in wartime they could, and did, come under the control of the US Navy. Eventually, some cutters in the Revenue Marine were deployed to the Great Lakes where the question arose as to whether they were permitted by the Rush-Bagot Agreement. From the notes exchanged by the United States and Great Britain as the Rush-Bagot Agreement was being negotiated, the United States understood that revenue cutters would fall within the scope of the agreement. At least, that would appear to have been the intentions of President Madison and Secretary of State Monroe. However, as time progressed, a different interpretation took hold in the United States and ultimately the United States came to view its revenue cutters as falling outside the scope of the Rush-Bagot Agreement, which the United States contended was solely designed to restrict the number and armaments of naval vessels on the Great Lakes. Representations about the purpose and number of US revenue cutters on the Great Lakes were made by Great Britain in 1857 and 1858 but went unanswered until at least 1864, when US Secretary of State William H. Seward demurred from the suggestion that revenue cutters were within the scope of the agreement[19]. Later however, in 1865, Seward conceded that the armament of US revenue cutters on the Great Lakes would conform to the stipulations of the Rush-Bagot Agreement[20].

Events south of the border now moved inexorably towards a cultural clash between northern and southern Americans. The Harpers Ferry raid mounted by abolitionists in 1859, and the subsequent hanging of its ringleader, John Brown, raised opposition to slavery in the north, as well as southern defensiveness towards the institution, to a fever pitch. American politics fractured in the ensuring 1860 election cycle with separate northern and southern candidates seeking election for the Democratic Party and a new party, the Constitutional Union Party, formed from the declining Whigs also contesting the election along with the Republican Party. The Republican candidate, Abraham Lincoln, prevailed in the electoral college and became President but without any support in the deep south. His election caused the secession of South Carolina in December 1860, and thereafter a breakaway nation-state, the Confederate States of America, rapidly took shape as one southern state after another seceded from the union.

Lincoln came to office in March 1861 and immediately took the view that the constitution of the United States did not permit the unilateral secession of the states, and he indicated that he was prepared to enforce that view by deploying the army. The

---

19. Callahan, *The Neutrality of the American Lakes*, 148. Secretary Seward expressed this view in correspondence with the US Secretary of the Treasury, Salmon P Chase, who exercised control over the US Revenue Marine.
20. Ibid, 13, 133-34.

prospect of civil war led to the secession of a few wavering states such as Virginia and the battle lines were soon drawn in what became the most costly (in terms of lives lost) and traumatic war in the history of the United States. United States military forces were ripped apart and although the (now northern) United States seemingly had the advantage over the south in population and industrial development, many of the best general officers in the army and navy were from the south, and they left the US forces to lead the southern military forces. The south obtained several notable victories particularly in the first years of the Civil War. Over time, however, the dreadful cost of the war hardened minds on both sides of the border between the USA and the CSA. After the Union Army secured a tactical victory over the Confederate army at Antietam in the autumn of 1862 President Lincoln issued the Emancipation Proclamation in January 1863, which abolished slavery in the revolting states. In so doing the Lincoln Administration recast the war in moral terms as a fight against slavery, thus seeking to bolster support for the federalist cause at home and abroad.

Britain and France both initially favoured the Confederate States of America in the struggle. Britain, as the world's leading textile manufacturer, obtained its cotton from the southern states where large amounts were grown on southern slave plantations. Both Great Britain and France, then the leading world powers, had reason to fear the growing strength of the United States. The US share of the world's gross domestic product was growing exponentially in the middle of the nineteenth century and would in fact match Britain around 1870, and then exceed it. With growing economic power would come growing military and geopolitical power and the European powers understood this. The formation of a successful secessionist state in US territory would arrest that trend and possibly derail the path to worldwide power of the United States. Therefore, the European powers adopted a risky strategy of outwardly maintaining neutrality while favouring the south in practice. The Confederacy was recognized as a belligerent, rather than as a rebel regime, in May 1861 and in November 1861 a major diplomatic crisis erupted when a US Navy vessel stopped a British passenger ship on the high seas, boarded it, and took away two Confederate diplomats who were en route to Europe to serve as the Confederacy's resident commissioners in London and Paris. Great Britain took strong umbrage to the boarding of a British-flagged ship on the high seas and the seizure of its passengers and for a while it appeared that war might break out between the United States and Great Britain over this insult to the British flag. Ultimately, however, the crisis passed as Lincoln had no desire for a foreign war amidst a civil war, and the imperial government softened its stance under the direct influence of Prince Albert, the prince consort to Queen Victoria. The crisis passed with the subsequent release of the Confederate commissioners by the United States.

A growing anxiety about the waxing power of the Union was not dissipated however, and steps were taken by the imperial government and the colonial government to strengthen Canada's defences. Imperial troops were sent to Canada and some 18,000 would eventually be stationed in Canada during the US Civil War. In addition, the Canadian volunteer militia was increased to a maximum strength of 35,000 men[21].

The US Civil War did not leave individual Canadians unaffected. Most Canadians supported the US Government's efforts to abolish slavery and there were also substantial commercial and family ties between Canadians and the residents of the northern border states. Union Army recruiters were active in Canada during the US Civil War and it is estimated that between twenty and fifty thousand Canadians and other residents of British North America served in the Union army

21. David Ross and Grant Tyler, *Canadian Campaigns 1860-70* (Oxford: Osprey Publishing, 1992) 8, 9.

in the US Civil War[22]. In addition there were some Canadians who, as with the imperial government in London, sympathized with secessionists either from geopolitical reasoning or out of a sympathy for the aristocratic society that the Confederacy embodied. An unknown number of British North Americans served with the Confederate forces during the war but the total is thought to have been considerably below the number of those who fought with the union.

The Confederate States of America was itself active in Canada during the American Civil War, basing a commissioner in the country to look after its interests, and sending a parade of spies and secret insurgents into the country to foment trouble along the border as a distraction for the union forces. A substantial focus of Confederate activity was the union army prisoner of war camp on Johnson's Island in Sandusky Bay, Ohio. The Confederacy twice prepared plans to seize the *Michigan* and use that ship to strike at Johnson's Island to free the confederate prisoners. The first plan, in 1863, was formulated by Lieutenant William H. Murdaugh, an officer in the Confederate States Navy. He envisaged boarding a Canadian steamer in Canadian waters for the transit of the Welland Canal and then seizing the ship when it reached the open water on Lake Erie[23]. The plot was foiled when rumours of it reached the ears of colonial government officials who took steps to increase watchfulness on the Welland Canal, and issued a public warning of the plot. Steps were also taken to warn the US Government. The US promptly ordered the *Michigan* to proceed to Sandusky to protect the Johnson's Island POW camp. The confederate officer in command of the effort now recognized that it would not be possible to proceed with a successful attack and the strategy was abandoned[24].

22. Ibid, 11.
23. Rodgers, *Guardian of the Great Lakes*, 85.
24. John Bell, *Rebels on the Great Lakes: Confederate Naval Commando Operations Launched from Canada 1863-1864* (Toronto: Dundurn, 2011) 35, 36.

As the noose around the Confederacy tightened, increasingly desperate attempts were undertaken by the confederate forces to disrupt the Union and to damage northern morale. In naval terms the Confederacy could not compete with the power of the US Navy which grew much stronger during the war as it enforced a blockade of southern ports. Consequently, the Confederacy turned to asymmetrical warfare on the high seas, investing in blockade runners, ocean-ranging commerce raiders, and even a rather primitive submarine[25]. On the Great Lakes confederate commandoes renewed their scheme to free the prisoners on Johnson's Island in 1864. In the new plan, a confederate band planned to capture the US passenger steamer *Philo Parsons* on its regular run between Detroit, Michigan, and Sandusky, Ohio, and use it to mount an attack on the *Michigan*, while it was anchored near Johnson's Island. The plot would also have included a planned prisoner uprising at the POW camp. The freed prisoners would hopefully be able to find their way back to the Confederacy via Canada[26].

On September, 19, 1864, a senior officer of the Confederate strike team boarded the *Philo Parsons* at Detroit as the ship began one of its scheduled runs to Sandusky. He persuaded the master to stop at Sandwich, Canada West, to embark three other passengers including the disguised Acting Master John Yates Beall of the Confederate States Navy, and two others. The *Philo Parsons* made a regular stop at Amherstburg, Canada West, and took on other passengers, including 16 men who were disguised confederate insurgents. After crossing the international boundary, the master left the ship in the care of the first mate at Middle Bass Island in Lake Erie and repaired to his home

25. Both the Confederacy and the Union invested in new technologically innovative ironclad warships for coastal and riverine warfare. At the Battle of Hampton Roads March 8-9, 1862 the ironclads *CSS Virginia* (formerly the *Merrimack*) and the USS *Monitor* duelled to a draw that proved the worth of iron-hulled warships and resulted in the death-knell for the era of wooden-hulled warships.
26. Ibid, 73.

on the island. Under the command of the first mate, the *Philo Parsons* made one other stop at Kelleys Island before setting out for Sandusky. After leaving Kelleys Island the confederate raiders launched their attack by taking over the ship at gunpoint and then steaming near Sandusky to spy out the *Michigan* at anchor[27]. Fearing a lack of fuel Beall, now in command of the ship, returned to Middle Bass Island to obtain wood. The master of the *Philo Parsons* attempted to rejoin the ship at that point and was made a prisoner. While that was happening, another passenger steamer, the *Island Queen*, made port at Middle Bass Island. Union soldiers from the 130th Regiment from Toledo were aboard the *Island Queen* which caused great alarm amongst the confederates[28]. Beall quickly decided to seize that ship which was accomplished after a minor scuffle with its crew[29].

After putting the passengers from his prizes ashore Beall departed Middle Bass Island with the *Philo Parsons* and the *Island Queen*. He ordered the *Island Queen* to be abandoned and scuttled and then proceeded in the *Philo Parsons* to Sandusky for the attack. However, when the *Philo Parsons* reached Sandusky Beall's crew caught cold feet, fearing that an attack would be a suicide mission, and mutinied. Without a loyal crew there could be no successful attack on the *Michigan* and so Beall was forced to set a course back to the Detroit River, with the *Philo Parsons* now flying the Confederate naval standard. The *Philo Parsons* put into Sandwich and Beall and his erstwhile crew departed from the ship[30]. Although Beall did attempt to scuttle the *Philo Parsons*, the ship's owner had the ship pumped dry and back in service the next day[31].

It was probably best for Beall and his raiders that no attack took

27. Ibid, 77.
28. Rodgers, *Guardian of the Great Lakes*, 89.
29. Bell, *Rebels on the Great Lakes*, 78.
30. Ibid, 90.
31. Rodgers, *Guardian of the Great Lakes*, 91.

place as the US authorities had been warned of the specific plans for the attack. The *Michigan* subsequently searched for the *Philo Parsons* but the ship had made good its escape back to Sandwich. However, the *Michigan* did find the *Island Queen* wrecked on the Chiconolee Reef[32]. So ended the one naval attack undertaken by the Confederate States Navy on the Great Lakes during the American Civil War. It ended without achieving any of its objectives, and only succeeded in wrecking one civilian passenger steamer. However, the raid did create sense of consternation and panic along the American side of the Great Lakes and the US Government was pressed to raise its lake defences.

The *Michigan* remained the only US naval vessel on the Great Lakes and the only other marine forces present were revenue cutters from the US Revenue Marine, although the number of cutters varied and shortly after the outbreak of the war their number was reduced to one following the withdrawal of five of the cutters for blockade service in the Atlantic[33]. The Confederate naval activities however, together with some land-based raids on a train near Buffalo,[34] and an attack by Confederate cavalry raiders on the town of St. Alban's, Vermont, raised alarms along the northern US border and anger in Washington. After Beall's raid Congress authorized more revenue cutters for service on the Great Lakes and for a brief period the Lincoln Administration imposed passport requirements on visitors to the United States from Canada, rescinding that requirement only in March 1865 after the colonial government agreed to reimburse the United States for the monies that were stolen by the confederate raiders in the

---

32. Bell, *Rebels on the Great Lakes*, 92.
33. Callahan, *The Neutrality of the American Lakes*, 139.
34. Acting Master Beall was a ringleader of the Buffalo train raid to free Confederate generals being transported by train from Johnson's Island. The raid was a failure and Beall was subsequently captured, tried as a spy and brigand under military law, convicted, and hanged.

St. Albans raid[35]. The colonial government was naturally very concerned about the insurgent raids, and the American reaction to them, and the colonial government requested that the imperial government once again deploy Royal Navy vessels on the Great Lakes[36].

More serious than these pinpricks along the northern border however were the depredations of the Confederate States Navy's oceanic commerce raiders. When civil war broke out southern military strategists realized that the Confederacy could not instantly produce a navy to compete with the Union, and the army took priority with respect to military materiel. Consequently, the Confederate States Navy relied heavily on the use of oceanic commerce raiders to wage an economic war by sea on the Union. Great Britain made the error of permitting southern agents operating in the country to contract with British shipbuilders for the building, or conversion, of ships for the purpose of commerce raiding. After the outbreak of the war, James Mallory, the Confederate Secretary of the Navy, sent a civilian navy department employee, James Bulloch, to Great Britain where he worked assiduously to procure oceanic commerce raiders for the Confederacy. Although the British *Foreign Enlistment Act* prohibited British Subjects from building, equipping, or operating a warship for a belligerent such as the Confederate States of America, Bulloch was able to circumvent that Act by a combination of deception and legal manoeuvres[37]. In particular, Bulloch commonly arranged for Confederate vessels to depart Great Britain as a merchantman and only when it was upon the high seas would the putative Confederate raider

35. Robert Bothwell, *Your Country, My Country: A Unified History of the United States and Canada* (New York: Oxford University Press, 2015) 116. The confederate raiders had been released from custody by a magistrate and were allowed to keep the money they had stolen which caused considerable outrage in the Union.
36. Bell, *Rebels on the Great Lakes*, 65. By the time of the US Civil War era the imperial government did not maintain any naval vessels on the Great Lakes (Rodgers, *Guardian of the Great Lakes*, 170).
37. Angus Konstam, *Confederate Raider 1861-65* (Oxford, Osprey Publishing, 2003) 9.

meet a second ship carrying its armaments[38]. In doing so, Bulloch avoided the creation of a warship within British jurisdiction in contravention of the *Foreign Enlistment Act*.

Bulloch arranged for both the purchases of existing vessels for conversion into oceanic raiders as well as contracting for the construction of new vessels intended to be raiders. All of this was readily apparent to the United States and the American Minister protested repeatedly to the British Government. While the British Government did take steps to impede the construction or conversion of vessels for the Confederacy, its efforts were lackadaisical and ineffectual. For example, when the American Minister protested about the British-built vessel *Enrica* (subsequently commissioned as the *CSS Alabama*) the request was referred to the Foreign Secretary's legal advisor who was absent due to illness, allowing an official sympathetic to the southern cause to warn Bulloch who immediately sent the *Enrica* to sea[39] to avoid impoundment by the British Government. Undoubtedly, the overall British response to American protests reflected the underlying tilt of British policy in favour of the creation of the Confederate States of America as an independent state. Out of Great Britain the Confederacy obtained the oceanic raiders *CSS Florida, CSS Alabama, CSS Georgia, CSS Rappahannock* and *CSS Shenandoah* which would take a cumulative total of 150 Union prizes during the American Civil War. The depredations of the Confederate raiders could not affect the outcome of the war strategically but they caused great economic loss and forced huge increases in marine insurance premiums. Many American shipowners were forced to re-flag their vessels in Great Britain and Canada to avoid losses[40].

The failure of the British authorities to prevent their shipyards from being used by the Confederacy can be contrasted

38. Ibid, 10.
39. Ibid, 13.
40. Ibid, 20.

unfavourably with the efforts in other countries to prevent the same results. In France, Bulloch contracted for the construction of four oceanic raiders but all four were seized by the French Government before they were even launched and no Confederate oceanic raiders were sourced from France during the Civil War[41]. In Canada, following the failure of the attempted raids on Johnson's Island, the Confederate navy decided to try and create a lake raider to attack Union shipping on the Great Lakes. For this purpose the 350-ton steamer *Georgian* was purchased through the intermediary of a Kentucky seafarer who was a resident of Canada West, for conversion to a raider. Subsequently, ownership was transferred to prominent Canadian lawyer and Confederate sympathizer, George T. Denison[42]. However, the plans for the lake raider came to nought because the *Georgian* needed work on its propulsion system and rumours of the ship's intended use came to the attention of the colonial government, which placed the *Georgian* under intense scrutiny[43]. Two American spies from the *Michigan* were put aboard the *Georgian* and they reported on the *Georgian's* efforts to reach operational status[44]. During the winter of 1865 the *Georgian* was fitted with a ram which caused the United States to immediately complain to the colonial government, which then seized the vessel[45]. The confederate plot had to be abandoned and, eventually, after the conclusion of the US Civil War, the *Georgian* was transferred to the US Government as confiscated Confederate States naval property, over the strenuous legal objections of Denison[46].

Perceiving that the British Government had not done enough to forestall Confederate asymmetrical attacks, and irritated by

41. Ibid, 39.
42. Bell, *Rebels on the Great Lakes*, 96.
43. Ibid, 98.
44. Rodgers, *Guardian of the Great Lakes*, 92.
45. Ibid.
46. Bell, *Rebels on the Great Lakes* 156.

the perceived bias in Great Britain towards the southern secessionists, the Union resolved to strengthen its northern marine defences. The American view was reinforced by continuing concerns in Congress regarding the purposes of the canal system that had been constructed on the St. Lawrence (and on the Rideau River) which, to American eyes, could be used to insert British gunboats into the Great Lakes, thus negating any military advantage that might have accrued to the United States through the limitations contained in the Rush-Bagot Agreement[47]. Consequently, early in 1865, the Lincoln Administration gave the formal six-months notice required under the terms of the Rush-Bagot Agreement for its termination, an action that was given legislative approval in a joint session of Congress held in February 1865[48]. At the same time, pending the termination of the Agreement, the Lincoln Administration sent a diplomatic note to Great Britain stating that it would increase its naval forces on the Great Lakes beyond the existing legal stipulations as a defensive measure and relied on the precedent of the Patriot War when the colonial government had also temporarily exceeded the stipulations in the Agreement due to insurgency[49]. The Congressional Act that gave approval to the executive actions of the Lincoln Administration cast the termination in terms of the overwhelming need of the United States to protect its northern border, stating: "...the peace of our frontier is now endangered by hostile expeditions against the commerce of the lakes and by other acts of lawless persons, which the naval force of the two countries, allowed by the existing treaty, may be insufficient to prevent; ...[50]." Two Great Lakes steamships, the *Hector* and *Winslow* were chartered by the US Government to increase its ability to monitor marine activities on the Great Lakes[51].

47. Callahan, *The Neutrality of the American Lakes,* 150.
48. Fitzpatrick *An Address Delivered by the Rt. Hon. Sir Charles Fitzpatrick*, 14.
49. Ibid.
50. Act of Congress, February 9, 1865.
51. Callahan, *The Neutrality of the American Lakes*, 152.

Faced with a diplomatic *fait accompli* that clearly resulted from Great Britain's own high risk diplomatic strategy of tilting towards the secessionists in the early phases of the war, all that Great Britain could do was to accept the termination gracefully. The imperial government expressed the hope that the United States and Great Britain could return to the former arrangements after the conclusion of the US Civil War[52]. Nevertheless, the pending termination of the Rush-Bagot Agreement alarmed both the imperial government and the colonial government and there was a great concern that the termination of the Rush-Bagot Agreement was a precursor to a possible attack on Canada.

The inexorable conquest of the south by the Union armies continued through the first months of 1865 and the Confederacy, now cut off from European supplies by the Union naval blockade, and lacking an extensive industrial and population base, was slowly strangled. In April 1865, the capital at Richmond was taken by union forces under General Ulysses S. Grant and shortly thereafter Grant forced General Robert E. Lee to surrender the Army of Northern Virginia. Confederate resistance quickly collapsed as the remaining field commanders in the Confederate States Army surrendered to Union army commanders. By May, after the surrender of the western forces of the Confederacy, the rebellion collapsed and the Civil War was over. The last shots were fired from the oceanic raider *CSS Shenandoah* in June 1865 when the *Shenandoah* attacked US whaling vessels in the north Pacific before sailing for Great Britain and internment.

As victory neared, the United States began to have second thoughts about the termination of the Rush-Bagot Agreement. The people of the United States looked forward to an end to war and the termination of the Agreement seemed to run counter

52. Fitzpatrick *An Address Delivered by the Rt. Hon. Sir Charles Fitzpatrick*, 14.

to the general desire for peace. As a result, on March 8, 1865, the United States formally notified Great Britain that it was withdrawing the notice of termination of the Rush-Bagot Agreement prior to the expiration of the notice time period of six months set out in the Agreement[53]. The United States advised Great Britain that it wished the Agreement to remain in force, as a practical matter, which both parties subsequently took to mean that the Rush-Bagot Agreement would continue to be regarded as an international agreement that was in force[54]. Notably, however, no action was taken to reverse the earlier congressional approval of the notice of revocation. Nor did the US action represent a lessening of Union bitterness towards the European powers, including Great Britain, that had supported the Confederacy. On August 4, 1865, victorious General Ulysses S. Grant, the Union commander in chief in the field and his staff, were hosted aboard the *Michigan* which conveyed the party on a reconnaissance mission in Lake Erie[55]

The withdrawal of the US termination of the Rush-Bagot Agreement was welcome news for Canada and Canadians could breathe a sigh of relief as the American action suggested that perhaps the border tensions created by the Confederate insurgents operating from Canada might not survive the conclusion of peace. The American change of heart was also well received in Great Britain where the threat of revocation had led to two serious debates in the House of Commons about the implications of that action for imperial defence[56]. Although the

---

53. Callahan, *The Neutrality of the American Lakes*, 164-65.
54. Fitzpatrick *An Address Delivered by the Rt. Hon. Sir Charles Fitzpatrick*, 15. The ambiguity of Seward's advice of March 8th prompted the imperial government to write to the US Secretary of State to ask for a clarification as to whether the Rush-Bagot Agreement was to continue in force or whether the state parties were merely to conduct themselves in a reasonable manner in the future. On June 16, 1865, Seward replied that the Notice of Withdrawal was itself withdrawn and prompted by a subsequent note from the British Minister dated August 19, 1865, Seward reaffirmed that the Rush-Bagot Agreement would continue in force unless a fresh notice of withdrawal was issued by one of the parties to the Agreement (see Callahan, *The Neutrality of the American Lakes*, 166).
55. Rodgers, *Guardian of the Great Lakes*, 105.

American revocation effort in 1865 was the most serious threat to imperil the Rush-Bagot Agreement, the sudden collapse of the Confederacy in 1865 had removed the potential threat to the United States of insurgent raids from Canada and, consequently, had saved the Rush-Bagot Agreement. No new revenue cutters were constructed by the United States and by 1867 the United States had withdrawn its existing revenue cutters on the Great Lakes, leaving only the now aging *Michigan* to patrol those waters.

56. Callahan, *The Neutrality of the American Lakes*, 163.

1865-1890 THE FENIAN RAIDS, THE CHICORA INCIDENT, AND MANIFEST DESTINY

The American Civil War forever changed the geopolitical landscape of North America. From a country riven by sectarian divisions the United States emerged as a single political unity, although it would take many years for the hard feelings engendered by the Civil War to be laid to rest. During the war many young men who had never travelled far from their home saw the vast country to which they belonged and they developed a new appreciation for it, giving rise to a new national consciousness. The United States emerged from the war as a major industrial power – in fact it was the major industrial power in the Americas – and it was on course to challenge the economic supremacy of Europe. Its army and navy were large and battle-tested. In 1865 the United States Navy was second in strength only to the Royal Navy and could deploy 671 warships, including 71 ironclad vessels which were useful in riverine conflict[1]. The combination of industrial power and large battle-hardened military forces now allowed the United States to give effect to two aspects of its national narrative, the Monroe Doctrine, and Manifest Destiny.

Earlier in the nineteenth century President Monroe had articulated the Monroe Doctrine which forewarned European powers that the United States would not tolerate European

---

1. Black, *Fighting for America*, 350.

powers colonizing or intervening in the affairs of states in the Americas, existing colonies excepted. At first, and for many years thereafter, the European powers did not feel threatened by the Monroe Doctrine since the United States lacked the military or economic power to enforce it. Indeed, its practical enforceability in the first part of the nineteenth century depended upon the tacit backing of Great Britain's Royal Navy to prevent European powers from attempting to intervene in the Americas. At the end of the US Civil War however, the power of the American army and navy gave the country the ability to compel European powers to bend to the will of US foreign policy in the Americas.

Manifest Destiny, the companion to the Monroe Doctrine, grew out of a sense held by Americans of American exceptionalism. Their nationalistic break with the British Empire and their establishment of a democratic form of government (albeit imperfect in some respects) created a sense that the United States of America, as a country, was a wholly different conception than a European state. The Revolutionary War had been fought in part over access to the land beyond the Appalachians and land hunger drove the American population farther west. Awareness of the breadth of the continent was brought to public consciousness by the explorations of the intrepid explorers Lewis and Clark, and the imaginations of the American public were fired with thoughts of possessing all of the North American continent, as the manifest destiny of the American republic. Although the concept of Manifest Destiny, unlike the Monroe Doctrine, was never articulated as official government policy it animated the American political objectives in the nineteenth century with respect to both the acquisition of new territories from European empires and neighbouring states, as well as the suppression of the aboriginal first nations in the west. Many Americans considered that the Canadian territories would inevitably become part of the United States. After the US Civil War informed opinion in the United States increasingly thought that the admission of Canadian territories would occur voluntarily, at the request of the Canadian population, and thus the possibility of a further war of conquest receded from public consciousness.

During the Civil War Great Britain and France had made the strategic error of supporting the southern secessionists as a means of weakening the natural growth in economic and military might of the United States. The government in Washington, now headed by President Andrew Johnson following the assassination of President Lincoln, began to square its accounts with the European powers. Five imperial powers maintained an active presence in North America and its adjacent waters at the conclusion of the Civil War; Great Britain, France, Spain, Russia and Denmark. The implied threat to the European powers from the newfound strength of the United States was a pithy one – recede from North America – and depending upon the subtlety of the government of each European power that is more or less what each of them (other than Denmark) eventually did with more or less prompting by the United States, as the circumstances required.

The first European power to feel American pressure to recede from North America after the conclusion of the US Civil War was France. While the United States was distracted by the Civil War France had taken advantage of the power vacuum in North America to intervene in Mexico. Emperor Napoleon III hoped to create a French-influenced monarchical state in Mexico and he promoted the candidacy of Archduke Maximilian of Austria-Hungary as Mexican Emperor. Heavily supported by French troops and conservative elements in Mexico but opposed by Mexican liberals, Maximilian ascended the throne of Mexico in 1864[2]. However, resistance to his regime was widespread and a civil war broke out in Mexico. The United States regarded his

2. A Mexican general served as regent in 1863-64 while Napoleon III arranged for Maximilian's accession.

regime as illegitimate, and a violation of the Monroe Doctrine, but could do nothing about it while the Civil War raged in the United States. Following the end of the Civil War the United States had the power to force France out of Mexico. The Johnson Administration sent General Philip Sheridan with 40,000 troops to the US border with Mexico along the Rio Grande River, making plain the US displeasure with French attempts to control Mexico. Although Sheridan's troops did not advance across the border, the message to France was plain enough. Sheridan's forces engaged in a large logistical operation in support of the Mexican liberal resistance to Maximilian's French-supported monarchical regime[3].

Faced with the threat of American intervention and the prospect of a major war in Mexico with the United States, Napoleon III realized that he could not achieve his goal of a protected Mexican state subservient to France and announced in January 1866 that France would withdraw from Mexico. As a face-saving measure Napoleon stated as his reason for the withdrawal of French forces that the monarchical regime in Mexico had been stabilized and could survive on its own, which was false[4]. The final withdrawal of French forces from Mexico took place from Veracruz on March 16, 1867, and the Mexican anti-monarchical resistance quickly overcame Maximilian's forces. A victorious liberal Mexican regime stood Emperor Maximilian before a firing squad and executed him on June 19, 1867. Thus ended the last French attempt at empire-building in North America.

The second European power to withdraw from North America in the aftermath of the Civil War was Russia. Russian America, now known as Alaska, was imperial Russia's only overseas colony. It had been largely run by default through the Russian-American Company rather than by the imperial administration and Russia came to see it as a problematic appendage to the

3. Black, *Fighting for America*, 352.
4. Ibid.

empire. Furthermore, the vulnerability of the colony had been exposed during the Crimean War (1853-56) when Russia had fought against an alliance of powers that included Great Britain. Although a local truce had been declared between the Russian-American Company and the Hudson's Bay Company, the long frontier with the British North-Western Territory emphasized the difficulty of Russian America's defence. In addition, the United States became increasingly active along the west coast of North America following its conquest of Mexico's Pacific territory of California and the resolution of the Oregon Territory dispute with Great Britain. Towards the end of the 1850's the commander of the Russian Pacific fleet prepared a report for his government in which he emphasized that the American doctrine of Manifest Destiny would inevitably cause the United States to seize Russian America[5].

During the American Civil War Russia, alone amongst the major European powers, tilted towards the Union, sending a Russian naval squadron to the east coast on a goodwill mission. The United States remained favourable to Russia owing to its moral support during the Civil War. Tsar Alexander II's emancipation of the serfs in 1862 compared favourably to President Lincoln's emancipation of American slaves in the Emancipation Proclamation of 1863, and the subsequent passage of the 13th Amendment to the US Constitution. Although some discussions occurred between the two countries over the fate of Russian America before the Civil War, nothing certain resulted.

After the conclusion of the Civil War Russia became more inclined to sell Russian America to the United States before Manifest Destiny propelled Russia into a conflict with the United States over the territory. American attention had been drawn to Russian America in the final stages of the Civil War by the depredations of the Confederate oceanic raider *Shenandoah*. The

---

5. Richard Kluger, *Seizing Destiny: How America Grew from Sea to Shining Sea* (New York: Alfred A Knopf, 2007) 513.

last of the Confederate Navy's raiders procured by James Bulloch in Great Britain had been engaged in commerce raiding during the last days of the Civil War. On its wide-ranging voyage the *Shenandoah* had entered the Bering Sea and devastated the US whaling fleet that was operating in Russian American waters[6].

In early 1867, to prevent future conflict and to retain American goodwill the Russian Government instructed its ambassador in Washington to negotiate the sale of Russian America to the United States. Secretary of State Seward was receptive to the Russian overture because he realized that possession of Russian America could prevent future losses to American merchant fleets at the hands of oceanic raiders like the *Shenandoah* if the United States possessed the territory[7]. Seward also saw that despite the obvious desire of the United States to expand into the northern half of the continent the creation of a new country closely allied to Great Britain across the northern border was now a certainty, and American Manifest Destiny would be forestalled from its northward expansion. However, there was still the possibility of acquiring all of the Pacific coast of the continent because the colony of British Columbia had not yet declared in favour of union with Canada, and the quick annexation of Alaska might yet result in the incorporation of what had formerly been the northern half of the Oregon Country into the United States. Even if that were not possible it seemed obvious that Canada would eventually desire Russian America for itself to maximize the new country's Pacific coastline. Seward acted very quickly after the Russian ambassador arrived in March 1867 with the Russian proposals. The negotiations were conducted in secrecy so that Canada and Great Britain would not learn of them and they resulted in a treaty that was drafted in the middle of night and signed at 4:00 A.M. on March 30, 1867. By 10:00 A.M. on the very same day the draft treaty was approved by President

6. Konstam, *Confederate Raider 1861-65*, 37; Kluger, *Seizing Destiny*, 515.
7. Kluger, *Seizing Destiny*, 515.

Johnson and was sent to the Senate of the United States for its constitutional advice and consent, which was subsequently obtained[8]. The formal transfer of sovereignty occurred in the autumn of 1867 and the Russian Empire withdrew from North America.

The position of Great Britain in North America was a complex one. The early United States of America had defined itself by rebellion against the British Crown and war against Great Britain. Imperial authorities in London had remained resolute in defence of the remaining North American colonies although they perceived the growing danger of war in North America with a country rising in power and population. In the first half of the nineteenth century Great Britain needed to retain British North America for reasons of imperial prestige, for the opportunity it presented to influence the policies of the United States, and, in the era of wooden capital ships, for lumber and masts to preserve Britain's control of the oceans[9]. However, the Civil War settlement had changed the political equation in British North America. The growing dominance of the United States in North America could no longer be ignored and Great Britain's political tilt towards the south in the Civil War had antagonized the government in Washington, and inflamed American public opinion. Furthermore, the naval operations conducted in the Civil War showed conclusively that technological change had rendered obsolete wooden warships propelled solely by the wind. Canadian timber was no longer required by the Royal Navy as a strategic resource, and the imperial authorities recognized the potential blow to imperial prestige should Great Britain be forced to wage a potentially unsuccessful war with the United States. The need for a political accommodation with the United States in North America now became an imperative of British foreign policy.

8. Ibid, 530, 535.
9. Richard A Preston, *The Defence of the Undefended Border: Planning for War in North America 1867-1939* (Montreal/London: McGill-Queen's University Press, 1977), 11.

The United States had advanced major claims for compensation against Great Britain as a result of the depredations of the Confederate oceanic raiders built in Great Britain, especially the *CSS Alabama*, the most successful of the raiders, under its dashing master, Raphael Semmes. Some politicians in the United States called for the annexation of Canada to the United States as compensation for the damage done to US interests by Great Britain's support of the Confederate States of America. The United States cancelled the 1854 Reciprocity Treaty, which many in the United States felt had been overly favourable to Canadians. The loss of reciprocity put economic pressure on Canada, although by forcing Canada to stand on its own, it probably lessened the risk that Canadian popular opinion might be swayed into accepting union with the United States.

Further pressure on Great Britain, and on its North American colonies, was now provided by the activities of the Fenian Brotherhood, an association of Irish-Americans formed in New York as a secret society in 1858, and linked to the Irish Republican Army in Ireland. The Fenians were dedicated to the cause of Irish independence, a goal which they thought could be advanced through attacks on British North America, as it had proved to be impossible for them to foment a successful rebellion in Ireland itself. Fenian leaders hoped to seize Canada and use it as a base of privateer operations against British shipping, or to foment hostilities between Great Britain and the United States, an event that they thought could promote a successful Irish rebellion[10]. The United States government, of course, did not officially support the objectives of the Fenians. However, the pressure that the Fenians placed on the colonial government and through it on Great Britain was useful to the United States as it attempted to negotiate a satisfactory resolution of the Alabama Claims with the British government. As at least one American historian has pointed out, the Fenian insurgency did not outlive

10. Rodgers, *Guardian of the Great Lakes*, 108.

the settlement between Great Britain and the United States over the US Civil War claims[11].

By 1865 there were 10,000 civil war veterans in the Fenian Brotherhood in the United States and many of them were eager to smite Great Britain for the cause of Irish nationhood. For the first time since the Patriot War Canada faced a border insurgency emanating from the United States. The colonial government infiltrated the Fenians with secret agents to tap into the Fenian's planning strategy. The first attempted Fenian raid occurred in April 1866 when a Fenian force threatened Campobello Island in New Brunswick. Quick action by the imperial military authorities in Nova Scotia forestalled the attempt at an invasion and the crisis passed.

More substantial attacks were planned on Canada East and Canada West. The Fenian strategy was a proposed three-pronged assault. The first attack would be launched north from St. Albans, Vermont, along the traditional Lake Champlain-Richelieu River invasion route. A second prong was to move north from Potsdam, New York, while a third major attack (which never materialized) was to be mounted east by water from Lake Michigan to Goderich on Lake Huron, and to Sarnia at the north end of the St. Clair River. Lesser forces would engage the British and Canadians from mobilization points at Detroit, Michigan, Cleveland, Ohio, and from Buffalo and Ogdensburg, New York[12]. By this point in time railways and telegraphs had become important components of civil and military defence and the Fenians understood that disrupting rail and telegraph networks would assist them by hampering the ability of the colonial government to respond to their attacks.

US authorities along the border did take some steps to prevent the Fenians from mounting an attack on Canada but they were

11. Ibid, 109.
12. Ibid, 110.

unable to forestall the attacks. On the night of May 31, 1866, Colonel John O'Neill crossed the US-Canadian border unopposed at Niagara with approximately 800 Fenian soldiers who were landed in Canada from two steamers and four barges near Fort Erie, Canada West, threatening both the Welland Canal and nearby railway lines. Although *Michigan* was present in the area, the Fenians were able to prevent the ship from interfering with their crossing by the simple expedient of suborning the ship's pilot with liquor and female companionship[13]. The colonial government had been forewarned that an attack was likely and had mustered 20,000 men from the colonial militia to defend the province[14]. Under the *Militia Act* of 1862 seven naval companies of sixty men each had been created on the Great Lakes, five on Lake Ontario (Toronto, Hamilton, Oakville, Gardner Island, and Kingston) and two on Lake Erie (Dunnville and Port Stanley). The naval militia hired boats and steamers to defend the province[15].

Colonel O'Neill's invading Fenian force moved inland and was met by a Canadian troop column near the small town of Ridgeway. As Canadian militia advanced the Fenians began to fall back but in the confusion of battle the militia was ordered to prepare for a defence against a cavalry charge by forming a square. That manoeuver astounded the experienced Fenian veterans of the Civil War who stopped their retirement and commenced sustained firing into the square. Under such an attack the militia lines broke and the militiamen fled pell-mell from the scene of the debacle, leaving Colonel O'Neill and his Fenian insurgents in possession of the field. After crushing the militia at Ridgeway O'Neill led his troops back to Fort Erie which they took after a short sharp battle with the Dunnville

---

13. Ibid, 113.
14. Ross and Tyler, *Canadian Campaigns 1860-70*, 13.
15. William Johnston, William GP Rawling, Richard H Gimblett, John MacFarlane,, *The Seabound Coast: The Official History of the Royal Canadian Navy 1867- 1939* (Toronto: Dundurn Press, 2010) 4.

naval company and the Welland Canal Field Battery[16]. However, O'Neill was now determined to retreat back into the United States and his men boarded a barge to cross the Niagara River. The Dunnville naval company had also embarked on the steamer *WT Robb* and after picking up stragglers from the militia force that had been defeated at Fort Erie they pursued and arrested some of the Fenian stragglers before retreating to Port Colborne at the end of the day[17]. The American authorities had meanwhile dispatched *Michigan* and had also employed two tugboats armed with guns from the *Michigan* to police the border, and to prevent the Fenians from reinforcing their invasion force[18]. As the Fenians retreated, the American force led by *Michigan* was waiting and when the Fenian barge reached American territory *Michigan* and the armed tugboat *Harrison* captured it and arrested everyone aboard for violation of US neutrality laws[19]. The colonial forces suffered 41 casualties (killed and wounded) at Ridgeway and six wounded at Fort Erie[20].

A second attack occurred on June 7th at Pigeon Hill, Canada East, when a Fenian insurgent force under Brigadier General Samuel Spier moved up the Lake Champlain invasion route and entered the country. Militia forces met them and after a short engagement the Fenians retreated with several men killed and 16 men taken prisoner. A repeat engagement at Pigeon Hill on June 22nd was farcical, with the Fenians firing on the Richelieu light infantry before fleeing[21].

The final Fenian assaults occurred in 1870. Colonel (now General) O'Neill assembled a force opposite entrenched militia positions on Eccles Hill near Stansbridge, Quebec. Up to 400 Fenian soldiers commenced an assault and firing broke out as the

16. Ross and Tyler, *Canadian Campaigns 1860-70*, 18.
17. Rodgers, *Guardian of the Great Lakes*, 116.
18. Ibid, 114.
19. Ibid,, 119.
20. Ross and Tyler, *Canadian Campaigns 1860-70*, 18.
21. Ibid, 19-20.

Fenians approached the border. When the Fenians attempted to bring a field gun into action a rapid advance to the border by militia troops caused the Fenians to break and scatter[22]. This largely completed the Fenian Insurgency although a comic-opera assault on the customs house near Pembina, Manitoba, in 1871, was foiled by US Army troops. (It was subsequently discovered that the customs house attacked by the Fenians had mistakenly been placed in the United States, so technically the assault did not occur on Canadian territory.)

Nevertheless, the Fenian Insurgency caused great alarm in Canada, and renewed requests were made to the imperial government to provide for a naval defence on the Great Lakes. Acting on the requests of the colonial government, the Royal Navy's Commander in Chief on the North American and West Indies station dispatched three warships to Canada, the 35-gun wooden steam frigate *Aurora* to Quebec, and the 21-gun wooden steam corvette *Pylades* and the wooden steam sloop *Rosario*, of 11 guns, to Montreal. Three gunboats were also provided by the Royal Navy and four gunboats were provided by the colonial government with crews drawn from the *Aurora* and the *Pylades*[23]. The four gun *Royal* was sent to Cornwall to patrol between Cornwall and the western terminus of the Beauharnois Canal, while the four gun *St. Andrew* was stationed at Prescott to guard the upper St. Lawrence River between Prescott and Kingston, and the two gun *Heron* was ordered to Toronto to patrol Lake Ontario. The two-gun *Rescue* and the similarly armed *Britomart* were sent to Lake Erie to patrol the lake from Fort Erie to Maitland, and from Maitland to Amherstburg respectively. The *Michigan* (a two-gun armed gunboat of the colonial fleet − not to be confused with the American warship of the same name) was posted to Windsor to guard the Detroit River, Lake St. Clair, and the St. Clair River, and finally the innocuously named *Cherub*

22. Ibid, 33.
23. Gilbert Norman Tucker, *The Naval Service of Canada* (Ottawa: King's Printer, 1952) 43.

(also armed with two guns) was sent to Goderich to protect Lake Huron between Sarnia and Collingwood[24]. The naval force established during the Fenian insurgency once again exceeded the limits prescribed by the Rush-Bagot Agreement. Including the two gunboats stationed at Cornwall and Prescott, the colonial government could muster three warships on Lake Ontario, which exceeding the legally-prescribed limitation by two vessels, and those vessels exceeded the numerical restriction on armaments by a total of nine guns.

The unhappiness of the United States with Great Britain's role in the Civil War had naturally affected relations between the United States and Canada. As a result, Canadian politicians, particularly Sir John A. Macdonald, began working in the 1860's towards a unification of British North America into a single country in order to avoid being swallowed up by a new and powerful American state following the conclusion of the American Civil War. Encouraged in this endeavour by the imperial government, colonial politicians from the provinces of Canada (Canada East and Canada West) New Brunswick, Nova Scotia, Prince Edward Island and Newfoundland met at various dates at Charlottetown, Quebec City, and finally London, England, to hammer out the terms of union between the British North American colonies. The imperial government supported those efforts from a realization that Great Britain must retreat politically and withdraw militarily from North America in the face of the waxing postwar American power. Queen Victoria, who was fully briefed on the subject, noted in her diary the ". . . impossibility of our being able to hold Canada . . ."[25].

Great Britain assigned officers to analyse the defence needs of

24. Ibid.
25. Queen Victoria, The Letters of Queen Victoria - vol 1, (ed) George Buckle (New York: John Murray, 1926) 250. However, notwithstanding the British perception that Canada could not be defended against the United States, the Queen did go on to state "... but we must struggle for it."

Canada during the American Civil War and the results indicated the enormous challenges that a successful defence would present to the country's defenders. Captain William Noble RN assessed the harbors and fortifications in Canada and reported in November 1861 that in a war with the United States the colonial forces must cut the American lines from the interior to the New York frontier along the St. Lawrence River, necessitating the seizure of Fort Montgomery at Rouses Point, as well as the American fortifications at Niagara and Mackinac[26]. Further, the Royal Navy must establish a naval squadron on Lake Huron[27]. Noble also emphasized the need to defend both the Beauharnois and Welland canals[28]. Captain Richard Collinson reported that in the event of war communications would likely be cut along the shared boundary of the St. Lawrence River and therefore small warships must be rushed to Kingston without delay to assist in maintaining lake supremacy. Collinson also stated that the Royal Navy must establish a naval squadron on Lake Huron[29]. An 1864 report by Lieutenant Colonel William Jervois emphasized the need for the Royal Navy to retain control of the lower St. Lawrence River between Quebec and Montreal. Jervois thought that 90,000 troops would need to be based in the country between Quebec and Kingston to maintain a solid defence[30].

A further report by Captain Lindesay Brine RN in 1870 was somewhat more optimistic in suggesting that offensive naval operations on the Great Lakes by Canada (or the threat of such operations) might forestall an attack from the south and, if deterrence failed, Quebec could be held and the Royal Navy should be able to dominate both banks of the lower St. Lawrence River[31].

26. Preston, *The Defence of the Undefended Border* 27.
27. Black, *Fighting for America*, 328.
28. Preston, *The Defence of the Undefended Border* 27.
29. Ibid, 28.
30. Black, *Fighting for America*, 329.
31. Preston, *The Defence of the Undefended Border*, 50.

Far from reassuring British politicians these analyses underscored the precarious position that Great Britain found itself in following the Union success in the Civil War. The Great Lakes were particularly exposed and it was obvious that the Americans would both seek to and likely succeed in cutting off communications west of the St. Lawrence River, thus isolating Canada West from the main imperial military post at Quebec. The defence of Canada, and indeed all of British North America, would be fraught with difficulties and risk. To the imperial authorities, the new geopolitical reality compelled a British retreat from North America. Freedom from major defence responsibilities in North America would also allow Great Britain to expand its trade and empire in other areas of the world, as the US Navy was primarily a coastal force during the latter part of the nineteenth century, and the destruction or re flagging of much of the US merchant fleet in the Civil War had discouraged it from seeking oceanic supremacy[32].

Accordingly, on July 1, 1867, with strong imperial encouragement, British North America became one country under the name of Canada, and was organized as a federation that was internally autonomous within the empire but not yet externally independent. The new country retained its constitutional links to the British Crown and remained subject to the foreign policies of the imperial government. However, the new constitution of Canada explicitly provided that the national government would have responsibility for its own defence, and while it was understood that Canada would remain under British protection as part of the empire, internal security would no longer be an imperial responsibility. At its beginning Canada consisted of the province of Canada, now once again split into two provinces, Quebec and Ontario, together with New Brunswick and Nova Scotia. Prince Edward Island opted out of joining in 1867 but reversed itself and joined in 1873 while

32. J R Hill (ed.) *The Oxford Illustrated History of the Royal Navy*, 164.

Newfoundland remained aloof and did not enter the confederation until 1949. Thus, at its inception, Canada remained an eastern North American country but that would change almost immediately.

The vast western prairie had long remained the exclusive preserve of the Hudson's Bay Company which, according to its royal charter granted in 1670, governed the lands around Hudson's Bay that were known as Rupert's Land together with the far-off North-Western Territory as an exclusive domain. However, its licence to govern had expired shortly before the American Civil War and following that war, as Great Britain sought to make a respectable and face-saving retreat from North America, the imperial government required the company to surrender its lands in 1869, following which the Great Britain proceeded to transfer both Rupert's Land and the North-Western Territory to Canada in 1870. At a stroke, Canada's geographical reach extended from the Atlantic ocean to the Rocky Mountains.

However, one part of the vast western territories presented the federal government[33] with an immediate challenge. Part of the territories along the Red River had been colonized by both the Metis[34] and by Scottish immigrants during the Hudson's Bay Company's long administration of those lands. Inhabitants of the Red River settlements wanted to ensure that their own interests would not be overlooked in the transfer of their territory from the company's administration to Canada's administration.

33. At this time, and for many years afterwards, Canadians would have described their national government as the Dominion Government, because the new country was constituted as the Dominion of Canada (an attempt to name it as the Kingdom of Canada failed over concerns about American sensitivities to monarchical forms of government in the Americas).
   However, the word "Dominion," over time, became associated with constituent states of the British Empire having limited national sovereignty, and thus fell into disfavour, and ceased to be used. The modern term federal government is used today and is also used throughout this text to describe the national government of Canada in the post-confederation period.
34. The Metis are a mixed people of aboriginal First Nations and European ancestry who are particularly well-represented in western Canada.

Therefore, in the period after the surrender of the Hudson's Bay Company's royal charter but before Canadian political control could be actively asserted, a Provisional Government for the settled portion of the territory known as Manitoba was established under the Metis leader Louis Riel.

The federal government negotiated terms for the admission of the Red River settlements as the Province of Manitoba in 1870. Disturbances associated with the provisional government interregnum however, motivated the federal government to send out a military expedition to Manitoba to ensure that federal authority would be respected. The expedition was placed under the command of a British Army officer, Colonel Garnet Wolseley, and consisted of both British and Canadian militia troops. Part of the journey to the west undertaken by the troops was via a steamer on Lake Huron and Lake Superior and it is that passage which created an important precedent for the use of the Great Lakes waterways for military purposes.

To move the troops between Collingwood, Ontario, and Fort William, Ontario, the federal government chartered several steamships. Given the United States antagonism towards Great Britain following the Civil War, there was a concern that the US authorities might not permit the use of the US-owned canal at Sault Ste. Marie, which allowed navigable passage between Lake Huron and Lake Superior. That assumption was to prove correct despite the fact that US government vessels had been allowed to transit Canadian canals, including the Welland Canal, during the American Civil War[35]. As to the use of canals it had been the practice that where a vessel that was owned by one of the state parties to the Rush-Bagot Agreement wished to transit one of the connecting canals permission would be sought from the country that owned the canal by the country that owned the ship. Thus, as early as 1848, the United States had sought

35. George F G Stanley, *Toil and Trouble: Military Expeditions to Red River* (Toronto: Dundurn, 1989) 97.

permission from the colonial government for the passage of US revenue cutters from the Great Lakes to the Atlantic Ocean using the St. Lawrence River canals[36].

During this period the Soo Locks at Sault Ste. Marie, Michigan, were owned by the state of Michigan. The Governor of Michigan sought instructions from Washington about how to respond in the event that a formal request was made by Canada to allow some government vessel carrying arms or troops to transit the Soo Locks. The Grant Administration advised that no foreign military expedition should be permitted to transit an American canal without authorization from Washington. Accordingly, American authorities moved to restrict the use of the canal to deny passage for war materiel or troops. But the US Government kept its instructions about the use of the canal secret, and a delay by the army in telegraphing officials at Sault Ste. Marie, Michigan, aided the initial movement of British and Canadian forces[37]. On Lake Huron the steamer *Algoma* departed Collingwood with military stores on May 3, 1870, and making good progress it arrived at the American locks at Sault Ste. Marie and quietly passed through before heading to Fort William to deliver its cargo. The next transport would not have an easy passage however. The *Chicora* was a former Confederate blockade runner that had made passages between the Bahamas and the Confederacy and was known to American authorities. To minimize the chances that it would be stopped the Canadian authorities determined to remove military supplies and the advance party of troops that the *Chicora* carried and to march the troops with their supplies across Canadian territory to Lake Superior while the ship proceeded *sans* cargo through the American canal. After transiting the canal the troops and military supplies could be re embarked for the voyage to Fort William. However, when American inspectors boarded the

36. Callahan, *The Neutrality of the American Lakes*, 130.
37. Preston, *The Defence of the Undefended Border*, 48.

Chicora they found cargo that they considered military materiel and the *Chicora* was prevented from accessing the canal[38]. US authorities also refused permission to the gunboat *Prince Alfred* to pass through the canal, even with its guns removed[39].

The British Minister, Sir Edward Thornton, interceded with the US Government explaining that the *Chicora* would not carry war materiel through the American canal and that, in any event, the federal government had resolved its differences with the inhabitants of Manitoba through peaceful negotiations with the representatives of Riel's Provisional Government. Therefore, the Red River Expedition was wholly peaceful in its intentions. The US accepted that position and Bancroft Davis, the Acting US Secretary of State, instructed the Governor of Michigan that President Ulysses S. Grant authorized the passage of vessels chartered by the Canadian government for the purposes of the Red River Expedition, provided that the ships did not carry troops and munitions through the US canal[40]. The *Chicora* incident crystallized the precedent of prior permission for the movement of all government vessels transiting any of the American or Canadian canals and locks on the Great Lakes. It also established a precedent for the denial of passage where vessels carried troops or war materiel to respond to internal dissension or rebellion within the state seeking a right of passage.

Meanwhile, the federal government had been negotiating with the Metis through Donald Smith, who was a partner in the Hudson's Bay Company, and an amicable political settlement had been reached that was subsequently embodied in the *Manitoba Act,* which created the new province of Manitoba[41]. Consequently, when Garnet Wolseley's force arrived at Lower Fort Garry in Manitoba he found that Riel and his Provisional

38. Stanley, *Toil and Trouble*, 98.
39. Preston, *The Defence of the Undefended Border*, 48.
40. Stanley, *Toil and Trouble*, 100.
41. Granatstein and Oliver, *The Oxford Companion to Canadian Military History*, 364.

Government was not in open rebellion against the Crown. In fact, Riel advised Wolseley's intelligence officer that he would hold his Provisional Presidency only until the new federal authorities arrived[42]. When Wolseley arrived with his force at Upper Fort Garry on August 24, 1870, he found that the Provisional Government had dissolved itself and the fort was abandoned. The authority of the federal government was quickly established and Manitoba entered confederation as Canada's newest province. In September, with a new provincial Lieutenant Governor in place, and the political situation stabilized, Wolseley withdrew from Manitoba. The British Army's 60th Regiment left Winnipeg on August 29th, taking with them in their boats a black bear which they had adopted as a regimental mascot. The regiment arrived in Ontario on October 18th and a few weeks later Wolseley and the regiment left Canada. They were the last regular British Army troops to be stationed as garrison forces in Canada[43].

Events were now moving rapidly towards a denouement of the British saga in North America. With confederation in 1867 Canada had been established as a country and by 1870 it encompassed most of the northern half of North America. Given American antagonisms towards Great Britain for its role in lending support to the southern secessionists in the Civil War British policy makers were anxious to avoid the risk of war with the United States by withdrawing as much as possible from the continent. At this time there was also considerable pressure from the British population to reduce the expenditures of the government on imperial military garrisons and thus the withdrawal of all British forces in Australia also occurred in 1870[44].

42. Stanley, *Toil and Trouble*, 156.
43. Ibid, 175. Except for the troops garrisoning the Royal Navy bases at Halifax, Nova Scotia, and Esquimalt, British Columbia.
44. Black, *Fighting for America*, 377.

The policy of withdrawal reached its climax through negotiations and the signing of the Treaty of Washington on May 8, 1871, in which, for the first time, a Canadian political figure in the person of Prime Minister Sir John A. Macdonald participated as a member of the official British negotiating committee. The treaty resolved all of the outstanding issues concerning Great Britain's relations with the United States, including issues concerning Canada and the remaining British North American territories. Britain settled American claims made against it for the Civil War depredations by the Confederate Navy's oceanic raiders, especially *Alabama*, by agreeing to arbitration of the American claims. The final award from that arbitration amounted to 3.2 million pounds sterling. Britain also agreed to submit a border dispute between the colony of British Columbia and the United States with respect to the ownership of the San Juan islands in the Strait of Juan de Fuca to the German Emperor (who ultimately ruled in favour of the United States). Fishing rights off the Newfoundland coast were satisfactorily dealt with and, importantly for Canada, a right was conferred in perpetuity upon the United States for shipping access on the St. Lawrence River, which otherwise might be closed to it by the actions of Canadian authorities[45]. Canadians (i.e., British Subjects) were given navigation rights on Lake Michigan (subject to limitations)[46]. Although the Treaty of Washington resolved outstanding practical issues, the more subtle result was a recognition by Great Britain of American primacy in North America, and the end of a 250-year British attempt to dominate the continent.

The British Army's withdrawal in 1870 was preceded by the withdrawal of the Royal Navy. In early 1868 the station ship at Montreal was withdrawn and although crews from *HMS Constance*, the station frigate at Quebec City, continued to supply

45. Ibid, 376.
46. Callahan, 173.

gunboat crews on the Great Lakes through the summer of 1868 to counter the Fenian threat by the autumn of that year naval authorities considered that the real danger had passed. Accordingly, the gunboat crews supplied by the Royal Navy were withdrawn from the Great Lakes and they never returned. The following year, when Admiral Rodney Mundy departed from his position as commander in chief on the North American and West Indies Station, he suggested that if naval protection on the Great Lakes was required in the future it should be the responsibility of the new Canadian government[47]. After more than a century of involvement with the naval defence of Canada the Royal Navy quit the Great Lakes forever.

As Great Britain withdrew from the Great Lakes, the federal government made some efforts to provide for naval security in the interim because of the continuing threat of the Fenian Insurgency. Two of the private steamers that had been outfitted by the militia naval companies during the Fenian Insurgency, the *Rescue* and *Michigan* (now renamed the *Prince Alfred*), were purchased by the federal government as the first naval vessels of the new Dominion of Canada to guard the Great Lakes in compliance with the Rush-Bagot Agreement[48]. Later, the two armed ships were used to transport troops assigned to the Red River Expedition but afterwards the federal government took both vessels out of service and the naval militias that had been created in the communities along the Great Lakes were allowed to lapse[49].

During the 1870's and the 1880's both the governments of Conservative Prime Minister Sir John A. Macdonald (1867-1873, 1878-1891) and Liberal Prime Minister Alexander Mackenzie (1873-1878) concentrated on the internal consolidation of Canada. After the collapse of the reciprocity

47. Tucker, *The Naval Service of Canada*, 44.
48. Johnston, Rawling, Gimblett, MacFarlane, *The Seabound Coast*, 5.
49. Ibid, 6.

treaty with the United States in 1866 it became imperative to erect tariff barriers to protect and encourage domestic industry and that became national policy. The annexation of Rupert's Land, the North-Western Territory, and the entry of British Columbia and Prince Edward Island into the confederation placed new stress on the construction and completion of railway lines to link the country from east to west and that also became a key policy of nineteenth century national governments. In the west, the incorporation of new territories with substantial aboriginal first nation populations required negotiations to resolve land claims and the creation of reserves, and a series of treaties were entered into with first nations as the century progressed. That did not occur without conflict however, and the army was deployed in the west once again in 1885 against the Metis and aboriginal First Nations during the North-West Resistance. Subsequently, however, large scale immigration and migration into the west did occur. In 1880 Great Britain transferred the arctic archipelago to Canada and afterwards only Newfoundland and its Labrador dependency remained outside of the confederation.

The emphasis on internal consolidation in Canada was also replicated south of the border, in the United States, where the 1870s and 1880s saw the US Army involved in multiple Indian Wars and the often forcible transfer of the US aboriginal population to reservations. Massive immigration and migration into the US west continued and the industrial economy grew commensurate with the country's burgeoning population. Relations between Canada and the United States remained cordial as each sought to consolidate their territory and to develop their own economy. Although British troops were no longer present in Canada's interior Canada retained the British security shield by virtue of its continued position as a constituent part of the British Empire, which reached its apogee towards the end of the century. Additionally, the Royal Navy continued to maintain its naval bases at Halifax, Nova Scotia, and Esquimalt, on Vancouver Island. British troops also continued to garrison both of those bases.

On the Great Lakes shipping and commerce grew apace without naval conflict of any sort between Canada and the United States. The now aging American guard ship, *Michigan*, continued to ply the Great Lakes but without engendering any fears on the part of Canadian authorities. The *Michigan* often visited Canadian ports, particularly Sarnia, where the seamen could obtain cheap liquor and tobacco products and where it was welcomed by Canadian merchants[50]. The United States also continued to provide for the civil enforcement of its customs laws by the presence of the Revenue Marine vessels of the Treasury Department's Revenue Marine service.

In Canada, the Federal Government took stock of the lessons learned from the *Chicora* Incident and undertook the construction of an all-Canadian canal between Lake Huron and Lake Superior at Sault Ste. Marie. The canal was built between 1887 and 1895 on St. Marys Island, a distance of about one and half miles, including a 900-foot long lock. The canal and lock ensured that the Federal Government would be able to pass Canadian government-owned ships into Lake Superior without incurring any future difficulties with the American authorities.

As Britain withdrew from the continent, following Russia and France, the other two remaining colonial powers in North America, Denmark and Spain, showed little movement towards a continental withdrawal. Greenland, which was owned by Denmark, was simply too remote for most Americans to express much interest in it. However, Secretary of State Seward was enthusiastic about acquiring Greenland, as was a former Treasury Secretary, Robert Walker, who advised in the forward

50. Rodgers, *Guardian of the Great Lakes*, 124.

to a report prepared for Seward that Greenland's purchase would out flank Canada on the northeast and complement Seward's coup in purchasing Alaska from the Russians, which had compressed Canada's Pacific coast between Alaska and Washington[51]. Walker saw the acquisition of Greenland as potentially increasing the pressure on Canada to submit to annexation by the United States. However, Seward had sought and failed to purchase the Danish West Indies, a group of islands in the Carribean Sea, souring relations with Denmark. That, and the difficulties in obtaining approval from Congress for the purchase of Greenland in the final year of Seward's term of office, was simply too much for Seward to undertake[52]. Greenland's potential acquisition was left to another day[53].

Finally, there was Spain, an imperial power that had long been ousted from the mainland of North America but which still retained the island of Cuba only 90 miles from the southern coast of the United States, an island long coveted by Americans. (Spain also retained the smaller island of Puerto Rico but that was of much less interest to the United States.) Spain simply did not comprehend that its geopolitical position in North America was unwelcome to the new rising imperial power in North America, which was the United States. Caught up in its own internal political difficulties at home Spain maintained an oppressive colonial policy in Cuba that spurred rebelliousness among the island's inhabitants. Increasingly, American policy makers considered Spain's retention of its North American possessions as untenable. As we will see later, when conflict between Spain and the United States became inevitable in the 1890's that conflict would have spillover effects on the arms limitation regime spawned by the Rush-Bagot Agreement.

51. Charles Emmerson, *The Future History of the Arctic* (New York: Public Affairs, 2010) 79.
52. Ibid.
53. The United States revived consideration of a purchase of Greenland from Denmark in 1946 but nothing came of it. The Danes remained unwilling to transfer sovereignty.

PART THREE: THE WATCHFUL PEACE ON THE LAKES, 1890-1931

1890-1900 THE RISE OF THE UNITED STATES, THE STONE BATTLESHIP, AND THE JOINT HIGH COMMISSION

By the 1890's Manifest Destiny had run its course across the United States between the Canadian border and the Rio Grande River. The US Army had been extensively deployed in the west in the years following the Civil War, at first to pressure the French to leave Mexico, and afterwards to suppress the aboriginal tribes fighting against the settlement of the west. The last major aboriginal uprising in the USA occurred in 1891 and after its suppression the army was redeployed, with many US troops repositioned near the border with Canada[1]. The year before, in 1890, the US Census Bureau had officially declared that the frontier had been eliminated and for the first time the entire country was considered to be settled. That development had important implications for American self-perceptions and caused some, notably the American historian Frederick Jackson Turner, to wonder if American dynamism and the particular political culture of the United States would be compromised by the lack of tension between a settled America and a wilderness frontier. That discussion animated the debate around the Manifest Destiny of the United States, and the potential for expansion beyond the existing political borders of the country.

1. Preston, *The Defence of the Undefended Border*, 118.[2] Alvin C Glueck, "The Invisible Revision of the Rush-Bagot Agreement, 1898-1914,"*The Canadian Historical Review Vol LX (1979)* (Toronto: University of Toronto Press, 1979) 469.

Hitherto, the US Navy had essentially been a brown-water navy, focussed on coastal protection but with a limited capacity to project force at a great distance abroad. In the early 1890's the Harrison Administration undertook a policy of naval renewal that essentially called for the construction of new warships to support the activities of a blue-water fleet. The Harrison Administration called for the construction of battleships and cruisers and one torpedo boat. American shipyards on the Great Lakes could not construct the larger vessels due to the physical constraints of the Great Lakes and the connecting rivers and canals, which would frustrate passage to the sea. However, the construction of a torpedo boat was well within the capabilities of the Great Lakes shipyards and the rivers and canals would pose no restraint on its movement to the ocean.

Nevertheless, when a Bay City, Michigan firm bid on the torpedo boat contract and provided the lowest bid it lost the contract because of the provisions of the Rush-Bagot Agreement, despite the support of Benjamin Tracey, President Harrison's naval secretary[2]. In April 1892, Senator James McMillan of Michigan publicly called on the Secretary of State, James Blaine, for an explanation of why Michigan firms were prevented from bidding on naval contracts. Blaine was in ill-health, and was approaching the end of his tenure as Secretary, so he waffled on the subject suggesting at first to the imperial government's Minister, Sir Julian Pauncefote, that he would not propose any change to the Rush-Bagot Agreement and then subsequently suggesting that it should be amended to allow warships to be built on the Great Lakes before finally withdrawing even that suggestion[3]. However, the US Government did propose to build two new armed revenue cutters for Great Lakes service and that was permissible according to the established practices concerning the implementation of the Rush-Bagot Agreement[4].

---

2. Alvin C Glueck, "The Invisible Revision of the Rush-Bagot Agreement, 1898-1914," 469.
3. Ibid.
4. At this point in time the United States Revenue Marine maintained three armed revenue

Blaine's successor as Secretary of State, John Foster, maintained that the Rush-Bagot Agreement did not prevent the parties from building warships on the Great Lakes provided that the warships were not deployed on the lakes but he left office along with the Harrison Administration early in 1893 before that issue could be satisfactorily resolved[5]. Interestingly, Foster also addressed the subject of the continuing validity of the Rush-Bagot Agreement. Senator McMillan had questioned whether the Rush-Bagot Agreement was still in force in light of the notice of withdrawal that had been issued by the Lincoln Administration and then quickly recalled towards the end of the Civil War. Congress had passed a joint resolution agreeing to the US withdrawal from the Agreement before the executive branch of the US Government recalled the notice. McMillan questioned whether the recall of the notice of withdrawal by the Lincoln Administration was valid after the Congress had approved the withdrawal notice and he noted that there was no subsequent action by Congress to ratify the withdrawal of the notice. Some officials in the Treasury Department also took the view that the failure of Congress to ratify the withdrawal of the notice meant that the Rush-Bagot Agreement was no longer in force[6]. While Secretary Blaine had not offered any opinion on this question his successor Foster stated that it was "a nice argument" but it was not material, and the United States considered that the agreement remained in force[7]. Secretary Foster also confirmed that the US regarded revenue cutters, which were not under the operational control of the US Navy, and whose purposes were directed at law enforcement rather than naval defence, to be outside of the scope of the Rush-Bagot Agreement[8].

cutters on the Great Lakes, one each at Erie, Detroit and Milwaukee (Callahan, *The Neutrality of the American Lakes*, 178).

5. Ibid.
6. Callahan, *The Neutrality of the American Lakes*, 179.
7. Don Courtney Piper, *The International Law of the Great Lakes*, 107.
8. Ibid.

In Canada, the federal government at this juncture preferred not to raise any issues regarding the Rush-Bagot Agreement, or to make any plans for the possible defence of the country against a potential American attack. The Conservative Ministry was in some disarray during the early 1890's and experienced five Prime Ministers in five years. Two (Sir John A. Macdonald and Sir John Thompson) died in office, one (Sir Mackenzie Bowell) was forced out in a cabinet revolt, another (Sir John J C Abott) retired, and the last (Sir Charles Tupper) was defeated in the 1896 general election, and replaced by Wilfrid Laurier of the Liberal Party. Nevertheless, Canadian military officials remained concerned about the potential threat represented by the United States and any possible upgrading of American naval forces on the Great Lakes. Major General Herbert, the commander of the Canadian army and militia forces, recommended planning for a pre-emptive strike on the Great Lakes should relations with the United States move towards war in order to counterbalance the superior resources that the United States could quickly deploy on the Great Lakes but the government demurred. The Federal Government insisted on maintaining the status quo (no changes to the agreement and no formal diplomatic objections to American activities) as the best approach in the circumstances[9].

The Royal Navy was of a similar mind as the federal government with respect to any possible changes to the Rush-Bagot Agreement and the consequential need to establish a naval defence on the Great Lakes. Having given up its responsibilities on the Great Lakes at the time of confederation, the Admiralty was averse to any suggestion that it should accept any further responsibilities for lake defences on behalf of the imperial government. An Admiralty note dated June 29, 1892, from Captain (later Admiral) Cyprian Bridge, then the Director of Naval Intelligence at the Admiralty, described the defence of the

9. Preston, *The Defence of the Undefended Border*, 120.

Canadian land border as a military issue but noted that unlike the American Revolutionary War, and the War of 1812, the naval control of the Great Lakes was of much less importance owing to the influx and distribution of settlement in Canada, and the improvement in transportation and communications wrought by the development of Canadian railways. Bridge noted that the Agreement was not a formal treaty and either side could renounce it by notice. However, it was important for Great Britain that the Agreement be maintained in force since it gave the imperial government a straightforward reason to resist any demands by Canada for naval protection on the Great Lakes. British military planners at the end of the nineteenth century clearly saw that it was no longer possible for Great Britain to effectively protect Canada by the deployment of imperial forces within the country. The sensitivity of the issue was readily apparent from Captain Bridge's comment that should the US place warships on the Great Lakes it would be difficult to resist a request for naval defence on the Great Lakes from the Canadian federal government, and "injudicious" to act on such a request[10].

In a subsequent minute to the Undersecretary of State for the Colonial Office on behalf of the Lords of the Admiralty, Evan MacGregor, the Permanent Secretary of the Admiralty, described the Rush-Bagot Agreement as an arrangement that had worked in Great Britain's favour for many years. The Agreement had allowed the Royal Navy to withdraw from the Great Lakes where deployment had represented an inefficient distribution of British forces. MacGregor thought that the Admiralty lords should extol the virtues of the Agreement to the Colonial Office by emphasizing that the existence of the Rush-Bagot Agreement had not presented "real difficulty" to Canadian authorities in stopping the depredations of confederate raiders in the Civil

10. Cyprian A. G. Bridge (Capt. RN), Directorate of Naval Intelligence, Admiralty, "Memorandum", June 29, 1892, (Ottawa: Library and Archives Canada, Department of the Naval Service, Inland Waterways and Canals, Naval Control of the Great Lakes).

War, nor had it stopped US authorities from suppressing the subsequent attacks made on Canada by the Fenians[11].

Relations between Canada and the United States remained cordial although a jarring note was introduced in 1895 when a diplomatic crisis erupted between Great Britain and the United States over the application of the Monroe Doctrine. The issue concerned the border between British Guiana, a Crown colony in South America, and Venezuela, and the dispute inadvertently involved Canada because Canada remained constitutionally tethered to Great Britain. A large part of British Guiana was claimed by Venezuela but Great Britain did not recognize the validity of the Venezuelan claim. An agent for the Venezuelan government lobbied in Washington for the application of the Monroe Doctrine to the dispute and the Cleveland Administration responded sympathetically. The United States sided with Venezuela on the need for international arbitration of the dispute and on the scope of that arbitration. Great Britain's refusal to accede to the US view provoked the Cleveland Administration. What was initially a far-off diplomatic dispute quickly escalated when the United States determined that Great Britain was not recognizing the predominant role of the United States in affairs in the Americas. For a time it actually seemed possible that war between the United States and Great Britain would break out before cooler heads prevailed. Ultimately, the dispute was submitted to arbitration and the scope of that arbitration met American demands. Thus, the immediate crisis passed.

The fallout from the Venezuelan Affair was worrisome to the federal government which had felt compelled at the time of the crisis to rearm the Canadian militia with newer and more

11. Evan MacGregor, Permanent Secretary to the Admiralty, "Memorandum to the Undersecretary of State, Colonial Office," (Ottawa: Library and Archives Canada, Department of the Naval Service, Inland Waterways and Canals, Naval Control of the Great Lakes).

modern rifles as a precautionary measure[12]. Orders-in-Council were also passed to permit the formation of naval reserve companies on the Great Lakes at Toronto and at Guelph[13]. The Canadian Pacific Railway sought a subvention to permit it to construct a special rail car that could be used to transport small naval craft into the Great Lakes but the British Admiralty advised that the money would be better spent in expanding the locks to permit the passage of larger warships that could command the lakes in the event of a war with the United States[14]. War planning by military officials was given a greater urgency. At a meeting of the Joint Naval and Military Committee in early 1896 it was pointed out that a Canadian defence against the United States must attempt to protect Montreal, Quebec, and Toronto, while keeping open the St. Lawrence River to Lake Ontario and retaining the Welland Canal[15]. To do all of that required that the Canadian army's main force (consisting of the small permanent force together with the militia) be deployed south of Montreal and Quebec, where the main force could hopefully mount an offensive towards Albany and Troy, New York. Meanwhile a St. Lawrence Field Force would be charged with occupying Oswego, New York, as well as important railway junctions at or near Moers Junction, Watertown, and Malone, with a possible offensive move against Rouse's Point. Provision for the defence of Ottawa would also be made but western Ontario would not be defended, nor would the canal located at Sault Ste. Marie be defended, and western Canada would be used as a diversion to absorb large bodies of American troops. It was considered likely that the Canadian Pacific Railway (then the only Canadian

12. Stacey, *The Undefended Border*, 13.
13. William Johnston, William GP Rawling, Richard H Gimblett, John MacFarlane,, *The Seabound Coast: The Official History of the Royal Canadian Navy 1867-1939*, 49.
14. Ibid, 47.
15. Author Unknown, "Canadian Defence; Notes taken at the Preliminary Meeting of the Joint Naval and Military Committee, March 30, 1896" (Ottawa: Library and Archives Canada, Department of the Naval Service, Inland Waterways and Canals, Naval Control of the Great Lakes).

transcontinental railway line) would be severed by an invading American force[16].

However, by 1897 Prime Minister Laurier, in consultation with the Admiralty, came to the conclusion that there was little risk of war developing between Canada and the United States and therefore there was not a sufficient reason to invest in naval protection on the Great Lakes[17]. Military officials were not so reassured. A report by Colonel Lake, the Quartermaster General, highlighted the potential need to arm the government's three fisheries vessels, CGS Petrel, CGS Curlew and CGS Acadia with the rapid-fire twelve and six-pounder guns purchased in 1896 following the Venezuelan crisis and held in storage at Quebec City[18]. Although the Rush-Bagot Agreement precluded such armaments as permanent fixtures, nothing in the agreement stopped Canada from holding such armaments in storage for rapid deployment in the event of a crisis[19]. Colonel Lake's report led to an inquiry into defence needs within Canada (the Leach Commission)[20] and two reports commissioned by the British War Office[21].

The Leach Commission concurred with the views on naval matters put forward by Colonel Lake, and emphasized that a Royal Navy officer should be placed in authority for the purpose of rallying whatever Canadian vessels would be available on the Great Lakes at the commencement of hostilities, with the intention of keeping the lakes open until Royal Navy vessels could arrive to assist[22].

16. Ibid.
17. William Johnston, William GP Rawling, Richard H Gimblett, John MacFarlane,,
    The Seabound Coast: The Official History of the Royal Canadian Navy 1867-1939, 48.
18. Percy Lake, "Memorandum to the General Officer Commanding (Canada), February 28,
    1898" (Ottawa: Library and Archives Canada, Department of the Naval Service, Inland
    Waterways and Canals, Naval Control of the Great Lakes).
19. William Johnston, William GP Rawling, Richard H Gimblett, John MacFarlane,
    The Seabound Coast: The Official History of the Royal Canadian Navy 1867-1939, 50.
20. Ibid, 51.
21. Glueck, "The Invisible Revision of the Rush-Bagot Agreement, 1898-1914," 473.

In the United States around this sensitive time Senator McMillan took the opportunity to renew his efforts to secure warship construction contracts for Great Lakes firms. McMillan pestered the Cleveland Administration with demands for explanations why a Detroit shipbuilding firm had not received any of the six new contracts for gunboat construction despite being a competitive bidder. The Cleveland Administration was forced to concede that the Rush-Bagot Agreement prevented a Great Lakes shipbuilding firm from receiving a contract to construct a warship[23].

Meanwhile, American critics of the Rush-Bagot Agreement's prohibition on the construction of new war vessels on the Great Lakes were partially satisfied by the construction at Great Lakes yards of three new revenue cutters for service on the Great Lakes. The first of those vessels, the *Gresham*, was 900 tons in displacement and was armed with modern weaponry causing Canadian officials to become alarmed, although British officials remained calm[24]. In 1897, the United States followed up on the launch of new revenue cutters for lake service by sending an old wooden-hulled steam bark, the *Yantic* into the Great Lakes as a training ship for the Michigan naval reserve[25]. The US had not sought Canadian permission to bring the *Yantic* into the Great Lakes and it was only due to the *Yantic's* collision with a Canadian government vessel during its passage that its presence was brought to the attention of the federal government[26]. The *Yantic* was old, and its journey through the Great Lakes canal had caused further damage so it was not much of a threat and the Laurier Ministry decided not to raise an issue about the presence of the ship despite concerns about the direction that the US

22. William Johnston, William GP Rawling, Richard H Gimblett, John MacFarlane, *The Seabound Coast: The Official History of the Royal Canadian Navy 1867-1939*, 52.
23. Glueck, "The Invisible Revision of the Rush-Bagot Agreement, 1898-1914," 470.
24. Ibid.
25. Ibid.
26. Ibid.

Government was taking with respect to naval forces on the Great Lakes.

Sir Wilfrid Laurier saw the need for a North American detente and he proposed to Great Britain and the United States that a joint commission meet to debate and resolve all outstanding issues between the countries. Perhaps alarmed at how close they had come to conflict over the Venezuelan Affair, both Great Britain and the United States concurred with the Canadian suggestion and a Joint High Commission involving the three countries began meeting in the spring of 1898.

The year 1898 was also a critical year in the emergence of the United States as a world power. Manifest Destiny had morphed into a sentiment that the United States should acquire overseas possessions like the other great powers both for American international prestige and as a sort of substitute for the now closed western frontier. American expansionists came into the ascendant and began exploring what potential gains the United States might exploit.

Foremost among the potential acquisitions that America sought was Canada. However, the United States remained strongly protectionist in outlook and the US government had rebuffed Canadian overtures for reciprocity in the aftermath of the McKinley tariff of 1890, causing the prospects for economic integration in North America to dim, and depriving the annexationists of an important economic tool to promote annexation. Nonetheless, resolutions were introduced into Congress in both 1891 and in 1894, which sought approval for the US government to enter into negotiations with Canada for its entry into the union of the United States[27]. All such efforts came to nought as there was no political support for the concept in Canada.

---

27. Preston, *The Defence of the Undefended Border*, 121.

Although many Americans now thought that the United States should expand abroad as so many European powers had done in recent years an anti-imperialist sentiment among the American public still obtained some credence. Hitherto, the United States had not sought territory outside of North America although, exceptionally, it had acquired the Midway Islands in the central Pacific in 1867 as a potential naval harbour. Now, other tropical islands entered into American calculations. Americans had played a prominent role in the political life of the Kingdom of Hawaii for most of the nineteenth century and strong links existed between the two countries. In the post-Civil War era reciprocity had given a gigantic boost to the Hawaiian kingdom by making it into a substantial purveyor of sugar to the United States. Wide scale social change had created new pressures in the internal politics of the kingdom, and the withdrawal of reciprocity by the McKinley Tariff caused political instability. In 1893 a political dispute over constitutional change boiled over and the American-led political class mounted a putsch against the royal government with the active connivance of the American Minister, who arranged for the deployment of US Marines from a US warship stationed at Honolulu. The rebel leaders of the provisional government sought annexation by the US and the Harrison Administration, which had encouraged the rebels, attempted to secure annexation but the Harrison administration left office before annexation could be consummated. The incoming administration of President Cleveland opposed annexation on the grounds that US officials had improperly aided the Hawaiian rebels and a political stalemate resulted in the islands.

Frustrated, American annexationists turned their attention to a tropical island much closer to home – Cuba. US presidents from the time of Thomas Jefferson had sought to add Cuba to the United States by purchasing it from Spain but the intransigent Spaniards had always refused, sometimes contemptuously[28]. In the post-Civil War political settlement in North America which had seen all of the European powers more or less withdraw from the continent the Spanish remained in Cuba and Puerto Rico despite growing US power and dominance in the Americas. Rebellions in Cuba in the 1890's followed by Spanish repression intensified American concerns about the future of the island, and encouraged annexationists to once again think about its acquisition by the United States.

In 1898, during the Cuban revolt against Spain, the United States dispatched one of its battleships, the *USS Maine,* to Havana to look after US interests in the islands. While *Maine* was anchored in Havana harbour an explosion (the cause of which has never been conclusively determined) destroyed the ship on the night of February 15, 1898, with the loss of two-thirds of its crew. The print media of the day played up the loss of the *Maine* as the result of Spanish perfidy and the slogan "Remember the *Maine"* was spoken everywhere in the United States, inflaming public opinion against Spain. Those who favoured a war with Spain as a prelude to the acquisition of Cuba now maneuvered to bring the US into war. The resulting Spanish-American War of 1898 changed the United States from a continental power to a world power as the United States took Cuba, Puerto Rico, Guam, and the Spanish Philippines by force of arms. Previous concerns about the conduct of American officials in promoting the overthrow of the royal Hawaiian Government were now swept aside as the strategic importance of Hawaii was underscored by the Philippines acquisition, and the Hawaiian islands were also now annexed by the United States.

Canada had acted to accommodate the United States during its belligerency against Spain, perceiving that to be the wisest course in dealing with the rising new world power. When the United States sought permission from Canada to move its revenue

28. Kluger, *Seizing Destiny*, 544.

cutters on the Great Lakes through the Canadian canal system in order to transfer them from the Great Lakes to the Atlantic for operations against Spain Canada readily acceded to the request, accepting diplomatic assurances from Washington that the cutters would undertake no warlike actions before reaching the Atlantic[29]. Canada actually gave its permission on the same day that permission was sought by the United States, which prompted Spain to complain that Canada was acting improperly, and had breached its neutrality[30].

The war ended quickly and before long the United States sent its revenue cutters back into the Great Lakes but they were not the same ships that had departed the lakes for war service. The new revenue cutters were somewhat smaller although had the Rush-Bagot Agreement limitations applied to them they would have exceeded the limitations in the Agreement. Canada had also deployed a cutter on the Great Lakes. The *Petrel* was a steam ram-bowed gunboat used for fisheries enforcement and protection on Lake Erie and Lake Huron beginning in 1894. Although the United States took the view that revenue or law enforcement cutters were exempt from the limitations imposed by the Rush-Bagot Agreement Canada was careful to ensure that the *Petrel* complied with it. The *Petrel* was armed with one twelve-pounder gun, ten rifles, ten revolvers, and ten cutlasses[31].

During the spring of 1898 Canada began meeting with Great Britain and the United States in the Joint High Commission which Canada had proposed as a means of resolving outstanding issues between Canada and the United States. The Rush-Bagot Agreement was number nine on the list of issues to be considered by the three parties. When the Agreement came up for discussion, the United States asked that it be changed to

29. Preston, *The Defence of the Undefended Border*, 138.
30. Ibid, 139.
31. William Johnston, William GP Rawling, Richard H Gimblett, John MacFarlane,
    The Seabound Coast: The Official History of the Royal Canadian Navy 1867-1939, 21.

accommodate the construction of new war vessels for employment outside of the Great Lakes, as well as the positioning of vessels for naval training purposes at Great Lakes ports. When the Canadian and British delegates indicated their potential support for the American position, the McKinley Administration made its position explicit: no more US warships would be stationed on the Great Lakes but the US would be allowed to place two armed vessels of up to 1000 tons for naval training and, as well, the US would still maintain up to six revenue cutters with both size and armament limitations. Further, the US would be able to build ships for both Great Lakes service as well as service on the oceans provided that the ships were a) built sequentially, b) removed from the Great Lakes before construction began on another vessel, and, c) no armaments or ship armour would be installed until after the newly constructed vessels departed from the Great Lakes[32].

Laurier, the principal Canadian delegate on the Joint High Commission, was agreeable to the American proposal, sensitive as he was to the growing power of the country's southern neighbour. Laurier realized that if the United States was not satisfied it could abrogate the Agreement and achieve its objectives outside of negotiations. The imperial government was more reserved than the federal government concerning the proposal but it ultimately agreed with the Canadian position[33].

At the end of 1898 a draft revised agreement had been prepared under which each of the United States and Canada would have each been allowed to keep two naval training vessels of up to 1000 tons armed with a maximum of two four-inch guns, together with a secondary armament of no more than six smaller weapons. In addition, each country would have been allowed to maintain up to six revenue cutters not to exceed 900 tons with one six-pounder gun as their primary armament. The revised

32. Glueck, "The Invisible Revision of the Rush-Bagot Agreement, 1898-1914," 471.
33. Ibid, 472.

draft would also have permitted each nation to construct warships on the Great Lakes for service elsewhere provided that they were constructed sequentially one at a time and were subsequently transferred to the ocean as soon as practicably possible. For passage to the sea all such newly constructed warships would have the right to transit intermediate waterways[34].

Ultimately, however, the efforts made in the Joint High Commission to negotiate formal amendments to the Rush-Bagot Agreement were not successful, as the commission broke down over differences between Canada and the United States relating to the demarcation of the Alaskan boundary, which the two countries were unable to bridge. Nevertheless, the commission process was a useful one. Over time, however, propositions advanced in the Joint High Commission process would come to be accepted as practical adjustments to the original Agreement[35].

A great concern of the Laurier Ministry was a new American initiative to bring US navy vessels into the Great Lakes as training vessels for its naval militia. With the growth in American power and prestige following its victory over Spain in the Spanish American War there was a growing interest by young middle and upper class American men in establishing a connection with the navy. The naval militia provided them with such an opportunity and the presence of training vessels on the Great Lakes meant that they would not have to travel very far to participate in summer manoeuvres. When he addressed the

34. Ron Purver, "The Rush-Bagot Agreement: Demilitarizing the Great Lakes, 1817 to the Present," *Encyclopedia of Arms and Control and Disarmament, Vol. 1* (New York: Charles Scribner's & Sons) 581, at 587.
35. Glueck, "The Invisible Revision of the Rush-Bagot Agreement, 1898-1914," 472. Revenue cutters were henceforth accepted as being outside of the Agreement and the US refrained from basing a new naval warship on the lakes as a successor to the *Michigan*. New construction on the Great Lakes did not occur at this time because the shipbuilding program of the US Navy concentrated on large warships that, owing to their size, could not be built on the Great Lakes and transferred to the ocean. Canada remained opposed to warship construction on the Great Lakes until World War One.

Lawyers Club in New York City on the subject of the Rush-Bagot Agreement in later years, Canadian Chief Justice Sir Charles Fitzpatrick commented on the motivation for this phenomenon, stating: "I suspect that many of the summer manoeuvres are organized to enable handsome young Americans to visit the Lake watering places and display their natty uniforms for the benefit of their lady friends[36]."

Taking advantage of the public's new fascination with the navy American officials sponsored the construction of a battleship on Lake Michigan for the World Exposition held in Chicago, Illinois, in 1893. However, this was not an ordinary battleship. At a cost of $115,000.00, the *Illinois* was constructed as a full-scale replica of the planned US battleships *USS Indiana* and *USS Massachusetts*. Unlike the latter two battleships however, the *Illinois* was a fake ship built of bricks encased in concrete to give the appearance of armour with a wooden superstructure that was coated in cement[37]. It was equipped with four artificial 13 inch guns and eight artificial 8 inch guns but the remainder of its armament, which included four 6 inch guns, twenty six-pounder guns, six one-pounders, two Gatling guns, and six torpedo tubes, were all real enough[38].

Although it has been suggested that the construction of an artificial battleship was intended to avoid the restrictions of the Rush-Bagot Agreement, the Agreement does not appear to have played any role in determining the construction of the replica. While the *Illinois* was an artificial construction, it was similar to the vessels planned by the US Navy and many parts of the structure were real, including the decks, masts, funnels and secondary armament. It was equipped with engines, a boiler,

36. Fitzpatrick, *An Address Delivered by the Rt. Hon. Sir Charles Fitzpatrick*, 17.
37. Cecil Adams, "Did Chicago Once Have a Brick Battleship?", *Chicago Straight Dope*, April 22, 2010 (http://chicago.straightdope.com/sdc20100422.php, accessed 2011/07/15).
38. Author Unknown, "Battleship Illinois (replica)," *Wikipedia: The Free Encyclopedia*, (http://en.wikipedia.org/wiki/Battleship_Illinois_replica, accessed 2011-07-15).

boats, anchors, lights, and winches like any other vessel and its cabins, bridge, and mess were all perfectly real[39]. So was the crew, as the US Navy detailed personnel to man the *Illinois* during the world fair. Its true purpose was to promote the creation of a blue water navy commensurate with the role of the rising great power that was the United States in the 1890's.

After the close of the Exposition the US Navy gave the *Illinois* to the state for use in training its naval militia. In a scene that seems to support the observation made by Chief Justice Fitzpatrick about the true purpose of the naval militias, the *Illinois* became very popular among the young social set in Chicago. It was reported that in 1894 a formal soiree was held with an orchestra playing on deck while officers and men in dress uniforms and their beautiful female companions graced the *Illinois*, decorated for the occasion with oriental lanterns and military paraphernalia[40].

However, in a unit established more for the pursuit of social status rather than military skills, internal squabbling soon took a center stage and the US Navy was forced to disband the ship's naval militia unit. A lone ship-keeper watched over the now desolate *Illinois* while efforts continued to move it to a more suitable location along the Chicago waterfront. In the end, all efforts failed and the winter ice on Lake Michigan broke it apart. By 1896 the *Illinois* was a forgotten wreck[41].

The difficulties with the naval militia and the loss of the *Illinois* did not stop efforts by the US Navy to increase its training efforts on the Great Lakes in subsequent years. In addition to the *Yantic*, and the ancient *Michigan*, the United States positioned four naval vessels on the Great Lakes for training purposes from 1900 to 1905, each time with the permission of the Canadian federal

39. Cecil Adams, "Did Chicago Once Have a Brick Battleship?"
40. Ibid.
41. Ibid.

government, which required the US Government to send its ships through the Canadian canal system unarmed[42]. Prime Minister Laurier remained concerned about the increasing US naval training presence on the Great Lakes but thought that any pressure from Canada to reduce the American naval training presence could result in the United States withdrawing from the Rush-Bagot Agreement. The United States simply assumed that the consensus achieved in the Joint High Commission on the permissibility of naval training vessels was accepted in Ottawa and London as an informal corollary to the Agreement, which in fact it was, or became, through Canadian reserve in not protesting the increasing naval training presence.

The construction of new war vessels on the Great Lakes for the US Navy oceanic services did not occur. American expansion beyond North America had forever changed the missions of the US Navy. Now, being much less concerned with coastal defence, the US Navy began its rise to a world-girdling blue-water navy. As a result, the types of ships that it now sought from builders could not be produced on the Great Lakes owing to the size of the new ships, which could not be accommodated by the existing Great Lakes canal and lock systems.

Consistent with its new missions and policy the US Navy laid down the keel for a new battleship in 1897. That battleship became the *USS Illinois* and it carried forward the proud name of the country's only stone battleship. Like its namesake it spent the last three decades of its service tied to a wharf where it served variously as a training ship, barracks, and hulk until 1956, when it was finally sent to the scrapyard.

---

42. Glueck, "The Invisible Revision of the Rush-Bagot Agreement, 1898-1914," 472-73.

1900-1914 IMPERIAL RETREAT, THE NASHVILLE INCIDENT, AND BRYCE'S TRAVAILS

As one century turned into another, Canada began to stand on its own and to take a larger share of responsibility for its relations with the United States, including the responsibility for its own defence posture. Larger forces now began to exert an influence on the course of Canada's evolution into an international actor. Although historical development is often the result of the interaction of large forces bearing upon the behaviour of states and societies it is also true that individuals can have a substantial effect on the course of history. In the late nineteenth and early twentieth centuries such an individual influence was present on the world stage in the form of the German Emperor, Kaiser Wilhelm II, who succeeded to the throne of imperial Germany in 1889.

Europe in the late nineteenth century was a largely monarchical continent, with France and Switzerland being the only two substantial states possessing a republican form of government. The European states that were monarchies ranged from constitutional monarchies such as Great Britain, where the sovereign's constitutional role was limited by democracy, to absolute monarchies such as Russia, where the Tsar held sway as the absolute political master of the Russian Empire. On the spectrum between absolutism and constitutional monarchy, Wilhelm's Germany fell somewhere in the middle, possessing a parliament that controlled the appropriation of public funds for government purposes but with an executive branch that was responsible only to the sovereign, and not to Parliament. This divided and limited autocratic government worked best when the monarch was an unassertive man of reserved temperament, as was the case with Wilhelm's father and grandfather. However, when the sovereign was a vain man of mercurial temperament, and one who had a pronounced sensitivity to real or imagined slights, such as Wilhelm II, the form of the German government presented a real risk to the peace of Europe.

In the nineteenth century it was common for the royal families of Europe to arrange marriages between the children of the various royal houses to ensure a social separation between the rulers and the ruled. This phenomenon had a stabilizing influence in Europe through the development of a shared outlook. The influence of Great Britain's royal family became significant owing to astute marriages made by the British royal family, which was reinforced by the paramount authority of Britain as the world's nineteenth century superpower. Presiding over the royal families of Europe was Queen Victoria, who came to the British throne in 1838 and reigned until 1901.

Wilhelm II was the child of Prince Frederick Wilhelm of Germany and Princess Victoria, the eldest daughter of Queen Victoria and Prince Albert. Through that marriage the Queen hoped that Germany would develop as a country along the liberal lines that were followed in Great Britain. However, while Prince Frederick Wilhelm was a liberal-minded man his son Wilhelm was not. Wilhelm was strongly influenced by conservative tutors as well as by his grandfather, Kaiser Wilhelm I, and the German Chancellor, Prince Otto von Bismarck. He was also affected by a deformity to his left arm which made it a challenge for Wilhelm to succeed at the martial arts that German society cultivated. Wilhelm developed an aggressive bearing wrapped in a reactionary political philosophy. His accession to the throne in 1889 at a relatively young age and before he was equipped by experience to take on the role of a semi-autocrat, together with his assertive and mercurial temperament and personal vanity, boded ill for European political stability.

At first, Wilhelm was kept in check by his grandmother, Queen Victoria. Although Wilhelm detested his mother, he adored his grandmother. Queen Victoria looked askance at her grandson but accepted Wilhelm as a member of the royal family and sought to encourage her ideal of a monarch in him, a model based in large part on the memory of her restrained, intelligent, and diplomatic late consort, Prince Albert.

While Wilhelm greatly admired his grandmother, Queen Victoria, he feared and despised her heir, his uncle Prince Edward, the Prince of Wales. Edward was everything that Wilhelm was not. A *bon vivant* in his younger (and even in his older) days he was a cosmopolitan man of the world who moved smoothly through upper European and British society and was well liked everywhere. As Prince of Wales he visited Canada in 1860 in a well remembered and highly regarded visit that helped to sustain loyalty to the royal family. Prince Edward looked down on Wilhelm as an uncouth youth and may have resented Wilhelm's treatment of his mother, who was Edward's sister.

Great Britain at the beginning of the twentieth century remained the predominant military power in the world and the Royal Navy was the backbone of the power of the British Empire. Britain had much in common with Germany as both states were northern European protestant countries with strong industrial economies. Both countries had strong scientific resources in academia and industry, a strong trade union movement, the rule of law, and developed commercial linkages. The royal family of Great Britain had Germanic roots in the old Kingdom of Hanover and many figures in upper British society were Germanophiles. Further, Great Britain's imperial rivalries did not involve Germany, rather, it was Russia that posed a potential threat to British control of the Indian subcontinent, the jewel in the British imperium. France was Britain's rival in the scramble for colonial territory in Africa which almost brought the two counties to blows in the Fashoda crisis in 1898. Nevertheless, Great Britain and Germany would soon come to follow opposing courses in Europe and around the world. How did this come about? While many factors influenced the course of diplomacy in the years before World War I, a key element was the naval policy followed in Germany in the years before that war.

After succeeding to the German throne in 1889, Wilhelm, possessed of a firm belief in his own capabilities, forced the retirement of the German Chancellor, Prince Otto von Bismarck, who had dominated the reigns of his grandfather and father. Bismarck was a shrewd strategist in the political manoeuvring for dominance in Europe in the late nineteenth century. His crowning diplomatic achievement had been the political and military alliance among the three reactionary empires of central and eastern Europe, Germany, Austro-Hungary, and Russia. Wilhelm, however, allowed the treaty with Russia to lapse leaving an opening for France, still nursing bitterness towards Germany over the loss of the provinces of Alsace-Lorraine following the 1870 Franco-Prussian War, to reach an alliance with Russia against Germany. That opened up the prospect for German military planners that in any European war Germany might face a two-front war which the German military staff regarded as a nightmare scenario.

Great Britain had remained aloof from European alliances but general British policy since the Napoleonic era had always been to oppose any power which sought hegemony in Europe. Many in both Great Britain and Germany thought that a friendship or alliance between the two countries made perfect sense but those hopes were dashed by Wilhelm's naval policy. Always desiring to dominate, and fuelled by a cutting realization that he was little appreciated by the British royal family to which he belonged,

Wilhelm, egged on by his naval minister, Grand Admiral von Tirpitz, resolved to develop a blue-water navy that could compete with the Royal Navy. In this way, Wilhelm sought to compel respect for Germany by Great Britain and respect for himself by the members of the British royal family, especially his uncle King Edward VII, who finally succeeded Queen Victoria in January 1901.

Starting in 1898 and continuing forward for a number of years, a succession of German naval funding bills allowed the construction of a blue-water fleet that was capable of challenging the Royal Navy for the command of European waters. This development struck at the heart of British military policy which had always relied on the Royal Navy for its national defence. The British standard was to maintain the Royal Navy at a strength that was equal to the next two largest naval powers. To maintain that standard while the German navy grew, Great Britain was forced to embark on a new shipbuilding program of its own, which came at a very substantial cost to the public treasury.

The ambitions of the German naval armaments program and the potential harm that it posed to British maritime supremacy isolated Great Britain in Europe. British officials now pondered whether they should join the European system of defensive alliances as a means of protection against the potential German naval threat.

Hitherto Britain had only needed to worry about its capacity to defeat a combination of the French Navy and the US Navy, the two largest secondary fleets. The French Navy was divided between its Atlantic and Mediterranean fleets and the United States had to maintain naval forces on both its east and west coasts. The new German fleet however, would be concentrated in its entirety at bases along the North Sea, and was within direct striking distance of Great Britain. That constituted a new and much more serious potential threat.

King Edward VII, a nineteenth century monarch in outlook and temperament, was perhaps the last British sovereign to play an active political role in the formation of public policy. A noted Francophile, he moved assiduously to foster a new and closer relationship between Great Britain and France. Although he may not have been acting in an official capacity in his efforts to promote a rapprochement between France and Great Britain, Edward saw himself as a promoter of peace through a balance of powers. An official visit by Edward to France in 1903, following the end of the Boer War, was a personal triumph for the King and it smoothed the way for Great Britain and France to establish an *entente cordiale* between the two countries in 1904. The resulting informal alliance between the two countries was deepened by subsequent military discussions between the two nations which increasingly meant that in any future European war Great Britain might not be able to remain aloof from it as it had remained aloof from European wars throughout the nineteenth century.

King Edward also visited his nephew by marriage, Tsar Nicholas II, in 1908. Russia was a close ally of France by treaty. Edward was the first British monarch to visit the Russian Empire and he hosted the Tsar and Tsarina on their reciprocal visit to Great Britain in 1909. Both visits helped to smooth over past difficulties between Russia and Great Britain whose interests in Asia had promoted the "great game" of imperial rivalries in west and south Asia. The King's efforts complemented the formal British diplomacy of the period so that by the end of Edward's reign in 1910 Europe was increasingly divided, much to Wilhelm's chagrin, between Germany, Austro-Hungary and Italy, which formed the Triple Alliance, and the Dual Alliance of Russia and France to which Great Britain was informally joined through the *entente cordiale* with France. As European royalty, diplomats, and politicians sleepwalked through one recurring international crisis after another, Europe moved almost inevitably towards the precipice of a world war. Meanwhile, the ruinous naval arms race that Wilhelm had started continued when a whole new British design for a big-gun battleship, *HMS Dreadnought*, sparked more expensive efforts to establish dominance in the North Sea.

European developments had consequential effects for relations between Canada and the United States and ultimately on the application of the Rush-Bagot Agreement. The role of Great Britain in North America began to change as Britain faced up to the challenge of a rising Germany in Europe. That, in turn, began affecting Canadian relations with the United States and Canada's defence posture and responsibilities within the wider imperial political framework.

In 1897, shortly after he became Prime Minister, Wilfrid Laurier determined that there was little likelihood of a conflict between Canada and the United States and no real concern from Canada's perspective about the country's defensive posture on inland waters. Later that year, at the Colonial Conference held in conjunction with the Queen's Diamond Jubilee, Laurier characterized any difficulties between Canada and the United States as mere family squabbles, and he eschewed any suggestion that Canada needed to invest in either its own naval forces or the Royal Navy[1].

In 1902 Lieutenant Colonel C V F Townshend reported to London that the Great Lakes were without any adequate defences and the historic invasion route along the Lake Champlain corridor was guarded only by a single Canadian soldier, who watched over Fort Lennox on *Isle aux Noix*[2]. A subsequent 1904 report by Lieutenant Colonel G M Kirkpatrick for the War Office in London noted that the United States held

1. Johnston, Rawling, Gimblett, MacFarlane, *The Seabound Coast*, 48.[2] Glueck, "The Invisible Revision of the Rush-Bagot Agreement, 1898-1914," 473.
2. Glueck, "The Invisible Revision of the Rush-Bagot Agreement, 1898-1914," 473.

indisputable naval dominance within the waters it shared with Canada and only the deployment of the Home Fleet from Great Britain could redress the imbalance[3]. Obviously, with the growing naval might of Germany in the North Sea Great Britain would not be able to deploy the Home Fleet, or any substantial part of it, to North American waters while the potential threat from Germany remained.

At this juncture a dispute over the Alaska boundary disrupted Canadian-American relations and had repercussions for Canada's relations with the imperial government as well. A treaty of 1825 between Great Britain and Russia had defined the boundaries between the North-western Territory, which had been administered by the Hudson's Bay Company, and Russian America in a general way without providing a clear demarcation of the border between the two territories. The location of the border remained uncertain after the United States obtained possession of Alaska by purchasing it from Russia in 1867. This issue would probably have been of little consequence but for the fact that gold was discovered in the Klondike region of Canada's Northwest Territories in 1898, sparking a huge gold rush that led directly to the severance and formation of the Yukon Territory from the larger Northwest Territories. The gold rush captured the imagination of Americans as well as Canadians and there was a population surge into the Klondike region. The Yukon Territory lacked easy access to a Pacific port on Canadian soil and a domestic port on the seacoast was much desired by the territory's inhabitants for the economic development of the Yukon. Canada interpreted the vague treaty with the Russians very liberally to achieve the outcome of giving Canada access to the Pacific through possession of the headwaters of one of the arms of the sea in the Alaskan panhandle. The United States naturally interpreted the language of the treaty quite differently, and to its advantage, and claimed the whole coast inland to the

3. Ibid.

heights of the mountain chain, which deprived Yukon of its access to the Pacific. In hindsight, many historians who have examined the matter have concluded that, notwithstanding the vagueness of the Anglo-Russian Treaty, the United States had the better legal case. Domestic politics in Canada however drove the issue to the forefront of Canadian-American relations.

Efforts to negotiate a satisfactory compromise between Canada and the United States failed. The Joint High Commission which Prime Minister Laurier had been instrumental in establishing after taking office in the late 1890's, and upon which he had personally laboured, had failed because of this very issue. The United States rejected Canadian efforts to place the issue before the Permanent Court of Arbitration at the Hague and insisted on a separate arbitration process. President Theodore Roosevelt had little time for the Canadian claim. Roosevelt was a high-energy president and a remarkable figure in American history. At times both self-righteous and belligerent he was also highly intelligent with a firm grasp of naval policy and the role that it could play in enhancing the appearance and reality of great power. More than any other political figure in his times he pushed the United States firmly into the centre of world politics from its former, and rather aloof position in the New World.

Now, as President, Roosevelt decided to send US troops to Alaska to reinforce the American claim line. To reflect his irritation for the arbitration process, he appointed as American representatives the Secretary of War in his own cabinet, Elihu Root, and two sitting United States Senators, Henry Cabot Lodge, and George Turner, all of whom were regarded (at least in Canada) as non-jurists who would be incapable of holding an open mind on the subject. Canada named two lawyers, the Lieutenant Governor of Quebec, and a lawyer from Toronto. The sixth member of the tribunal was Baron Alverstone, the Lord Chief Justice of England and Wales.

Regardless of the merits of the respective cases larger issues formed an important back-drop to the process of the arbitration. The growing industrial and naval might of Germany was a major concern to British political leaders and would soon place enormous strain on British finances as Great Britain strove to maintain a 2:1 ratio advantage over the Imperial German fleet. Reports from British military officials identifying the strategic exposure of Canada to attack from the south, and the near impossibility of mounting an effective defence of Canada without denuding the home islands of their necessary defences, was decisive in shaping British views on the future course of relations with the United States. The imperial government considered it acceptable, if necessary, to sacrifice Canadian interests in order to avoid antagonizing the United States. Lord Alverstone would have been aware of the politics surrounding the arbitration, and the pressing interests of Great Britain in the face of growing German naval power[4]. In the resulting arbitral award issued in the autumn of 1903 he sided with the Americans against the Canadian members of the tribunal, who then refused to sign the arbitral award[5].

There was outrage in Canada at what was seen as a betrayal of Canada by Great Britain. However, the merits of the arbitration aside, British international political instincts were correct. The growing might of Germany's naval power directly threatened Great Britain's crucial defence perimeter and the British would need the future goodwill of the United States to protect Great Britain's hemispheric interests in the New World while it faced the rising German threat in Europe. Canada was important to the empire but it was no longer central to it – the Near and Mid-East, and India, were the critical areas for British imperial control. Finally, Great Britain could no longer afford to protect Canada militarily from the United States even if it had the

4. Bradford Perkins, *The Great Rapprochement, England and the United States, 1895-1914*, (New York: Athenaeum, 1968) 170.
5. Ibid, 171.

capacity and the political will to do so, which quite frankly it no longer had.

Accordingly, British officials soon decided that Great Britain would cease efforts to defend Canada from the United States using military force,[6] although this was not made explicit or publicised. When the Committee for Imperial Defence subsequently proposed to discuss US violations of the Rush-Bagot Agreement in 1905, the British Foreign Secretary, Sir Edward Grey, intervened to squelch all discussion of the topic, and, in 1912, when discussions between British and Canadian officials on military questions were in the offing, British Prime Minister Herbert Asquith was cautioned by British officials not to reveal to Canadian officials that Britain had decided to abandon any naval defence of the Great Lakes[7].

As part of this imperial realignment, Great Britain decided to withdraw its remaining military presence from North America. Following the Treaty of Washington in 1871 Great Britain had continued to maintain imperial forces at two important naval bases, Halifax in Nova Scotia and Esquimalt in British Columbia. Now, to emphasize its acceptance of American hegemony in North America, and to remove any lingering concerns on the part of the United States with respect to British intentions, Great Britain withdrew the garrisons at Halifax and Esquimalt in 1906, and the bases were turned over to the Canadian federal government.

Prime Minister Laurier had foreseen the results of the Alaska boundary arbitration due to the pressure he had received from London and no doubt he realized that the urgency of obtaining a Canadian seaport for the Yukon had passed with the petering

6. Ibid 162; Phillips Payson O'Brien, *British and American Naval Power, Politics and Policy, 1900-1936*, (Westport (Connecticut): Praeger, 1998) 28.
7. Gwynne Dyer and Tina Viljoen, *The Defence of Canada; in the Arms of the Empire, 1760-1939*, (Toronto: McClelland & Stewart, 1990) 196-197.

out of the Klondike gold rush. Nevertheless, he was able to use the results of the arbitration politically to advance the objective of greater autonomy from the imperial government in London. In so doing he began to prepare the population for the country's inevitable rise to full independence from autonomy within the empire. In 1909 Laurier created a small Department of External Affairs, which was closely attached to the Prime Minister, and which began to function as the federal government's foreign affairs department – the first step towards the country's eventual external independence.

The abandonment by the imperial government of serious military planning for the defence of Canada became increasingly clear to the federal government but it was not perceived as a devastating blow by the Laurier Ministry. In the first place, the political ties between Great Britain and Canada remained, and Canada could count on British political support at least where Britain's vital interests were not concerned. More important, Canadian leaders since Macdonald had all recognized that a military confrontation with the United States could only end in disaster for Canada. The United States was the predominant power in the New World and even the entire power of the British Empire might not be sufficient to stop an assault on Canada by its southern neighbour. Canadian political leaders recognized that the best defence of Canada against the United States should be based on political and diplomatic relations, rather than on purely military defences.

To those ends, Canada pursued good diplomatic relations with the United States. Early in the twentieth century the two countries negotiated (with Great Britain's acquiescence) a treaty to manage the waters along the international boundary between the two countries. The Boundary Waters Treaty of 1909 established a permanent International Joint Commission with commissioners appointed by both countries to monitor the boundary waters, and to resolve any disputes that arose concerning them[8]. That treaty also established the right of the citizens of either country to enjoy the right of free navigation throughout their boundary waters. That resolved a long-standing issue. The Treaty of Paris in 1783 had not conferred rights of navigation on Canadians or Americans on the Great Lakes within the territory of the other state. An effort had been made to permit free navigation by the Jay Treaty in 1794 but the system created by the Jay Treaty was abrogated by the War of 1812[9]. Partial efforts to deal with the problem were subsequently made in the Webster-Ashburton Treaty of 1842, which had resolved border claims in the maritime colonies, and in the Treaty of Washington of 1871, which permitted the citizens of the United States engaged in commerce to forever exercise navigation rights on the St. Lawrence River above the 45th parallel of latitude[10]. Now, in the Boundary Waters Treaty, it was agreed that Canadians and Americans and vessels belonging to them were to be guaranteed the right of navigation on all of the Great Lakes and on the canals that connected them. This resolved Canadian concerns about the right of Canadians to exercise an unimpeded right to navigation on Lake Michigan, and American concerns about the right of US citizens to transit the canals along the St. Lawrence River in Canadian territory[11]. There was one proviso to this agreement however. It was agreed by both parties that warships of either nation would still require the consent of the other government in order to access any of the canals connecting the waterways that were located in the territory of the other state[12]. In this respect, the Boundary Waters Treaty formed an important corollary to the Rush-Bagot Agreement in regulating the use of canals by naval vessels. By complementing the Rush-Bagot Agreement the Boundary Waters Treaty provided a means to monitor and partially enforce

8. Piper, *The International Law of the Great Lakes*, 6.
9. Ibid, 47.
10. Ibid, 55.
11. Ibid, 49.
12. Ibid, 57.

the provisions of the Rush-Bagot Agreement. As a final measure of enhanced Canadian and American cooperation on the Great Lakes in 1913, the maritime boundary between the two countries was formally delineated based on a median line that was approximated by some 270 straight baselines[13].

The development of new initiatives to manage US-Canadian relations and to ease the potential for tensions to emerge along the border emanated from a slate-cleaning exercise that Elihu Root undertook after he became Roosevelt's Secretary of State in 1905. Root wished to clear up the remaining issues between the United States and Great Britain as those two imperial powers grew closer together in geopolitical cooperation. Amendments to the Rush-Bagot Agreement were one of the outstanding issues. Building on the foundation of the agreement in principle that had been achieved by the three states in the Joint High Commission process that had been convened in the previous decade, Root now sought a consensus that would explicitly allow the building of warships on the Great Lakes with appropriate safeguards to govern their use. To press his points upon a reluctant Canada Root alluded to the pressure placed on the US Government by shipbuilders located on the Great Lakes[14]. Root also raised again the argument that Canada's canal system allowed the Royal Navy to quickly place warships on the Great Lakes.

Laurier was averse to this development and explained his opposition to James Bryce, the imperial government's Ambassador in Washington, who faithfully conveyed Canada's objections (which were supported by the imperial government) to Root. As a result, the negotiations between Great Britain and the United States moved onto other matters, and the Rush-Bagot

13. Ibid, 17. A baseline is a geographical surveying term which creates a line from which the maritime jurisdiction of a state can be achieved. Usually the low water line is sufficient but in a convoluted coastline straight baselines may be used.
14. Glueck, "The Invisible Revision of the Rush-Bagot Agreement, 1898-1914," 475.

Agreement was left unchanged[15]. Canada, for its part, ensured that when tenders were issued for the new Canadian Naval Service in 1911 those tenders specified that Canadian warships could not be built on the Great Lakes due to the provisions of the Rush-Bagot Agreement[16].

During this period, Canada faced multiple requests by the United States to allow the passage of redundant war vessels as naval training vessels in order to augment the naval training programs that had been adopted by state militias along the Great Lakes. Canada continued to insist that all such US requests for permission must be processed as separate permissions, refusing in the spring of 1908 an American request for an open-ended permission to use the Welland Canal to allow one naval vessel to transit repeatedly between Lake Ontario and Lake Erie[17]. Nevertheless, Canada did not deny any of the specific US requests. In two cases the naval training vessels were prizes taken from the Spanish by the US in the Spanish-American War which were sought by Michigan and New York for their state naval militias. Both ships were obsolete vessels (one was merely a schooner) and of little military value.

However, a request by the United States for the passage into the Great Lakes of the *USS Nashville*, an American built gunboat launched in 1895, heightened Canadian concerns because *Nashville* was a modern warship that had substantial military value. Nevertheless, following a now consistent policy of accommodation towards US naval interests on the Great Lakes, the Laurier Ministry granted permission in February 1908 for the *Nashville* to proceed into the Great Lakes under the usual stipulations that its armaments should be removed before

15. Ibid.
16. William Johnston, William GP Rawling, Richard H Gimblett, John MacFarlane,
    The Seabound Coast: The Official History of the Royal Canadian Navy 1867-1939, 171.
17. Purver, "The Rush-Bagot Agreement: Demilitarizing the Great Lakes, 1817 to the Present,"
    Encyclopedia of Arms and Control and Disarmament, Vol. 1, 588.

passage through the Canadian canals, and that the ship would be used solely as a training vessel[18]. Permission for the *Nashville* to enter the Great Lakes provoked some questioning of Prime Minister Laurier in the House of Commons but the issue quickly passed.

But the *Nashville* did not proceed into the Great Lakes as planned, and shortly after President William Howard Taft's administration took office in April 1909 the American request for the *Nashville* to pass into the Great Lakes was renewed. This time however, the US Government explicitly asked for permission to reinstall the warship's armament once it had reached its destination at Chicago. Why the United States chose to make an explicit request for something that hitherto had always been implicit between the state parties to the agreement is unclear. The new development delayed Canadian consideration of the US request and, in the absence of any timely objections from Canada, the United States assumed that Canada did not oppose the stationing of the *Nashville* on the Great Lakes. Therefore, stripped of its armament, *Nashville* was sent to Illinois in May, stopping briefly at Quebec City, and then subsequently at Buffalo, to reinstall her armament before proceeding to Chicago. The sight of this armed American warship on the Great Lakes suddenly raised significant public concerns in Canada and the Laurier Ministry, ever mindful of the political implications of Canadian fears about the US Navy's presence on the Great Lakes, decided to formally decline permission for her passage in July 1909[19].

The decision by the Laurier Ministry to deny the Nashville passage caused consternation for Ambassador Bryce in Washington. Why, he demanded, had this decision not been taken in May before *Nashville* proceeded into the Great Lakes?

18. Glueck, "The Invisible Revision of the Rush-Bagot Agreement, 1898-1914," 576.
19. Ibid, 478.

When he pointed out that the federal government had approved the passage of the ship the previous year and the only new aspect of the matter concerned its rearmament, which had always been implicit in previous permissions, the Laurier Ministry merely sent further instructions to the Ambassador reiterating its opposition. Bryce demurred from expressing the Canadian views to the US Government stating that he would only do so in a general way if it became necessary. Ambassador Bryce's refusal to file the Canadian objections probably spared the federal government a great deal of embarrassment with the United States (and possibly with Great Britain).

Ottawa, however, was not yet finished with the issue and the federal government despatched a spy from the *Corps of Guides*, a special unit in the Department of Militia and Defence, to watch *Nashville* participate in US naval manoeuvres on the Great Lakes. The officer that was despatched, Captain C F Hamilton, found the American ships, all training vessels, at Alpena, Michigan, and he surveyed them as they performed naval manoeuvres and drills with the now fully-armed *Nashville*. Subsequently, he filed a report on their activities with the federal government in Ottawa. Perhaps that would have been well enough if Hamilton had left it there but Hamilton was actually a reserve officer rather than a member of the permanent force, and his primary occupation was as a newspaper journalist for the *Toronto News*. Hamilton then proceeded to write a story for his newspaper that emphasized the power of the *Nashville*, which only served to increase the anxiety of the Canadian public about US naval intentions on the Great Lakes[20].

With the colonial secretary in the imperial government backing his views on the need to get past the *Nashville* incident, Ambassador Bryce came to Ottawa and conferred with Laurier in September 1909, and got the Prime Minister's permission

20. Ibid, 479.

to deal with the issue in an informal way. Meeting with the new President, William Howard Taft, and his Secretary of State, Philander Knox, Bryce succeeded in smoothing matters over by acknowledging that Canada would accept *Nashville's* passage but that the ship should not have been rearmed without Canadian permission. Furthermore, Bryce prevailed on the administration to adhere in the future to the Rush-Bagot Agreement limitations (including those previously established adjustments and corollaries that flowed from past practice). Bryce was encouraged by President Taft's peaceful attitude, and his evident desire for good relations with Canada[21]. As an example of President Taft's benign views towards Canada's concerns regarding naval forces on the Great Lakes a subsequent refusal by Canada in 1911 to permit the placement of a modern war vessel on the Great Lakes by the United States was accepted by the Taft Administration with equanimity[22]. The effect of this Taft-Bryce prewar *modus vivendi* stabilized the Rush-Bagot Agreement towards the end of the Edwardian Era[23].

Meanwhile, in Ottawa, the Laurier Ministry felt the need to clarify Canada's forward strategy with respect to the Rush-Bagot Agreement. After consideration, the federal government concluded that a wide interpretation of the Rush-Bagot Agreement should not be encouraged at that time[24]. Later that year, when the United States planned naval exercises for its training vessels on the Great Lakes, Prime Minister Laurier came under fire from the Opposition Leader in the House of

21. Ibid, 481.
22. Ibid.
23. The conciliatory attitude of the Taft Administration can probably be attributed to the desire of President Taft to conclude a new reciprocity agreement with Canada to lower import tariffs between the two countries. The Taft Administration favoured closer relations with Canada and some in the administration hoped that reciprocity would eventually result in Canada joining the union (Bothwell, *Your Country, My Country*, 153). The proposed reciprocity treaty was the main wedge between the Liberal and Conservative parties in the 1911 general election which resulted in the defeat of Laurier and his Liberal Party Ministry.
24. Department of External Affairs, Handwritten note "Relevant and current re Rush-Bagot Treaty" (author and date unknown), (LAC RG 25, D1, Volume 740.)

Commons, Robert Borden. Laurier asked Ambassador Bryce to prevail upon the Americans to refrain from the planned Great Lakes naval manoeuvres in the interests of good relations between Canada and the United States. Bryce made representations to American officials and succeeded in persuading the Taft Administration to cancel the naval training exercise[25].

As the two countries entered the second decade of the twentieth century, the Rush-Bagot Agreement had been stabilized by the Taft-Bryce *modus vivendi* reached in 1909. When Robert Borden defeated Laurier in the general election of 1911 over the issue of reciprocity with the United States, he continued Laurier's general approach to the Rush-Bagot Agreement. Like Laurier's government, the Borden Ministry remained averse to proposals from the United States to allow the construction of warships on the Great Lakes for subsequent oceanic service. An attempt in 1912 by the United States to obtain Canadian agreement that an American shipbuilder could accept a contract to construct a gunboat that would then be disassembled, and later reassembled on tidewater, was rebuffed by the Borden Ministry. Canada took the view that such warships could be left at the shipyard for extended periods and very easily and quickly reassembled in a crisis, and thus evade the limitations of the Rush-Bagot Agreement. The United States accepted Canada's view and its gunboat shipbuilding tenders were not opened to builders on the Great Lakes[26]. On the Great Lakes *Nashville* was replaced by a smaller vessel, and the ancient *Michigan* (now renamed the *USS Wolverine*) was decommissioned in 1912, though it remained a training vessel for state naval militias. By 1915, the US would still have nine reserve naval vessels in its Great Lakes naval training squadron[27].

25. Preston, *The Defence of the Undefended Border*, 185.
26. Purver, "The Rush-Bagot Agreement: Demilitarizing the Great Lakes, 1817 to the Present," *Encyclopedia of Arms and Control and Disarmament, Vol. 1,* 588.
27. Rodgers, *Guardian of the Great Lakes*, 126.

While the political interest in the Rush-Bagot Agreement now temporarily receded, military officials continued to develop strategies and plans for the contingency of a war between the United States and Canada. In the United States planning for an invasion of Canada began in 1912-13 by the Army War College and that planning formed the basis of the subsequent Red-Blue War Plan for the invasion of Canada[28]. However, planning proceeded somewhat haphazardly because US military challenges vis-a-vis Mexico were of more immediate importance. Suggestions were made in some of the preliminary papers filed with respect to the war planning that the United States should abrogate the Rush-Bagot Agreement[29] but nothing came of those views.

In Canada, the Department of Militia and Defence continued to address the potential for another war with the country's southern neighbour. For military officials there were profound concerns about the risk exposure of the country following Great Britain's strategic decision to no longer defend Canada from an attack by the United States. In early 1912, still hoping for at least some assistance in that increasingly unlikely event, federal officials on the Interdepartmental Committee of the Department of Militia and Defence corresponded with their counterparts in the imperial government's Colonial Interdepartmental Committee in London, concerning the prospects for assistance from the Royal Navy in assuring Canadian control of the Great Lakes in the event of hostilities with the United States.

The response from London was blunt with the Naval Secretary to the Colonial Interdepartmental Committee agreeing with his Canadian counterparts that a meeting to discuss the issue should be held but warning them that in light of "the existing international political situation it is considered very unlikely that any assistance either in personnel or materiel can be expected

28. Preston, *The Defence of the Undefended Border*, 188-89.
29. Ibid, 189.

on the Great Lakes from the Admiralty in case of war with the United States; consequently any action by Canada should be based upon that consideration[30]."

Canadian naval defence planners presumed that Montreal would be the objective of any American attack and that for the purpose of besieging Montreal the United States would send its troops north on the traditional invasion route along and adjacent to Lake Champlain[31]. To counter such an attack, Canadian planners gave the opinion that Canada must hold both banks of the St. Lawrence River and to do that it would be essential to maintain Canadian naval control of Lake Ontario, all of which was thought to be within Canada's military capabilities to achieve. It was also recognized that, as in 1813, the United States would have the advantage in establishing naval control on the upper lakes and were that to occur it would likely force the abandonment of western Ontario by Canada. A possible landing on the southern shore of Lake Huron or Georgian Bay by American forces could imperil Toronto from the rear[32]. It seems clear from the discussion that Canadian naval planners thought that maintaining Canadian naval control on the Great Lakes would be a daunting prospect. That the United States was considered at the time to be the only real threat to Canada in the minds of Canadian defence planners was revealingly disclosed by their observation that "... the United States is and always must be a dangerous enemy to Canada and although at the present time both Federal and Imperial relations with her are cordial, ... they will not necessarily always be so . . .[33] "

30. Naval Secretary, Colonial Interdepartmental Committee, "Memorandum Re Naval Control of the Great Lakes, March 21, 1912," (Library and Archives Canada, Department of the Naval Service, Inland Waterways Lakes and Canals).
31. Memorandum from the Director of Naval Gunnery to the Director to Naval Service, "Naval Control on Great Lakes," (Library and Archives Canada, Department of the Naval Service, Inland Waterways and Canals, Naval Control of the Great Lakes).
32. Ibid.
33. Ibid.

Unbeknownst or unacknowledged by the author of this 1912 naval planning memorandum was the more immediate threat of a European conflict and the very real possibility that Canada would be drawn into it. In Europe the competing military alliances finalized their plans against each other while the political leadership in each country lurched from one international crisis, or rivalry, to another in Europe, Africa, and in Asia Minor. Each country jockeyed for position and influence on the world stage. Meanwhile, the closely related royal families that occupied the many thrones of Europe continued their rounds of visits to each other, maintaining a thin veneer of civility and cooperation as their countries braced for the coming storm. The monarchs of the three greatest powers, Great Britain, Germany, and Russia last met together at the wedding of Kaiser Wilhelm's daughter in 1913, where Great Britain's King George V (who had succeeded King Edward VII in 1910) complained that it was difficult for him to have a private conversation with Tsar Nicholas II of Russia because the Kaiser was constantly watching both of them out of a fear that they were plotting against him[34].

At sea, Great Britain had won the North Sea naval arms race with Germany. At great expense the Royal Navy had succeeded in outbuilding the Imperial German Navy in battleships and battle cruisers. While the Royal Navy was not able to maintain its historic two-power standard of dominance, it was still the largest and most powerful navy in the world at the outbreak of the war, with twenty-nine *Dreadnought*-type battleships to Germany's seventeen. As the costs of the naval arms race mounted in the years before the war, Great Britain called upon its autonomous dominions to share the cost of the world-girding imperial fleet. While Australia and New Zealand responded positively to this request, Canada was much less enthusiastic about contributing to the expansion of the Royal Navy's battleship squadrons.

34. Catrine Clay, *King, Kaiser, Tsar, Three Royal Cousins Who Led the World to War* (New York: Walker Publishing Co., 2006) 302.

Rather than acceding to Great Britain's request for funds, the Laurier Ministry had embarked on a project to create a separate Canadian Naval Service to defend Canada, which eventually became the Royal Canadian Navy.

There were a number of factors that affected Canadian enthusiasm for imperial naval expansion. Apart from the desire not to become involved in an expensive naval arms race, Canada recognized that Great Britain had effectively ceased to plan for the defence of Canada. The Royal Navy had abandoned its great naval base at Halifax, Nova Scotia, as well as the British Pacific Fleet base at Esquimalt in British Columbia, and had recognized American hegemony within the Americas. Prime Minister Laurier calculated that Canada could rely on the United States for defence against the remote possibility of an attack by a European state on Canada[35]. Even when tensions with the United States were high, as they were during the Alaska Boundary dispute, Laurier never doubted that he could rely on the United States for aid in the event of foreign aggression against Canada. Laurier even stated to one British general who arrived to command the Canadian militia that, as Prime Minister, he did not have to devote much effort to the militia because Canada could rely on the Monroe Doctrine as a defence against potential European hostility[36]!

Prime Minister Robert Borden, who succeeded Laurier as Prime Minister following the 1911 general election was unenthusiastic about a separate Canadian Naval Service and was much more interested in participating in the funding of the Royal Navy. In the end, however, he continued the policy of maintaining a separate Canadian Naval Service. Canada possessed two old cruisers by the outbreak of the World War, one stationed at

35. The only Asian state with the potential capacity to pose a threat to Canada at that time was Japan. However, that country was in a formal alliance with Great Britain and so any potential threat from that quarter to Canada had been neutralized.
36. Stacey, *The Undefended Border*, 13.

Halifax and the other at Esquimalt. In reality Canada relied on others to provide it with naval protection – the Royal Navy in the Atlantic and the Imperial Japanese Navy in the Pacific (under the terms of the Anglo-Japanese alliance). Ultimately, however, the federal government understood that the United States was the true guarantor against aggression by third-party states on the North American continent.

By 1914 all of Europe was a powder keg waiting for a spark to set off a cataclysmic explosion. On June 28, 1914, the spark was lit when the heir to the throne of Austro-Hungary, the Archduke Franz Ferdinand, was assassinated at Sarajevo, Bosnia-Herzegovina, by Bosnian Serb terrorists. It took a month for the fuse to burn but the explosion came at the end of July when war broke out between Serbia and Austro-Hungary upon the failure of the former to agree to the terms of an ultimatum that was designed to be refused. Now the network of interlocking alliances that had earlier deterred a general European war worked to pull all of the great European states into the vortex of war. The Tsar ordered a partial mobilization against Austro-Hungary on July 29th and then a general mobilization against both Germany and Austro-Hungary on July 30th when military officials advised him that a partial mobilization was not possible under the existing Russian war plan. Germany then issued an ultimatum against Russia to stop its mobilization and when Russia did not comply Germany mobilized and declared war on Russia on August 1st. France was also given an ultimatum by Germany not to interfere and when a satisfactory response was not received Germany mobilized in the west as well, attacking Luxembourg on August 2nd and declaring war on France on August 3rd. The German war plan in the west called for a massive movement of the German Army's right wing through Belgium and Luxembourg and into France. German troops declared war and entered neutral Belgium on August 4th which then prompted Great Britain to declare war on Germany on the same day because Great Britain was a guarantor of Belgian neutrality by treaty. Although Italy was allied with Germany and Austro-Hungary it declared itself neutral. On August 6th Austro-Hungary declared war on Russia, and France and Britain declared war on Austro-Hungary on August 11th and 12th respectively. Late in August, responding to requests for naval assistance from Great Britain, Japan declared war on Germany and Austro-Hungary. To guard against the possibility of attacks on the west coast from elements of German Admiral Graf von Spee's Pacific squadron, the Japanese cruiser *Chikuma* cruised to Esquimalt. Finally, in November, the allied powers declared war on the Ottoman Empire, which had joined in alliance with Germany and Austro-Hungary.

When Great Britain went to war, Canada automatically found itself at war because Canada, although autonomous within the British Empire, was still a subordinate country lacking *de jure* independence within international law. Consequently, Canada remained subject to the decisions taken by the imperial government with respect to foreign relations, including decisions concerning war and peace. Canada now embraced the world struggle that would consume the old states of Europe over the next four years and would subsequently contribute, at enormous cost, to Canada's rise to full nationhood within the world community.

1914-1931 WORLD WAR ONE AND THE AFTERMATH; MACKENZIE KING GOES TO WASHINGTON

On August 4, 1914, Canada found itself embroiled in a general European war which had fallen on the country like a thunderbolt. Yet there was an immediate outpouring of genuine support for Great Britain and Canada's imperial ties to Great Britain would retain their strength throughout the conflict.

Canada was a young country that had quickly grown in population in the prewar period as a result of the promotion of immigration by the federal government. Although there had been extensive immigration from populations in central and eastern Europe, a substantial wave of immigration from the British Isles had ensured that family and emotional ties with Great Britain remained strong. The imperial ties had provided the Canadian public with a sense that the country was protected from foreign aggression by Great Britain. It was not generally perceived that Great Britain had shifted its strategic foreign policy objectives away from the protection of Canada and towards a rapprochement with the United States. Hence, given the strong ties to the empire it was a certainty that Canada would make a major contribution to the imperial war effort.

The scale of Canada's contribution to the war effort was enormous, given the fact that Canada's population in 1914 was only 7.8 million people. The Canadian Army enlisted 595,441 men between August 4, 1914, and November 15, 1918,[1] and the total personnel in the Canadian Expeditionary Force that was sent to Europe numbered 418,052 of which 54,545 lost their lives, while the total enlistment in the Royal Canadian Navy was ninety-six hundred, of which 150 seamen lost their lives[2]. In addition, Canadians served abroad in the Royal Navy, the Royal Air Force (21,169), the Imperial Motor Transport and Inland Water Transport (5411) and the Jewish Palestine Draft (42)[3]. Additionally, there was a huge industrial effort made by Canadian industry to support the war effort and the entire economy was subsumed into the titanic struggle against the Central Powers[4].

Canada fielded a full army corps consisting of four divisions on the western front in Europe but the slaughter in the trenches put a great strain on the ability of the army to maintain its strength through the induction of volunteers. The outpouring of patriotic volunteers into the army in 1914 had mainly consisted of recent immigrants to Canada from the British Isles and only 25% of the first overseas contingent despatched by Canada to Europe consisted of Canadians born in Canada[5]. Recruitment in Quebec among the Francophone population was even more difficult until the federal government created an exclusive Francophone unit (which eventually became the Royal 22d Regiment) after the intervention of Laurier, who now led the Parliamentary Opposition. Eventually, when the Borden Ministry determined that conscription would be necessary to sustain the army in the field the fragile unity of the country almost fractured, and the

---

1. *Canada in the Great World War, Vol. 6* (Toronto: United Publishers of Canada,1921) 376-77.[2] Tucker, *The Naval Service of Canada*, 221.
2. Tucker, The Naval Service of Canada, 221.
3. *Canada in the Great War, Vol. 6*, 376.
4. The Central Powers consisted of Germany, Austro-Hungary, the Ottoman Empire and Bulgaria.
5. Ralph Allen, *Ordeal by Fire Canada, 1910-1945* (Toronto: Doubleday Canada Limited, 1961) 131.

bitter 1917 general election left the country divided almost exclusively along linguistic lines.

Relations with the United States were also affected by the war. Immediately upon its outbreak the United States declared itself to be neutral and American neutrality was strongly bipartisan with both President Woodrow Wilson and his predecessor, William Howard Taft, opposed to American intervention[6]. Great Britain was under severe strain especially due to the depredations of the German submarine campaign, which threatened to starve the country of foodstuffs and other essential resources. The Royal Navy likewise blockaded the European coast and severely impacted Germany's ability to import necessary commodities to sustain its war effort. In the only major confrontation between the Royal Navy and the Imperial German Navy during the war, at Jutland in 1916, the German dreadnought battleships were forced to retreat after scoring a tactical victory. Great Britain was never directly threatened again by the German fleet in the war and thus Jutland proved to be a strategic success for the Royal Navy.

To maintain its naval edge, Great Britain was forced to work with US companies to evade US neutrality laws by arranging for the surreptitious importation of required naval components into Canada. The imperial government even facilitated the entry of US workers into Canada to complete work on US-designed patrol vessels, much to the consternation of Canadian federal authorities, who were not fully consulted about this initiative[7]. The Borden Ministry continued to take an uncompromising line with respect to the application of the Rush-Bagot Agreement during the war years and American desires for placing additional

6. Ibid, 85.
7. Patrick McManus, "Stability and Flexibility: The Rush-Bagot Agreement and the Progressive Modernization of Canadian-American Security Relations" (PhD diss., University of Ottawa, 2009), 72, Theses Canada (ISBN: 978-0-494-61273-6).

training vessels on the Great Lakes in 1916, and again in early 1917, were both unfulfilled due to Canadian intransigence[8].

After the entry of the United States into the war in 1917, circumstances changed. America entered the war following Germany's declaration of unrestricted submarine warfare against both belligerents and neutrals, and Germany's attempt to persuade Mexico to ally itself against the United States in the event of US belligerency in return for a German promise to restore the territories Mexico had lost to the United States during the Mexican-American War. The nature of the relationship between Canada and the United States was fundamentally altered by the US entry into the war and the two countries, for the first time, were together in a political and military alliance. At a meeting in 1917 between Prime Minister Borden and President Wilson the US agreed to provide economic assistance to Canada in the form of ordinance contracts that helped to sustain the Canadian war effort, and which resulted in a new cooperative spirit in the relations between the two countries[9]. As the relationship between Canada and the United States continued to develop American forces served under Canadian command on the east coast, and their militaries began sharing intelligence data[10].

In 1917, the federal government requested permission from the United States, within the framework of the Rush-Bagot Agreement, to place gun platforms and to build ammunition magazines into merchant ships that Canadian firms on the Great Lakes were building to assist the war effort. The United States granted Canada permission on the condition that it would be a temporary expedient which would not alter the terms of the

8. Purver, "The Rush-Bagot Agreement: Demilitarizing the Great Lakes, 1817 to the Present," *Encyclopedia of Arms and Control and Disarmament, Vol. 1,* 588.
9. McManus, "Stability and Flexibility: The Rush-Bagot Agreement and the Progressive Modernization of Canadian-American Security Relations" 75.
10. Ibid, 76.

Rush-Bagot Agreement, and that Canada would not retain the vessels on the Great Lakes[11]. As the war progressed, the United States also constructed war vessels on the Great Lakes, particularly at the Ford Motor Company's River Rouge complex at Detroit[12].

While the army struggled in Europe, Canada itself was secure. The German submarine campaign did not reach Canadian shores during the war and the first sightings of German submarines in transit only occurred towards the end of the war, in the summer of 1918. Halifax was the major port for the creation of convoys to Europe and it experienced a great deal of naval and merchant traffic. A collision between two vessels in December 1917, one of which was carrying a cargo of munitions, resulted in a massive explosion that destroyed parts of the city and killed or wounded approximately 11,000 people, mostly civilians, in the largest man-made explosion prior to the atomic age. On the Pacific coast the Imperial Japanese Navy continued to afford naval protection to Canada's west coast, and the Japanese exercised allied naval control in the North Pacific under the terms of the Anglo-Japanese treaty throughout the war. Meanwhile the Canadian Army achieved its greatest victory at the Battle of Vimy Ridge in 1917 which greatly contributed to the growing consciousness of a Canadian national identity separate and apart from the country's membership in the British Empire. That was reinforced the following year when the Canadian Army served as shock troops leading the advance of British armies in the final Hundred Days campaign of the war.

World War One had a cataclysmic effect on Europe and by the time the war ended on November 11, 1918, it had resulted in the destruction of the Russian monarchy and the subsequent defeat of Russia by Germany before the Central Powers themselves

11. Purver, "The Rush-Bagot Agreement: Demilitarizing the Great Lakes, 1817 to the Present," *Encyclopedia of Arms and Control and Disarmament, Vol. 1,* 588-89.
12. Ibid, 589.

were overwhelmed by the Allied Powers of Great Britain, France, Italy, the United States, and Japan. Canada, along with the other British dominions had played an important part in defeating the Central Powers and had suffered accordingly, with substantial numbers of its soldiers either dead or wounded. There was a sentiment among some parts of the population that the imperial government had not fully appreciated the extent of Canada's contribution to the imperial war effort, nor the sacrifices that had been entailed by the country. However, Great Britain had suffered terribly as well and an entire generation of young men had been lost in the war by Great Britain. Among the other allies France, in particular, had been bled white by the war and came close to breaking under the strain in 1917 with the outbreak of mutinies in the French Army that were put down with great severity. Indeed, Germany had almost succeeded in winning the war in 1918 after defeating Russia and redeploying its forces from the eastern front to the western front for a final offensive that once again threatened central France.

Had the infusion of fresh US troops and materiel not been available to help stem the tide of the German advance in 1918, it is possible that the war would not have ended in victory for the Allied Powers. Thus, in Canada, there was a new appreciation of the vast resources and great strength that the United States could deploy in an emergency. By comparison, it was now clear that the British Empire was much more limited in the resources that it could supply, although it continued to rule over a vast extent of the Earth. These changing perceptions of the relative strengths of Great Britain and the United States of America had strategic implications for Canada in the postwar world. Unfortunately, initial hopes that a new era of peace would now dawn were dashed when the United States refused to enter the new League of Nations established at the behest of President Wilson to help maintain world peace in the postwar world. Without the great political and economic strength of the United States the League was continually hampered in its efforts. Furthermore, the harsh peace imposed on Germany and the dissolution of Austro-Hungary created instability in central Europe. Russia was convulsed by revolution and civil war leading to the establishment of a Marxist Bolshevik regime which presented new challenges to the now victorious western powers.

The peace brought a new recognition of Canadian national identity which was reflected by the insistence of Prime Minister Borden that Canada must sign the Versailles Peace Treaty in 1919 separately from Great Britain in recognition of Canada's evolving status in the world, and the contributions that it had made to the allied victory. The signature of the Canadian Prime Minister on the Peace Treaty in 1919 signalled Canada's *de facto* sovereignty, and the beginning of the country's march to formal *de jure* independence in the postwar world.

But the postwar world did not usher in a new age of peace that so many fervently wished for. The peace treaty with the defeated powers was extreme. Both Germany and the Ottoman Empire were shorn of their territorial possessions and Austro-Hungary was dismantled in its entirety. Germany was forced to pay huge war reparations and found compliance with the Versailles demands impossible to meet. Even allied nations such as Great Britain and France were compelled to repay with great difficulty the onerous war loans extended to them by the United States, now the predominant economic and financial power in the world. Although the world had been transformed by the war certain prewar habits and attitudes reasserted themselves and this was especially true of the relations between Canada and the United States with respect to naval armaments on the Great Lakes.

In the spring of 1919 the federal government had quickly acceded to a request by the United States for the passage of a naval training vessel, the *USS Newport*, through the Canadian canals and into the Great Lakes for the purposes of a training cruise. However, Canada's permission was subject to a provision that *Newport* would have to return to the Atlantic Ocean before ice closed the navigation season on the Great Lakes and St. Lawrence River[13].

By the autumn of 1919 prewar Canadian suspicions of US intentions on the Great Lakes had returned, and government records contain a complaint by the federal government to the British charge d'affaires in Washington concerning the passage of armed US eagle boats, which were steam-driven, steel-hulled, patrol vessels built at Detroit, through the Lachine Canal without having obtained prior permission from Canada to transit the canal[14]). When the United States responded by stating that the Eagle boats were constructed as a wartime commitment of sixty such craft for Great Britain,[15] the federal government queried the British Ambassador about any contracts which Great Britain may have entered into for the construction of war vessels on the Great Lakes[16]. During the war there had been tensions around Canadian perceptions that Great Britain had taken advantage of its *de jure* sovereignty over Canada in the area of naval production by facilitating the completion in Canada of partially constructed American patrol boats without full disclosure to Canada of British activities,[17] and the sudden passage of the latest tranche of eagle boats heightened Canadian concerns. The British were dismissive of Canadian concerns stating that the

---

13. Duke of Devonshire, "Diplomatic Note", Governor General, to the British Charge d'affaires (Washington) June 12, 1919; (LAC R11336-5-6-E MG26-K, External Affairs, Rush Bagot Pol. Series, 6294).

14. L H Davies, "Diplomatic Note", Deputy of the Governor General to British Charge d'affaires (Washington); (LAC R11336-5-6-E MG26-K, External Affairs, Rush Bagot Pol. Series, 6298.

15. "Diplomatic Note" US Response, (LAC R11336-5-6-E MG26-K, External Affairs, Rush Bagot Pol. Series, 6300).

16. John Iddington, "Diplomatic Note" Deputy of the Governor General to British Ambassador (Washington) (LAC R11336-5-6-E MG26-K, External Affairs, Rush Bagot Pol. Series, 6318).

17. McManus, "Stability and Flexibility: The Rush-Bagot Agreement and the Progressive Modernization of Canadian-American Security Relations" 72.

Admiralty was not aware of any such contracts and after the American entry into the war as an ally there would have been no need for any formal agreements for work completed as part of the joint war effort[18].

Nevertheless, the movement of the eagle boats heightened Canadian concerns about the security of its southern maritime border with the United States. The Canadian military began assessing the security situation along the country's southern coast and a new report was prepared by Lieutenant-Colonel Luard of the Plans Division dated March 13, 1920[19].

Colonel Luard noted that Canada's southern water frontier extended approximately 1000 miles between Cornwall and the west coast of Lake Superior. The lake and canal system afforded passage for vessels up to 270 feet in length with a draught of 14 feet while the American canals allowed for the passage of ships of up to 300 feet in length drawing a draught of ten feet from New York via the Hudson River and New York canals. Given that any of the canals could now be attacked and rendered unuseable by the new weapons system of aircraft bombardment, Luard suggested that any new naval defence would have to be devised from ships already present on the Great Lakes when a crisis occurred. As always, the control of Lake Ontario would be critical to maintaining an effective Canadian defence which meant that the ability of Canada to control the Welland Canal would be essential. Canadian shipbuilding capacity on Lake Ontario and Georgian Bay could give it the capacity to control Lake Ontario, and the ability to contend for control on Lake Huron, although the United States could quickly dominate the

18. "Diplomatic Note," British Ambassador (Washington) to Governor General Lord Byng, October 17, 1921; (LAC R11336-5-6-E MG26-K, External Affairs, Rush Bagot Pol. Series, 6325).
19. Lieutenant Colonel Luard DSO, RMLI, Plans Division, General Staff, "Notes on the Defences of the Great Lakes, Some Naval Considerations", March, 1920; (Library and Archives Canada, Department of the Naval Service, Inland Waterways and Canals, Naval Control of the Great Lakes).

other lakes. Luard thought that if Canada could obtain control Lake Ontario and Georgian Bay that might assist the country's overall military position in a crisis.

The increased concern about the transit into the lakes of US warships without first seeking Canadian permission led the federal government to review its policy on canal usage. At a cabinet meeting on February 16, 1921[20], the Meighen Ministry[21] decided to reaffirm the requirement that any armed or unarmed vessel belonging to a foreign state must obtain the permission of the Minster of the Naval Service (Canada) on the application of the foreign government concerned[22]. As usual however, Canadian sensitivity to the power of the United States, and the risk that formal complaint might impel the United States to abrogate the Rush-Bagot Agreement, or to insist on amendments to the Agreement, forestalled any protest or complaint to Washington from Ottawa[23].

The United States, after being apprised of the formal views of the Meighen Ministry by the British embassy dutifully attempted to comply with the procedures outlined by Canada. Thus, on April 28, 1921, US Secretary of State Charles Hughes formally applied for permission for the US submarine *N-3* to proceed through the Canadian canals into the Great Lakes to attend a convention of the Loyal Order of the Moose at Toledo, Ohio, in the summer of 1921[24]. Canada permitted the passage subject to the proviso that

20. Purver, "The Rush-Bagot Agreement: Demilitarizing the Great Lakes, 1817 to the Present," *Encyclopedia of Arms and Control and Disarmament, Vol. 1,* 589.
21. Arthur Meighen succeeded Robert Borden as Prime Minister on July 10, 1920.
22. Minute of the King's Privy Council for Canada dated February 22, 1921; (LAC, Department of the Naval Service, Inland Waterways and Canals, Naval Control of the Great Lakes, 6308-09).
23. Purver, "The Rush-Bagot Agreement: Demilitarizing the Great Lakes, 1817 to the Present," *Encyclopedia of Arms and Control and Disarmament, Vol. 1,* 589.
24. Chas. F. Hughes, Secretary of State of the United States, "Correspondence dated April 28, 1921", (Library and Archives Canada, Department of the Naval Service, Inland Waterways and Canals, Naval Control of the Great Lakes, 6312).

the *N-3* land the warheads from its torpedos before transiting into the Great Lakes.

As 1921 passed into 1922 the Conservative-Unionist government of Prime Minister Meighen was replaced by a Liberal Ministry under Prime Minister William Lyon Mackenzie King, who would come to dominate political life of Canada during the middle years of the twentieth century. Mackenzie King was anxious to move Canada towards formal independence while maintaining the country's historical links to Great Britain, and to align Canada more closely with the United States, which was growing rapidly in power and influence on the world stage. King perceived that a political opportunity was available to advance those objectives by negotiating a revised Rush-Bagot Agreement with the United States without the substantive involvement of the imperial government.

Naval armaments were top of mind at the time that King took office in the waning days of December 1921. The Washington Naval Conference was coming to a successful conclusion and was widely popular in the Anglophone countries. World War One had demonstrated that the United States was the leading world power measured by industrial and financial strength. Its ability to marshal enormous resources was unmatched by any other power during the war and its size, population and wealth gave credence to the view that it would be the dominant world power in the future. Although Great Britain had emerged victorious from the war, it was now diminished in strength in comparison to the United States. Given its straightened financial circumstances British politicians in the immediate postwar period were appalled at the prospect of a new naval shipbuilding war with the United States if Great Britain were to retain its national policy of naval supremacy. British politicians realized that the cost of a new naval arms race would be unbearable and, ultimately, Great Britain would not succeed in holding on to its historic supremacy on the oceans of the world.

Imagine, therefore, the surprise of British officials when, at the outset of the Washington Naval Conference in November 1921, US Secretary of State Hughes proposed a ratio of naval strength among the five major naval powers (United Kingdom, United States, Japan, France and Italy) that resulted in naval parity in capital ships between Great Britain and the United States without Great Britain having to spend a single pound on the new construction of capital ships[25]. The price that Great Britain paid for avoiding a naval arms race with the United States was the sacrifice of the Anglo-Japanese alliance that had proved quite useful to Great Britain in the years preceding the world war, and during it. The United States feared and detested the Japanese (and some of that ill-feeling was at least partially motivated by racial prejudices) and could not accept the renewal of that alliance while maintaining cordial relations with Great Britain. Although the sacrifice of the treaty increased the risks to Great Britain, and to the dominions and British possessions in the Pacific, the friendship of the United States was the greater prize and it was obtained with the avoidance of any new expenditures towards the cost of new shipbuilding. Canada under the Meighen Ministry had played a crucial role in advocating for the termination of the Anglo-Japanese alliance, and the resulting placation of the United States in the Pacific[26]. For an astute politician like Mackenzie King, the political benefits of achieving a similarly satisfactory result in relation to the Great Lakes were very tempting.

In July 1921, King embarked on his quest by visiting the US Capitol with his Minister of Militia and Defence, George Graham, to discuss revising the Rush-Bagot Agreement with US Secretary of State Charles Hughes[27]. Speaking for the Harding Administration, Hughes expressed surprise at the Canadian push

---

25. In the end the British did lay down two new capital ships (*Nelson* and *Rodney*) with the agreement of the other parties because the Japanese obtained consent to retain its newest battleship.
26. O'Brien, *British and American Naval Power, Politics and Policy, 1900-1936,* 173.

for revisions to the Rush-Bagot Agreement but listened attentively as King described how the large number of US naval ships on the Great Lakes, ostensibly for training purposes, could engender demands from Canadians that the federal government should also expand its naval capacity on the Great Lakes, and thus undermine the agreement[28]. In an interview on July 13, 1921, with the *New York Tribune* Mackenzie King described his proposed new treaty as another landmark in Canada-US relations and referred to the existing agreement as a bedrock of goodwill and friendly relations between the two countries, in addition to the practical effects of its limitation in naval armaments[29].

The Harding Administration requested that Canada submit a draft treaty to the United States as a basis for discussions and Canada quickly complied, delivering a draft text to Hughes on November 7, 1922[30]. A draft of this treaty[31] in the federal government's records provides an interesting insight into Canadian interests during this period. The title makes it clear that it was to be a two-party agreement between Canada and the United States alone. Great Britain would no longer be involved despite the fact that Canada did not yet possess *de jure* independence from the British Empire at this point in time. The preamble called for the abolition of naval armaments on the Great Lakes and linked that concept to the earlier Rush-Bagot Agreement and to the newly-endorsed Washington Conference Agreement between the big five naval powers. The scope of the proposed draft agreement would have applied its contents to the

27. Purver, "The Rush-Bagot Agreement: Demilitarizing the Great Lakes, 1817 to the Present," *Encyclopedia of Arms and Control and Disarmament, Vol. 1, 589.*
28. Ibid.
29. "New York Tribune, July 13, 1922"; (LAC, Department of the Naval Service, Inland Waterways and Canals, Naval Control of the Great Lakes, 6287).
30. Purver, "The Rush-Bagot Agreement: Demilitarizing the Great Lakes, 1817 to the Present," *Encyclopedia of Arms and Control and Disarmament, Vol. 1, 589.*
31. "Draft Treaty Between Canada and the United States of America Regulating Naval Forces to be Maintained by Both Powers on the Great Lakes," (LAC, Department of the Naval Service, Inland Waterways and Canals, Naval Control of the Great Lakes).

same geographical area as the original Rush-Bagot Agreement but explicitly included the connecting straits between the lakes and extended the treaty obligations to the shared portion of the St. Lawrence River[32]. The second and third articles contained the substance of the agreement and they banned the maintaining of any war vessels on the Great Lakes and prohibited any war vessels from visiting the Great Lakes unless both states agreed to the visit. Consistent with the practice that had developed hitherto under the Rush-Bagot Agreement an exception was made for armed vessels to be used solely for revenue and police enforcement duties but the number, armaments, and specifications of such vessels were to be agreed-upon by the two parties[33]. However, no such vessel could be used for naval militia training, or engage in naval manoeuvres on the Great Lakes[34]. (But the proposed treaty did not purport to govern unarmed training vessels[35].) Naval vessels could be built in shipyards on the Great Lakes provided that the other party was informed of the project, the expected date of completion, and the size of the ship but no armaments could be installed while the vessel was on the Great Lakes, and every such newly-built ship would have to be taken out of the Great Lakes within six months of the date of its readiness for launching[36]. Article five allowed either party to suspend the restrictions on the building of new war vessels where that party was engaged in a war but such suspensions would terminate when hostilities ceased. A final clause allowed for the termination of the agreement with two-years notice but also provided that the parties would meet one year into the notice period, presumably to engage in a dispute

32. Ibid, Article One.
33. Ibid, Article 2, 3.
34. Ibid, Article 3.
35. Purver, "The Rush-Bagot Agreement: Demilitarizing the Great Lakes, 1817 to the Present," *Encyclopedia of Arms and Control and Disarmament, Vol. 1,* 589.
36. "Draft Treaty Between Canada and the United States of America Regulating Naval Forces to be Maintained by Both Powers on the Great Lakes," Article 4.

resolution process in order to find a way to keep the agreement in force.

This proposal was more restrictive than the original Rush-Bagot Agreement and reflected Canadian unease at the number of US naval vessels that had been brought into the Great Lakes for training purposes since the days of the Laurier Ministry, and perhaps the growing sense of inferiority that Canada now experienced in comparison to the economic and military strength of its neighbour. While neither party at this point in time was maintaining a naval vessel for naval defence on the Great Lakes[37] the United States had found it useful to provide for naval training on the lakes and so it was a reach for Canada to now seek to restrict the stationing of armed training vessels on the Great Lakes. An outright ban on maintaining warships on the Great Lakes would have likely caused concern in US naval circles if the proposal had gone any further. Notably, during this period, US naval planners were still planning for the possibility of a general war with Great Britain which would necessarily have involved Canada since Canada still lacked *de jure* independence from Great Britain. In the years before the Washington Naval Conference Agreement ended the prospect of future naval shipbuilding rivalry between Great Britain and the United States it was even thought possible by American military planners that Great Britain would launch a preemptive strike against the United States in order to maintain British naval supremacy[38].

In launching his proposal Mackenzie King was clearly attempting to renegotiate the Rush-Bagot Agreement in terms that would satisfy Canadian public opinion and alleviate Canadian fears over the prospect of an American militarization of the Great Lakes. As far back as the days of the Laurier Ministry Canadians had begun to express alarm over the growing

37. The *USS Wolverine*, formerly the *Michigan* was decommissioned in 1912 although it was still being used as a naval training ship on the Great Lakes.
38. O'Brien, *British and American Naval Power, Politics and Policy, 1900-1936*, 155.

presence of armed American naval vessels, and armed US revenue cutters, on the Great Lakes. Obtaining American agreement to a more restrictive approach to naval operations on the Great Lakes would have been a significant political coup for Mackenzie King, and would have been a notable achievement as the first foreign treaty negotiated by the Canadian state without the participation of the imperial government.

The negotiation of a new Rush-Bagot Agreement also fitted in with other efforts that Mackenzie King was making to advance Canadian independence on the world stage. In the autumn of 1922 a significant step forward was taken by the federal government when it refused to commit Canada's support to a possible military action by Great Britain against Turkey in the Chanak Crisis. The Chanak Crisis resulted from the collapse of the Imperial Ottoman Government following its defeat in World War One. The peace treaty imposed upon it allowed Greece to occupy portions of Ottoman territory which sparked an irredentist movement among some Turkish army officers, including Kemal Ataturk, who led a revolt that smashed the Greek occupation force and subsequently compelled the last Ottoman Sultan to abdicate and flee the country. A small British garrison at Chanak which was intended to enforce the peace established by the Treaty of Sevres was stranded and surrounded. Fearing a renewal of war in the Near East, Great Britain called on its dominions to support the British army with troops to enforce the peace arrangements that had been entered into with the Sultan and his government. So urgent was the need for troops that Great Britain publicly announced its request to its four dominions (Canada, Australia, South Africa and New Zealand) even before formal telegrams to each of the governments concerned had been received by them, which was a serious breach of the political conventions that governed relations between London and the four British dominions[39].

39. Allen, *Ordeal by Fire*, Canada 1910-1945, 237.

Mackenzie King struck a blow for Canadian independence by refusing the request of the imperial government and asserted that Canadian troops would only be sent if the Parliament of Canada consented to send them following a recommendation by the Canadian Ministry, which at that point was not prepared to make such a recommendation[40]. Mackenzie King's action was decried by the Opposition Leader, Arthur Meighen, but the population was generally supportive of King's actions. The sacrifices of World War One were all too recent in the public mind and no one wanted Canada to become embroiled in a new European war. The crisis eventually passed without bloodshed, and a new peace treaty was subsequently worked out with the Republic of Turkey, as the successor state to the Ottoman Empire. No imperial troops were ultimately required and the British garrison at Chanak was not attacked. Nevertheless, Chanak was a watershed development on the road to Canadian independence since it marked the first time that Canada had refused to follow the foreign policy lead of Great Britain, and the first instance where Canada asserted a political right to determine whether to commit the Canadian armed forces to a conflict.

While all of these developments were occurring at the political level, the Canadian military continued to busy itself with plans for the military defence of Canada in the event of a war with the United States. On January 24, 1922, the Chief of the General Staff wrote to his counterpart, the Director of the Naval Service requesting naval input from the Royal Canadian Navy on several questions relating to the lake defences. The navy obliged and in dealing first with Lake Champlain, which sits astride the traditional invasion route into Canada from the United States, the navy suggested that Canadian control of that lake would be impossible unless the army could control both banks of the lake. The United States was capable of placing larger vessels on the

40. Ibid, 239.

lake while Canada was restricted to small vessels because of the size restrictions of the Chambly canal. The navy thought that Lake Champlain would in all probability not become a naval theatre of operations in a modern war with the United States and that all Canada could hope to do there would be to bomb the American locks in the Champlain Canal[41].

On Lake Ontario the navy thought that the military situation would be more favourable to Canada because Canada had better harbours and facilities on that lake and Canada could bring larger vessels into Lake Ontario via the St. Lawrence River, assuming that the river route remained open for traffic. If not, Canada would be forced to use the Rideau Canal system, which would only allow smaller vessels to be brought into Lake Ontario. Canada could arm perhaps fifty merchantmen operating on Lake Ontario to help secure its control but it would be necessary for Canada to hold or destroy the Welland Canal, and to bomb and destroy the canal locks at Oswego and Rochester in New York in order to hold the lake[42].

On Lake Erie and Lake Huron it was suggested that the United States would quickly assume control, although if sea mines were available US control on Lake Huron might be forestalled for a time. Lake Superior could be held only if Sault Ste. Marie, Michigan, was occupied by Canadian forces. In the absence of an occupation of Sault Ste. Marie, Michigan, by Canada, control of Lake Superior would inevitably fall to the United States[43].

These plans were largely predicated on a short struggle, and on a war in which Canada could rely on assistance from its imperial cousins as well as Great Britain. However, those assumptions must have appeared questionable even in the 1920's. In fact,

---

41. Director of the Naval Service, "Memorandum to the Chief of the General Staff", Department of Militia and Defence, February 25, 1922, (LAC, RG 25, D1, Volume 740).
42. Ibid.
43. Ibid.

Great Britain had washed its hands of Canadian defence against the United States even before the outbreak of World War One. In all but the shortest of struggles Canada would likely be overwhelmed by the superior war capability of the United States and it would have been impossible to maintain naval control of any one of the Great Lakes, or Lake Champlain.

As Canada waited for the United States to respond to its draft of a revised Rush-Bagot Agreement, the federal government continued to maintain a watchful eye on the movement of US warships into or out of the Great Lakes. In the spring of 1922 Canadian naval intelligence reported on the impending replacement at Detroit of the old *Yantic* by the *Dubuque*, a former surveying vessel built in 1902, and the replacement of *Essex*, an older gunboat at Duluth, by the *Paducah*, which had been constructed in 1902. The United States had requested and received permission from Canada to move the two newer ships into the Great Lakes by transiting the Canadian canals subject to the usual Canadian stipulation that their armaments would be removed for the journey[44].

In a memorandum for the Deputy Minister of the Naval Service the naval intelligence division summarized the scope of US naval assets and other marine assets in the spring of 1922, noting that the United States had seven significant but obsolescent naval assets on the lakes as training vessels: *Commodore* (Chicago) *Essex* (Duluth) (to be replaced by *Paducah*) *Gopher* (Toledo) *Hawk* (Milwaukee) *Yantic* (Detroit) (to be replaced by *Dubuque*) *Wilmette* (Chicago) and *Wolverine* [*ex Michigan*] at Erie[45]. In addition there were six US Navy submarine chasers and three naval tugboats

44. W H Eves, Department of the Naval Service, Intelligence Division, "Memorandum for the Director of Naval Service", May 20, 1922, (LAC, RG 25, D1, Volume 740).
45. The *Wolverine*, formerly the *Michigan* made its last long-range lake voyage in 1923 during which its historic engines finally failed. *Wolverine* was laid up at Erie Pennsylvania for a number of years as attempts were made to preserve it but when all efforts to save the ship failed it was finally sent to the scrap yard in 1949, ending a century and more of service on the Great Lakes.

stationed on the Great Lakes. The United States Coast Guard[46] maintained four revenue cutters: *Morill* (Detroit) *Tuscarora* (Milwaukee) *Chillicothe* (Ogdensburg) and *Chippewa* (Sault Ste. Marie) and four patrol cutters (former sub-chasers) *Boyce* (Chicago) *Cook* (Duluth-Sault Ste. Marie) *Klingelhoffer* (Chicago) and *Knudson* (Chicago). Finally, the coast guard harbour launches *Advance, Javelin, Search, Sentinel, Vigilant* and *Voyager* were based at Sault Ste. Marie, Michigan[47]. This was a substantial force, even though the military utility of some of the ships was debatable.

When the United States eventually responded to the Canadian initiative to rewrite the Rush-Bagot Agreement in May 1923, the federal government discovered that the United States did not share some of the objectives that Canada had articulated in the draft treaty. Rather, the United States pressed for a naval advantage in any new treaty. The US Government proposed to allow armed naval training vessels on the lakes although with a stipulation that they would never be used against the other party for a hostile purpose – even if war broke out between them! Further, the number, size and armaments to be carried by such training vessels would be subject to the consent of both parties. For revenue and police vessels there would be no restrictions at all in relation to either their numbers or their armaments provided that the armaments were appropriate to the role of those vessels. And like the naval vessels that would not be used for hostile actions against the other party, even in the event of war, so too the revenue and police vessels would have no role in warfare. Finally, no state-owned ships, whether naval or civil enforcement vessels, would be required to obtain permission from the other state in order to enter the Great Lakes[48].

---

46. On January 28, 1915, the United States Coast Guard was formed by merging the US Revenue Marine with the US Life-Saving Service.
47. "Memorandum to the Deputy Minister of the Naval Service" May, 1922, (LAC, RG 25, D1, Volume 740).
48. Purver, "The Rush-Bagot Agreement: Demilitarizing the Great Lakes, 1817 to the Present," *Encyclopedia of Arms and Control and Disarmament, Vol. 1,* 589.

The United States did concede however, that warships constructed on the Great Lakes should be withdrawn from the lakes within six months of their launch readiness date, and such ships should only receive their armaments after they had left the Great Lakes[49].

The American proposals would have effectively eviscerated the Rush-Bagot Agreement as a mechanism to limit naval armaments on the Great Lakes. There would have been no real restrictions against basing naval vessels on the Great Lakes so long as they could be justified as training vessels, and there would have been no limitations on their passage to and from the lakes through the connecting straits and canals. Revenue vessels would continue to enjoy their existing exclusion from the Rush-Bagot Agreement and would now be free to move in and out of the Great Lakes using the canals and straits without any Canadian permission. Prime Minister Mackenzie King must have realized that the American approach was completely opposite to what he had hoped to achieve and that what was being proposed was a regressive outcome for Canada. Whatever hopes he may have had to sign a new naval arms limitation agreement with the United States as a sign of Canadian maturity on the world stage must have been dashed. Instead of a renewed Rush-Bagot Agreement that would modernize the 1817 provisions while allaying lingering concerns about American naval armaments on the Great Lakes the final outcome would have probably represented a retreat from the original principle of a system of lakes demilitarized of offensive naval weapons systems. The Prime Minister therefore set aside the initiative relating to the Rush-Bagot Agreement for the time being. Meanwhile, the time that the United States took to consider the Canadian proposals had by now robbed the Rush-Bagot revision of any possible place of honour as the first international treaty to be negotiated and signed by Canada in its own right, without

49. Ibid.

any involvement in the diplomatic process by Great Britain. The honour of being the first such treaty (which Mackenzie King would always consider to be one of his most important personal accomplishments during his time in office) would fall to the lowly Halibut Fishing Treaty of 1923, which was signed in March 1923[50].

The federal government took up consideration of the American draft of the proposed treaty to replace the Rush-Bagot Agreement in the autumn of 1924. Surprisingly, despite the fact that the American proposals were contrary to Canadian strategic objectives the Canadian military expressed no reservations and only asked for information concerning revenue cutters. Politically, Mackenzie King's cabinet expressed approval of the draft on October 8, 1924, but there must have been severe reservations in the cabinet over that result because on the very next day the Minister of National Defence deferred the response of Canada to the United States and the whole project was put on a permanent hold. Eventually, after a final follow-up inquiry from the United States in 1925, the third and final attempt to revise the Rush-Bagot Agreement was allowed to die a quiet death[51]. Doubtless, it was realized, probably by Mackenzie King himself[52], that agreeing to the American draft would render any restrictions ineffective and public knowledge of that fact would probably cost the government a substantial part of its political capital. Rather than accept criticism for agreeing to a poor result political discretion dictated that it would be preferable to live with the now antiquated Rush-Bagot Agreement rather than to strive for something more modern that would put at risk the benefits of the existing agreement.

50. Allen, *Ordeal by Fire*, 242.
51. Purver, "The Rush-Bagot Agreement: Demilitarizing the Great Lakes, 1817 to the Present," *Encyclopedia of Arms and Control and Disarmament, Vol. 1*, 590.
52. Mackenzie King's diaries, however, do not appear to shed any light on why the government changed its mind so suddenly.

As the decade wore on, Canada continued its march towards full membership in the community of nations. Already a member of the League of Nations, and now having negotiated and signed its first diplomatic agreement, the Halibut Fishing Treaty, it was time for a more formal understanding of the exercise of sovereignty within the international family that was rapidly transforming itself from the British Empire into the British Commonwealth. At the Imperial Conference in London in 1926 the role of the dominions and their relationship to Great Britain was discussed and a resolution was reached on November 15, 1926, expressed in the Balfour Declaration (which was named for Arthur Balfour, a former British Prime Minister who served in 1926 as Lord President of the Privy Council, and who developed the formulation adopted at the conference). The resolution, sponsored by both Prime Minister Hertzog of South Africa, and Prime Minister Mackenzie King of Canada, stipulated that from that time forward the previous indivisibility of the Crown which had pre-empted the creation of international legal standing for the dominions would no longer be recognized within the British Commonwealth. The conference recognized that the self-governing dominions were: ". . . autonomous communities within the British Empire, equal in status, in no way subordinate one to another in any aspect of their domestic or external affairs, though united by a common allegiance to the Crown, and freely associated as members of the British Commonwealth of Nations[53]."

That declaration was, effectively, Canada's declaration of independence, although it was issued as a pronouncement of an imperial conference. From that point forward in time the imperial government recognized the federal government of Canada as an equal, rather than as a subordinate government, and ceased to exercise the incidents of sovereignty over Canada.

53. Cited in *R v Secretary of State; ex parte Indian Association of Alberta*, [1982] 2 All England Reports 118 at 128.

The conference also recognized that the Governor General would thereafter be considered as an official of the national government in each dominion and would report directly to the King, and no longer serve in the dual function of both a Canadian and an imperial official. With these developments Canada was able to exercise an independent legal personality on the world stage and to engage in its own foreign relations. Beginning in the latter part of the twenties, Canada began to send its own accredited diplomatic representatives abroad, initially to Washington, Paris, and Tokyo. (Appointments of a Canadian High Commissioner as a representative of Canada to Great Britain, which did not require Canada to possess an independent legal personality separate and apart from Britain, had begun previously in the 1880's).

The last act in the ascendancy of Canada to full membership in the worldwide community of nations occurred after the Imperial Conference of 1930, where it was decided that a statute of the British Parliament would be enacted to give *de jure* legislative force to the legal independence of the dominions. The following year, the imperial Parliament enacted the *Statute of Westminster 1931* which codified the evolution to legal independence embodied by the Balfour Declaration of 1926. With the *Statute of Westminster* Canada achieved its formal legal independence from Great Britain although the Bennett Ministry (in office in 1931) decided to leave the machinery for amending the constitution of Canada in the British Parliament for the time being, since it was not then possible to obtain the agreement of all of the provinces on the acceptability of a domestic mechanism for constitutional amendments[54].

54. By constitutional convention the British Parliament after 1931 automatically enacted any requests for constitutional amendments requested by Canada and the use of the British Parliament for this purpose was not viewed as a restriction on Canadian independence. The role of the British Parliament as part of the Canadian constitutional machinery was removed by the *Canada Act*, 1982, c. 11 (RSC 1985, Appendix, no. 44) which was the final legislation enacted by the British Parliament in relation to Canada.

More importantly, from the perspective of treaties, Canada became the successor state to any treaties or international agreements that Great Britain had entered into relating to Canada before the grant of *de jure* sovereignty. That included the Rush-Bagot Agreement and therefore from December 1931 all legal responsibility for the Rush-Bagot Agreement passed from Great Britain to Canada, and the Agreement became an agreement solely of concern to the two state parties in North America, Canada and the United States of America.

PART FOUR: TOWARDS A NORTH AMERICAN ALLIANCE

1932-1945 AMERICAN UNILATERALISM, THE OGDENSBURG ACCORD, AND A WORLD WAR

As 1931 greeted 1932 Canada emerged on the world scene as a fully independent country, bound now to Great Britain only by ties of sentiment. In 1932 the world also began its slow-motion descent into the horrors of World War Two. The Mukden Incident in the autumn of 1931 led to a takeover of Manchuria by the Japanese armed forces. China was powerless to stop the occupation and Chinese forces ceased formal resistance to the Japanese advance at the end of February 1932. Japan then established a puppet regime in what it called Manchukuo and used the new territory as a base to advance its policy of further acquisition of Chinese territory. The Japanese incursion into Manchuria dealt a severe blow to the prestige of the League of Nations, and the hopes of many people at the end of World War One that a new principled international order would emerge from the chaos of the world war were dashed.

In North America political relations between Canada and the United States remained cordial, and the established commercial links between the two countries continued to contribute to an ongoing exchange of people and ideas. Although there were some cultural differences between the two countries, there were also many similarities. In politics, both President Herbert Hoover and Prime Minister Richard Bennett were conservative politicians who were ill-equipped by experience or temperament to deal with the agonies of the Great Depression which swept over North America from 1929 onwards. The economic dislocation produced by the depression, and the aversion to European politics resulting from the public remembrance of the losses and sacrifices of the world war, encouraged isolationism and retrenchment in both countries.

Military officials in the United States and Canada continued their various planning strategies which included the prospect of war with each other. While there was a complete absence of political stresses that would justify any consideration of hostile intentions by either country it was characteristic of military officials to prepare for any conceivable eventuality. A Canadian plan, Defence Scheme No. 1, originally prepared in the immediate aftermath of World War One envisaged the possibility of several limited Canadian advances along the border; from British Columbia south toward Seattle and Spokane, Washington, from the Prairies south towards Great Falls, Montana, and Fargo, North Dakota, in Ontario north towards Detroit as well as east across the Niagara frontier towards Buffalo, and finally an incursion from the Maritimes south into northern Maine. The purpose of such a plan would be to establish strategic depth, as Canada's population was and is located mainly in the southern border regions. The intention of the Canadian planners was to hold American bridgeheads until imperial troops could arrive to support Canadian forces, perhaps an unlikely prospect following the historic prewar rapprochement between Great Britain and the United States.

On the American side of the border, military planners were refining the famous American coloured war plans. War Plans Red and Crimson[1] developed a mirror image of the Canadian

---

1. War Plan Red envisaged a war between the United States, Great Britain and Canada while Crimson envisaged an active war only between the United States and Canada. There were a great number of other plans such as Black (Germany), Gold (France), Green (Mexico), Orange (Japan), Red-Orange (Japan and Great Britain). There was even a plan for the invasion of Iceland (Indigo). Elements of some of these plans were subsequently utilized in

plan. The US military envisaged strikes by American forces from Washington state to occupy Vancouver, British Columbia, advances from Grand Forks, North Dakota, to occupy Winnipeg, Manitoba, and to cut the transcontinental railway lines, an advance from Detroit, Michigan, into western Ontario towards Toronto, a move from Buffalo, New York into the Niagara frontier to disrupt the Ontario power grid by seizing the hydroelectric facilities built at Niagara Falls, an offensive from upper New York state and Vermont to capture Montreal and Quebec City, and the seizure of the great east-coast port and naval base of Halifax.

A more relevant development in the relations between the two states was the establishment of the International Peace Garden on the border of North Dakota and Manitoba in 1932, as a testament to the desire of people in both countries for a lasting peace between Canada and the United States. As the decade of the thirties progressed, political leadership changed in both countries with Mackenzie King returning as Prime Minister of Canada once again in 1935, and the election in 1932, and subsequent inauguration in 1933, of the remarkable Franklin Roosevelt as President of the United States. Both men, but especially Roosevelt, brought forward new ideas on restoring their countries' economies and lifting their populations out of the doldrums of the Great Depression. Accordingly, it was domestic politics that occupied the attention of both governments and little attention was paid to military defence for a time. But the foreign sky continued to darken with the rise of fascist and militaristic governments in Italy, Japan, Spain and Germany.

While diplomats debated, and the world spiralled down into the vortex of war the Rush-Bagot Agreement obtained very little attention from either Canada or the United States. In 1938

the next great war. Planning was also undertaken for the suppression of domestic uprisings in the United States (White) and the US Philippine Islands (Brown).

Canada found itself in the embarrassing position of having constructed a new warship, the minesweeper *HMCS Fundy,* at Collingwood Shipyards on Georgian Bay without having previously given any notice of that fact to the United States. After completion it was necessary to send the *Fundy* out of the Great Lakes to Atlantic tidewater and for that purpose it became absolutely necessary for Canada to seek permission from the United States after the fact of construction in order for the *Fundy* to traverse the territorial waters of the United States. The United States granted permission after Canada provided assurances that the situation involving the *Fundy* would not become a precedent for the future, and that Canada would give notice to the United States of any future construction of warships on the Great Lakes that were intended for oceanic service [2].

In the spring of 1939, as the war clouds gathered over Europe, the US State Department reviewed the Rush-Bagot Agreement with a view to its modernization in light of the deteriorating international situation. In particular, the United States wished to obtain some relief from the restrictions that inhibited the use of the Great Lakes by the United States to support wide scale naval operations that might be required of the US Navy in a future war. The impetus for this review was a letter to US Secretary of State Cordell Hull from Admiral Leahy, the Acting Secretary of the Navy, requesting the advice of the State Department on whether the Rush-Bagot Agreement would preclude the US Navy from mounting modern armaments, such as twin 4-inch guns, on its Great Lakes naval training vessels. That letter led to further substantive discussions between the two departments on the Rush-Bagot Agreement. Interdepartmental discussions focused on the number and size of the naval vessels permitted on the Great Lakes, the movement and concentration of naval vessels on the lakes, the functions permitted to the vessels (with

2. Author Unknown, "Note to File," (LAC, RG 25, D1, Volume 740).

particular reference to target practice) and the question of whether larger 4-inch guns were permissible, and finally the circumstances under which new construction of warships could take place on the Great Lakes. Ultimately it was determined that the United States should seek some additional flexibility from Canada with respect to the Agreement although Secretary of State Hull made it clear that he did not wish to abrogate the Agreement, as the Agreement had obtained, through venerable age, a special position in both American and Canadian public opinion.

Internal American discussions resulted in instructions to John Simmons at the American Legation in Ottawa to submit a draft letter from Cordell Hull to Admiral Leahy at the Navy Department for the review and receipt of comments by the Canadian authorities. In the covering letter to the American Legation the State Department pointed out that the United States had encountered conflicts between the modern needs of the US Navy and the antiquated provisions of the Rush-Bagot Agreement. The solution being proposed however, was not a new cycle of negotiations with the Canadians but rather a unilateral American interpretation of the Rush-Bagot Agreement which would satisfy the needs of the US Navy. Although the State Department did not propose to formally consult with Canada, it nevertheless wished to obtain the informal views of Canadian officials concerning the reinterpretation being contemplated in Washington. Hence the reason for the instructions given to the American Legation in Ottawa to run the US proposals past Dr. O D Skelton, the Canadian Undersecretary of State for External Affairs, for his reaction. The American Legation was specifically instructed to emphasize that the United States "... desire to act in perfectly good faith and [it is] our belief that there should be no written communication between the two Governments whatever on the subject[3]."

Despite protestations in the letter from the State Department concerning the good faith of the United States Mr. Simmons was advised that time was of the essence, as the US Navy wished to commence training with enhanced armaments, and the proposed letter from Secretary Hull to Secretary Leahy had already received all the necessary internal clearances required from both departments. Clearly, Canadian input was intended to be *pro forma* in the circumstances. Should Skelton or other Canadian officials prove recalcitrant, the State Department proposed in that event to despatch from Washington another career foreign service officer, James Bonbright, to help Simmons settle the issues with Canadian officials[4].

The draft letter from Secretary of State Hull to Secretary Leahy provided an interesting insight into the then current American thinking on the subject of the Rush-Bagot Agreement. After first noting that the Rush-Bagot Agreement was intended to solve issues in 1817, emanating from the (then) recent War of 1812, the draft letter then goes on to express the view that the Rush-Bagot Agreement was never intended to be a permanent agreement. It was now long out of date. However, the draft letter noted that despite its obsolescence the Rush-Bagot Agreement had achieved, through its longevity, a privileged symbolic position in the diplomatic relations between the United States and Canada, and therefore it ought to be preserved rather than replaced by a more modern agreement. The draft letter noted that both countries had violated the agreement, at least technically, at various periods in their history but had done so as a result of the press of events, and neither country had sought to violate the spirit of the Agreement. The draft emphasized that it was the spirit of the Rush-Bagot Agreement that the United States aspired to maintain as it was ". . . representative of the feelings of the Canadian and American people toward each other[5]." The

3. "Letter from Department of State, Washington to John Farr Simmons, American Legation, Ottawa, dated May 15, 1939", (LAC RG 25, D1, Volume 740, file 135).
4. Ibid.
5. Ibid, 3.

draft letter then proposed a unilateral reinterpretation of the treaty which in some respects reflected past discussions but in other respects was quite divergent from past practices in its approach.

Although the State Department recognized that the United States was actually in contravention of the Agreement by maintaining five warships on the Great Lakes, instead of the four warships mandated by the Agreement, it was noted that Canadian permission had been obtained for the stationing of four of the US warships. The exception was the *Wilmette*, which had been constructed on the Great Lakes as a merchant vessel and subsequently had been acquired by the US Navy during World War One. Operational necessity precluded the United States from removing one of its naval training vessels to comply with the Agreement because one-third of the US Navy's reserve personnel were residents in an area that was centred on Chicago,[6] and it was impracticable to move even a small number of reservists to the east or west coasts for their annual training. The draft American reinterpretation also expressed a lack of concern about the size of the vessels that were currently based in the Great Lakes. In particular, the 100-tons burden limitation contained in the Rush-Bagot Agreement had no practical application in the twentieth century. The passage of time, and the great advances in marine technology that had occurred had consigned wooden sailing ships to history, and their steam or oil-burning replacements were now of much larger dimensions.

The State Department also considered that the US ships on the lakes were not used as warships for the defence of the United States but for naval training purposes and a numerical limitation on training vessels went beyond the requirements of the Agreement. In this robust American reinterpretation of the

6. The Great Lakes Naval Station was authorized during the President Theodore Roosevelt's Administration in 1904, and was officially opened by President Taft in 1911. Its 39 buildings could accommodate approximately 2000 naval recruits per year.

Rush-Bagot Agreement the purpose of the Agreement when it was created was to limit the number of active warships. The draft letter also noted that the warships that the United States continued to maintain on the Great Lakes were unclassified, and therefore considered by the navy to be unfit for any purpose other than training. Finally, the State Department suggested that target practice was an integral part of naval training and it was noted that US forces conducted target practice on the Great Lakes in the years before 1923 and once in 1938 without generating any Canadian complaints.

The State Department analysis also addressed the question of where the United States could deploy warships on the Great Lakes. It was noted that in 1817 the Great Lakes did not form a continuous line of communication but were actually separate bodies of water from a navigational perspective. Ships on Lake Ontario were confined to that lake and a part of the St. Lawrence River. Ships on Lake Erie were, depending on their extent of their draught, confined to Lake Erie, Lake St. Clair, and the Detroit and St. Clair Rivers. With difficulty shallow-draught vessels could cross the obstructions at the confluence of the St. Clair River and Lake Huron, thus allowing passage into Lake Huron from the St. Clair River. Ships on Lake Huron could pass into Lake Michigan but could not enter into Lake Superior which in 1817 remained virtually impassable from Lake Huron for navigation purposes. Navigation on Lake Champlain was isolated by the rapids on the Richelieu River before the construction of the Chambly Canal in 1843. The Agreement had limited warships to specific lakes (one each on Lakes Champlain and Ontario and two each on the remaining lakes). Now, however, the Great Lakes were navigable between Montreal and Duluth and restrictions of vessels to specific lakes were obsolete. Therefore it was proposed that naval vessels of either country be permitted to deploy where necessary for operational reasons within the Great Lakes.

The question of armaments was more difficult to resolve. The Rush-Bagot Agreement limited the two countries to warships possessing one 18-pounder gun. As this criterion related to the weight of the shell it meant in the modern context warships on the Great Lakes were limited to one 3-inch gun because the shell weight of a 3-inch gun was approximately 14 pounds. However, a 3-inch gun was no longer the typical armament on a modern warship in the 1930's, and the US navy wanted to deploy the standard 4-inch guns that US seamen would use on modern destroyers and other high-seas warships. But the weight of a four-inch shell at thirty pounds would clearly exceed the limitations of the Rush-Bagot Agreement. In order to resolve this problem two options were suggested to Admiral Leahy by the State Department. The first option would involve the placing of only one 3-inch gun on naval vessels on the Great Lakes. So armed, the vessels would be free to engage in target practice in American waters. However, since that was not a feasible alternative, a second option was to place two 4-inch guns on each of three naval vessels on the Great Lakes, and then remove all other armaments and permit those vessels to conduct target practice confined to Lake Michigan, which was wholly within US territorial waters. No naval vessel would be permitted to leave the waters of Lake Michigan without dismantling its 4-inch guns. Finally all 4-inch guns would be dismantled except in the summer season during the normal period for the training of US naval reservists.[7]

The second option would obviously result in a significant departure from the Rush-Bagot Agreement since the phrase "upper lakes" in the Agreement had always been interpreted to mean Lakes Erie, Huron, Michigan, and Superior, notwithstanding the fact that unlike the other three lakes no portion of Lake Michigan was within Canada. Thus the new

7. Ibid, 7.

interpretation, if adopted, would alter the Agreement's reference to the "upper lakes" to exclude Lake Michigan.

Finally, on the question of new naval construction on the Great Lakes the State Department took the view that the subject of new construction was inextricably related to the isolation of the Great Lakes from Atlantic tidewater that had existed in 1817. Since any new construction on the Great Lakes in 1817 could only be for naval purposes within the Great Lakes, it was reasonable to restrict the parties from engaging in naval construction on the Great Lakes. However, with the construction of canals and the ability of ships in the 1930s to access the Great Lakes from tidewater it was now reasonable, in the US view, to permit new naval construction at Great Lakes shipyards provided that:

1) Canada and the United States provide full information to the other country concerning any new construction at Great Lakes shipyards;

2) Any newly built vessels were immediately removed from the Great Lakes; and,

3) The ships would not be armed until they reached tidewater[8].

The arrival of the letter from the American Legation on May 18, 1939, enclosing the proposed draft letter from US Secretary of State Cordell Hull to US Acting Secretary of the Navy Admiral Leahy, caused a flurry of activity in federal government circles. On May 22nd O D Skelton, the Undersecretary of State for External Affairs, wrote to his counterpart the Deputy Minister of National Defence, Major-General L R LaFleche, to apprise him of the American initiative. Skelton immediately expressed reservations about the concept of permitting a unilateral reinterpretation of the Rush-Bagot Agreement by the United

8. Ibid, 9.

States, while recognizing that it was both beneficial and necessary for Canada and the United States to reinterpret the Rush-Bagot Agreement from time to time[9].

Skelton suggested to LaFleche that instead of a comprehensive document to deal with all of the current American concerns it might be best to deal with the issues raised by the US draft separately, and sequentially, to avoid any suggestion that the Agreement was being formally amended. Skelton noted both the number of current US Navy vessels on the Great Lakes (which exceeded the limitations contained in the Agreement) and the fact that the Americans were proposing to replace one worn-out vessel of 375 tons, the *USS Hawk*, with a replacement vessel, the *USS Sacramento*, that displaced 1,140 tons, although *Sacramento* was similar in size to most of the other US naval vessels on the Great Lakes. As to the question of the dispersal or concentration of warships on the Great Lakes Dr. Skelton suggested that this matter need not be formally raised with the Americans, thus suggesting to General LaFleche that Canada could live with the American views on vessel deployments within the Great Lakes. Similarly, on the question of the proper function of naval vessels on the Great Lakes Skelton agreed with the American position that training was properly carried out by naval vessels on the Great Lakes, although he did not appear to realize that American training had in the past included target practice. As to armaments, he merely pointed out the American proposals to General LaFleche for his comment. Finally, Dr. Skelton noted that the American proposals envisaged the construction of new warships on the Great Lakes which were intended for oceanic service. Skelton suggested that in addition to the stipulations set out in the State Department draft it might be desirable to add a condition that the building party should formally request

9. Oscar D Skelton, Undersecretary of State for External Affairs "Memorandum to Major-General L R LaFleche, Deputy Minister of National Defence, May 22, 1939," (LAC RG 25, D1, Volume 740, file 135).

permission to move its ship through the territorial waters of the other party on its way to Atlantic tidewater[10].

The United States continued to pressure Canadian officials for a quick response to the proposed US draft. The very next day a memorandum was placed on the file, ostensibly from Dr. Skelton, in which he minuted continuing American pressure for results. John Simmons of the US Legation telephoned the Department of External Affairs on the morning of May 23rd to say that the "situation at Washington was a bit difficult and they would like to have some kind of understanding[11]. Simmons reiterated that Washington's preference was to have a unilateral American reinterpretation of the Rush-Bagot Agreement but if that concept presented difficulties for Canada an alternative would be for the United States to write to Canada stating the American interpretation of what was possible under the Rush-Bagot Agreement without any request for a Canadian endorsement of the US views. Simmons pressed Dr. Skelton to learn whether Canada had serious concerns with the American proposals, or only had reservations concerning the form of the reinterpretation that the United States was proposing.

Although Dr Skelton was sympathetic to Simmons' need for a quick response from Canadian officials he told Simmons that the Department of National Defence had only just been apprised of the American proposals the day before and it was much too early to state whether there would be any substantive concerns from a Canadian perspective. Skelton was now seeking a way to accommodate the driving American objective for a quick Canadian response and he suggested breaking out the American proposals individually and dealing with them one by one in priority, a suggestion that had initially been put forward by Loring Christie, the Canadian Minister in Washington. Skelton

10. Ibid.
11. O D Skelton (ascribed), "Memorandum dated May 23, 1939," (LAC RG 25, D1, Volume 740, file 135).

thought that approach could allow for a quick resolution of the armaments issue which, in Skelton's view, was the most pressing change being advocated by the United States. However, Skelton's memoranda do not record Simmons' reaction to his suggestion.

Simmons tried to focus the discussion on the need to build new warships on the Great Lakes for ultimate service on the oceans, and he brought up the fact that Canada had built a new minesweeper the year before on the Great Lakes without first informing the United States. Canada had subsequently been compelled to seek US permission in order for the new minesweeper to transit the Great Lakes for oceanic service. Skelton acknowledged those facts but pointed out that Canada had been embarrassed by its failure to inform the United States about the building of the *Fundy*[12]. However, Simmons suggested that the only embarrassment with respect to the *Fundy* concerned an *aide memoire* prepared by Sir Herbert Marler[13] in which Marler had characterized Canada's actions in relation to the *Fundy* as improper, which also implied that what the United States now proposed was also improper in the context of the Rush-Bagot Agreement.

Skelton succeeded in putting off the American request for a quick response and arranged for officials from the departments of External Affairs and Defence to meet to develop a unified Canadian position on the American initiative. That meeting took place on May 27, 1939. Officials noted their concurrence with the American viewpoint concerning the desirability of maintaining the Rush-Bagot Agreement in its unamended form, a significant departure from past Canadian efforts to formally revise and update the Agreement. Canadian officials now described the Rush-Bagot Agreement as of "... inestimable value in furthering the ideals of good neighbourhood in North

12. Ibid.
13. Sir Herbert Marler was the Canadian Minister to the United States between 1936- 1939.

America . . . " and suggested that it also served, in a limited way, as an example for countries in other parts of the world[14].

However, the Department of External Affairs also recognized that the Agreement was tainted by obsolescence and that it required a new malleability in order to satisfy modern conditions. A new approach was required in which any necessary modification to the Rush-Bagot Agreement that was consistent the objectives of the Agreement, and upon which both Canada and the United States were in concurrence, could be implemented by an exchange of letters between the two states even though the proposal being implemented did not conform to the strict terms of the original Agreement[15]. This meant however, that Canada would not agree with the United States proposal that the Rush-Bagot Agreement could be modified by a unilateral American declaration. Canadian officials took the view that the maintenance of public confidence in the Agreement, together with the necessity of abiding by the principle of restrictions on what would otherwise be characteristic sovereign actions, precluded resort to unilateralism in the interpretation of the Rush-Bagot Agreement. Furthermore, where modifications in the practical implementation of the Agreement could be countenanced by the two states the Agreement would be strengthened by a mutual action that was informal but which would also remain as a matter of record in the relations between the two countries[16]. Such an approach would also be consistent with a desire of Canadian officials that Canada and the United States should refrain from any wholesale reinterpretation of the Rush-Bagot Agreement in preference for an issue by issue consideration of the need for changes to the Agreement by the two states.

14. Department of External Affairs, "Summary of observation and interpretation of Rush-Bagot Agreement, May 27, 1939," (LAC RG 25, D1, Volume 740, file 135).
15. Ibid.
16. Ibid.

Faced with some intransigence by Canadian officials to the prospect of unilateral American action, the US State Department gave way and shelved the concept of a unilateral reinterpretation based on an exchange of correspondence within the US Government between the Secretaries of State and the Navy, and agreed on May 27th[17] that an informal exchange of letters between the United States and Canada on the issues raised by the United States would be the best way to proceed. As a result, on June 5th, Dr. Skelton apprised the Acting Secretary of State for External Affairs, Ernest Lapointe, of the US request and advised him that Rear Admiral Percy Nelles, the Chief of the Naval Staff,[18] had expressed no reservations about the US proposals from a Canadian naval defence perspective[19]. The formal views of the Royal Canadian Navy were transmitted the following day to Dr. Skelton by General LaFleche of the Department of National Defence, in which the RCN concurred with the preservation of the Rush-Bagot Agreement in its unamended form, and with the new procedure for dealing with any necessary changes through written exchanges between Canada and the United States. Furthermore, the naval staff expressed no substantive reservations to the changes being requested by the American Government and specifically noted that there were no Canadian naval objections to the deployment of 4 inch guns on US naval training vessels stationed on the Great Lakes, or their use in target practice within US waters during the summer training season on the Great Lakes[20].

It is interesting to note that by accepting the American request

17. O D Skelton Undersecretary of State for External Affairs, "Memorandum to Maj-Gen L R LaFleche Deputy Minister of National Defence dated June 5, 1939," (LAC RG 25, D1, Volume 740, file 135).
18. The title "Chief of the Naval Staff" replaced the former "Director of the Naval Service" in 1928.
19. O D Skelton to Rt. Hon. Ernest Lapointe K.C., "Rush Bagot Agreement of 1817, June 5, 1939," (LAC RG 25, D1, Volume 740, file 135).
20. L R LaFleche, Department of National Defence (Naval Service), "Memorandum to O D Skelton dated June 6, 1939," (LAC RG 25, D1, Volume 740, file 135).

for the mounting and use of 4-inch guns on their Great Lakes naval training vessels the subject of a possible restriction of US 4-inch gun target practice to the waters of Lake Michigan, and the resulting implication that Lake Michigan was not to be considered an "upper lake" within the meaning of the Rush-Bagot Agreement, was successfully avoided by Canada.

A memorandum dated June 12, 1939, summarized the internal views of Canadian officials concerning this American initiative. Canadian officials were completely averse to the concept of a unilateral reinterpretation of the Rush-Bagot Agreement by either the United States or Canada. Furthermore, they did not consider that an exchange of letters between Canada and the United States could constitute a formal interpretation of the Rush-Bagot Agreement. However, practical measures concerning the implementation of the Rush-Bagot Agreement, including departures from its strict technical terms, could be agreed-to by both governments where they were of the mutual opinion that the departure from its strict terms would not impair the underlying objectives of the Agreement. In such cases a technical departure could be mutually agreed-to by the two national governments through an exchange of letters. Nevertheless, such an exchange would not have the effect of a legal reinterpretation of the Agreement where the strict technical requirements continued to exist. Finally, officials were of the view that the practice of managing the Agreement through exchanges of letters between the two governments, when circumstances required a departure from the strict literal terms of the Agreement, should be observed *de rigueur* in the future, and without exception[21].

Negotiations to resolve the US concerns now rapidly moved to

21. Department of External Affairs, Memorandum Re: "Informal Exchange of Letters Dated June 9 and 10, 1939, Between United States Legation and Department of External Affairs, Respecting the Rush-Bagot Agreement of 1817, June 12, 1939," (LAC RG 25, D1, Volume 740, file 135).

a conclusion. The United States did not wish to break out the issues that had been contained in the original US draft letter and deal with each such issue sequentially, according to priorities, as Canadian officials had suggested. American officials wished to deal with the identified problem areas in one fell swoop. Accordingly, a version of the letter that was originally to be sent by US Secretary of State Cordell Hull to Acting US Secretary of the Navy, Admiral Leahy, was transformed into a letter from the US Minister to Canada, David Roper, to Canadian Under-Secretary of State Dr. O D Skelton. The revised letter retained the discussion about the importance of the Rush-Bagot Agreement in the diplomatic relations between the United States and Canada noting that it ". . . has assumed a symbolic importance in the eyes of our own and Canadian citizens" despite the fact that it was likely never intended to be a permanent arrangement and remained ". . . a symbol of the friendly relations between the two countries for over a century[22]." (Internally, and perhaps more truthfully, US State Department officials had said of the Rush-Bagot Agreement that; "Age is its main, if not its sole virtue[23].")

Minister Roper noted that the success of the Agreement was in large measure due to the tolerance each country had shown when exigencies compelled the other country to depart from the strict terms of the Agreement, and that both parties had always done their utmost to preserve the spirit of the Agreement even when it had proved impossible for them to adhere to the strict terms of the Agreement. The US letter noted the presence of five US naval training ships on the Great Lakes and the need for the US Navy to conduct naval training in close proximity to Chicago, which necessitated the retention of the five naval

22. David C Roper, Envoy Extraordinary and Minister Plenipotentiary of the United States of America to Canada, "Letter to Dr. O D Skelton, Under-Secretary of State for External Affairs, Ottawa, June 9, 1939," (LAC RG 25, D1, Volume 740, file 135).
23. State Department (ascribed) Memorandum entitled "Paraphrase"; LAC RG 25, D1, Volume 740, file 135.

vessels on the Great Lakes and Lake Champlain notwithstanding the historic (and much violated) limitation in the Rush-Bagot Agreement to four naval vessels for each country. The United States now proposed to replace the worn-out *Hawk* with the *Sacramento*, and Canadian permission for the transit of *Sacramento* would subsequently be sought by the United States. The US Legation noted that the size of the American vessels also exceeded the stipulations in the Rush-Bagot Agreement but noted that the size differential resulted from the enormous changes in naval technology that had occurred in the years following 1817, through the development of steam propulsion, and iron or steel-hulled vessels in place of wooden sailing ships. The effects of technological change on naval vessels had, of course, long been noted and accepted.

The United States also proposed to disperse its ships or to concentrate them as circumstances required on the grounds that the Great Lakes now formed a continuous line of marine communications and no longer constituted separate and distinct inland seas as they had when the Agreement was formulated in 1817. The US took the view that this reinterpretation would not be contrary to the spirit of the Agreement.

As to the functions of naval vessels on the Great Lakes, the US noted that the Rush-Bagot Agreement only restricted naval vessels of the parties from interfering with the activities of the other country's naval forces, and otherwise the assigned naval functions of warships on the Great Lakes were unrestricted. This meant that naval training would be within the scope of permissible activities and target practice on the lakes (within each nation's territorial waters) would also be permissible.

On the question of modern armaments the existing restriction in the agreement (now extrapolated to modern gunnery) to 3-inch guns was noted as well as the need for US naval crews to train with the new modern standard of 4-inch guns. The US proposed that two 4-inch guns could be placed on three naval training vessels on the Great Lakes and that all other armaments on those warships would be removed. The US would be permitted to train crews with the warships equipped with 4-inch guns provided that target practice was confined to US waters and that the 4-inch guns would only be deployed on the naval training vessels during the summer months when reservists were ordinarily trained[24]. All mention of the possibility of restricting US target practice training activities to Lake Michigan was dropped from the final letter.

The last element addressed by the US letter concerned the construction of new warships on the Great Lakes. In a view attributed by the American Minister to US Secretary of State Cordell Hull, the United States proposed that the restriction contained in the Rush-Bagot Agreement on new construction should be considered in light of the geographical isolation of the lakes that prevailed in 1817 – an isolation that was no longer present in 1939. Minister Roper stated that ". . . Mr. Hull believes that it would be entirely in harmony with the intent of the negotiators and the spirit of the Agreement for either country to permit naval vessels, unquestionably intended for tidewater service only, to be constructed in shipyards situated on the Great Lakes[25]." The United States suggested that three conditions should apply to the relaxation of the restriction on construction of naval vessels on the Great Lakes. Firstly, there must be full disclosure made to the other government concerning the intentions of the other country to build a war vessel on the Great Lakes, together with information about the proposed warship. Secondly, the newly built warship should be removed from the Great Lakes as soon as it was completed, and, finally, no armaments should be installed on the new warship until it

24. Ibid.
25. David C Roper, Envoy Extraordinary and Minister Plenipotentiary of the United States of America to Canada, "Letter to Dr. O D Skelton, Under-Secretary of State for External Affairs, Ottawa, June 9, 1939," (LAC RG 25, D1, Volume 740, file 135).

reached the east coast of North America[26]. Minister Roper concluded the letter by inviting Dr. Skelton to make any observations he wished concerning the American proposal to the US Legation.

Minister Roper did not have very long to wait for a reply from Canada because Dr. Skelton responded to the US letter on June 10, 1939, the very next day after the US letter was received. Skelton noted the desirability of preserving an agreement that had been of inestimable value, though technically obsolete, and emphasized Canadian concerns that any departures or exceptions to the Agreement should continue to be developed through an exchange of correspondence between the parties. Canada did not have any difficulty with the US maintaining five naval training vessels on the Great Lakes, nor was there any issue with respect to the substitution of the *Sacramento* for the *Hawk*.

Skelton stated that the deployment of naval vessels lawfully upon the Great Lakes in any configuration, whether concentrated or dispersed, was consistent with the underlying purpose of the Rush-Bagot Agreement, in the Canadian view. To some extent, this constituted a reinterpretation of an underlying principle of the Agreement, since it is easy to read an intention in the original agreement to prevent any sudden offensive descent by the naval forces of one country against the territory of the other country, and such an operation would be more likely to succeed, and to inflict sudden harm on the other country, if its naval forces could be concentrated for an attack. That Canada was now prepared to accept the concentration of naval forces on the Great Lakes illustrated that Canadian fears over American intentions, which had been quite real as recently as days of the Laurier Ministry, had now largely dissipated.

Canada also stated that it was prepared to acknowledge that

26. Ibid.

naval training, including target practice gunnery, was a permissible activity under the Agreement. On the question of naval armaments, a key concern of the US authorities, Dr. Skelton stated that Canadian naval authorities concurred with their American counterparts on the desirability of training with modern armaments, including 4-inch guns. In this context the Canadian government agreed that arming three ships with two 4-inch guns for summer training service in American territorial waters would be "consistent with the underlying purpose and spirit of the agreement[27]." Canada specified only two conditions; that Canada should be informed of which ships are fitted with the 4-inch armament, and that the US Government apprised Canada of any future changes to the armaments of the five US training ships stationed on the Great Lakes.

Lastly, Canadian officials agreed with the US proposals for new construction on the Great Lakes but added that upon completion the government that had built the warship should make a formal request of the government of the other state party to the Agreement seeking permission for the new warship to transit the territorial waters of the other party in order to reach Atlantic tidewater. Finally, Canadian officials claimed the same rights for Canada that the United States would receive under this *modus vivendi* for the implementation of the Rush-Bagot Agreement.

Canada had secured its interests in ensuring that any exceptions to the Rush-Bagot Agreement, then or subsequently, would only occur if both parties to the Agreement had reached a consensus on the nature of the exception. The Rush-Bagot Agreement could now be viewed as a framework agreement setting out broad principles for Great Lakes naval cooperation by the United States and Canada within the context of naval arms limitations but open to mutually-agreed upon exceptions and departures where particular circumstances required. The United States

27. Ibid.

obtained Canadian agreement to the main issues that were frustrating US naval operations on the Great Lakes, although it had to give way to Canadian desires for mutual consultation and agreement concerning any changes relating to the Rush-Bagot Agreement. As with other departures or exceptions from the original Rush-Bagot Agreement there was no public disclosure of the contents of the exchanges between the two countries although in Canadian memoranda the possibility of a future public release on the subject was at least acknowledged[28].

For both parties the symbolism of the Rush-Bagot Agreement had been preserved notwithstanding that the most significant changes to the framework of the Agreement since its inception in 1817 had been obtained. Those changes took place in the context of a cordial and friendly diplomatic environment between the two countries and provided proof to American officials, if any proof was needed, that it could work with Canada on questions of security, which was a growing concern as the international atmosphere darkened.

On June 13, 1939, Secretary of State Cordell Hull wrote to Admiral Leahy at the US Navy Department to apprise him of the resolution with Canada concerning the issues around the modern application of the Rush-Bagot Agreement. After referring to the recent bids that the US Navy had received from a shipbuilder in Bay City, Michigan, for the construction of a sub-chaser, Hull advised Leahy that, in Hull's opinion, which was also shared by Canadian officials, it would "be entirely consistent with the underlying objective of the [Rush-Bagot] Agreement for naval vessels to be constructed on the Great Lakes for use in oceanic service[29]."

Abroad, the international situation seemed to grow worse by the

---

28. Ibid.
29. Cordell Hull, Secretary of State of the United States, "Letter to Admiral Leahy, Secretary of the Navy, June 13, 1939," (LAC RG 25, D1, Volume 740).

day. Facing down the harsh peace treaty of Versailles, Germany's Adolph Hitler reacquired the Saar region by plebiscite in 1935, and subsequently marched German troops into the demilitarized Rhineland in 1936. The major European powers chose to back down rather than to confront him over that treaty violation. Italy's Benito Mussolini struck at the independent Ethiopian Empire in the autumn of 1935 and completed its conquest in 1936. The major European powers did not effectively forestall Italy's unjustified assault on Ethiopia, and Canada repudiated the efforts of its own diplomat at the League of Nations in Geneva, who had sought to impose economic sanctions against Italy for its invasion of a peaceful state. In 1937, a militarized Japan invaded the remainder of China (after its earlier conquest of Manchuria) which effectively marked the outbreak of World War Two in Asia. Hitler conducted a soft, uncontested, invasion of Austria in 1938 and afterwards incorporated it into Germany. European powers followed a policy of appeasement towards Hitler, a policy that the Mackenzie King Ministry in Canada supported, in the doomed hope that Hitler would cease his aggressive expansionist policy in Europe. In the Spanish Civil War (1936-39) both Germany and Italy supported the fascist movement of General Francisco Franco, who ultimately prevailed over the left-wing Spanish Republic. Canadian antifascist volunteers joined the Mackenzie-Papineau Brigade in the army of the Spanish Republic against an actively-enforced prohibition against such enlistments that was imposed by the federal government. On an official visit to Germany in 1937 Prime Minister Mackenzie King met with Hitler and afterwards thought him to be a man who would not pose a threat to world peace[30]!

In 1938 Hitler demanded the cession of the German-speaking Sudetenland from Czechoslovakia and Great Britain and France, to their shame, facilitated the dismemberment of Czechoslovakia

---

30. Allen, *Ordeal by Fire Canada, 1910-1945*, 357.

in the Munich Agreement after which Great Britain's Prime Minister, Neville Chamberlain, expressed the opinion that the Munich Agreement meant "peace in our time." Hitler, however, had other ideas. In March 1939 Hitler ordered the invasion of what remained of Czechoslovakia which he then incorporated into his growing German Empire. In the same month Hitler occupied the Lithuanian territory of Memel and incorporated it into Germany. In April 1939 Italy's Mussolini attacked and conquered the Kingdom of Albania which he linked to Italy in a personal union through the Italian monarch. By this point, Great Britain and France perceived that war with Germany (and perhaps Italy) was inevitable, and they sought to obtain an ally in the Soviet Union, as well as offering guarantees to the remaining states in central and eastern Europe. However, their efforts had come too late. The Nazis pre-empted France and Britain by negotiating a non-aggression treaty with the Soviet Union that provided for a partition of Poland in August 1939. On September 1, 1939, Germany attacked Poland and on September 3rd Great Britain declared war on Germany, as did France. The Soviet Union, while remaining neutral in the larger war, occupied the eastern portion of Poland in accordance with its non-aggression pact with Germany. World War Two, the cataclysmic event of the twentieth century, had begun.

Canada remained neutral for one week after the outbreak of war. On September 10, 1939, a week after Great Britain and France had declared war, Canada declared war on Germany. There was no doubt that Canada would enter into the war because of its lingering loyalty to Great Britain even though the two states were now fully independent of each other. However, Prime Minister Mackenzie King wished to reinforce the fact internationally that Canada was an independent state and thus he delayed the Canadian declaration of war against Germany until September 10, 1939. War with Italy would come the following year when Italy joined Germany in its attack on

France, and war with Japan, Germany's Asian ally, would come with Japan's Pacific offensive in December 1941.

The United States maintained a watchful neutrality. President Franklin Roosevelt took an active interest in the war, correctly perceiving that the United States would eventually be drawn into it as it had been in World War One, despite the efforts of American isolationists and the strong desire of the American people to avoid war. Even before the war, Roosevelt, perhaps prompted by US military leaders, was aware of the fact that Canada's defences were inadequate to protect the size of its territory and publicly stated that the United States could, and would, defend its own neighbourhood. Prime Minister Mackenzie King was sensitive to US concerns about the possibility of a foreign attack on the United States and Canada's own obligation, as a good neighbour of the United States, to take the necessary defence measures to ensure that its own territory was protected against foreign assault, to the extent that it could reasonably be made secure against subjugation[31]. King and Roosevelt enjoyed a warm personal relationship and their cordial relations facilitated the development of an alliance between the two countries under the pressure of the world war. Mackenzie King had spent time in the United States in his younger years and he held a generally positive view of Americans. King had also known Roosevelt's cousin Theodore, and it helped that Franklin Roosevelt liked Canada, to the point of maintaining a summer estate on Campobello Island in New Brunswick.

The impetus for alliance came in the spring of 1940 when the German army conquered the Scandinavian countries of Denmark and Norway and then swept across western Europe, easily conquering the low countries (Netherlands, Luxembourg and Belgium) and smashing the allied armies in France. France was crushed, and conquered, and the British extracted its army

31. McManus, "Stability and Flexibility: The Rush-Bagot Agreement and the Progressive Modernization of Canadian-American Security Relations," 86.

from France under great peril at Dunkirk. Afterwards, Great Britain stood alone in Europe against Germany and Italy, which had entered World War Two as Germany's ally. European war developments alarmed US military planners as well as the President in Washington. Great Britain had moved to occupy the Danish overseas territories of the Faeroes and Iceland but Greenland was exposed and the potential for a German occupation of Greenland was unacceptable to the United States. The US Government made an agreement with the Danish Ambassador in Washington that gave the United States a colour of right to assume the defence of Greenland. Later the United States also replaced Great Britain as the occupying power in Iceland. That still left the vast territories of Canada and Newfoundland exposed to the threat of German attacks. The Roosevelt Administration felt compelled to deal with that exposure to ensure the protection of the continental United States.

In August 1940, President Roosevelt met Prime Minister Mackenzie King on the border between the two countries at Ogdensburg, New York. There, the two men created the foundation for a continental military alliance in the Ogdensburg Agreement, which led to military cooperation between the then neutral United States and a belligerent Canada, including the establishment of a Permanent Joint Board on Defence[32]. The effect of this agreement, which represented a personal effort by both President Roosevelt and Prime Minister Mackenzie King, was to recognize that the United States exercised military hegemony in North America and that Canada would cooperate with the United States in the future to ensure the security of the continent. The Ogdensburg Agreement paved the way for a smooth defence relationship between the Canadian and American militaries. From this point forward, Canada and the United States jointly planned for continental defence against

32. Stacey, *The Undefended Border*, 14.

third nations and their respective militaries ceased to engage in planning for conflicts between each other. The two countries committed themselves to a permanent alliance.

The Ogdensburg Agreement also led to a measure of equality in planning between the Canadian and American militaries and ensured that Canadian interests would be considered despite the great discrepancy in power between the two states[33]. Ogdensburg marked the creation of a new framework for the engagement of militaries from both countries that was comprehensive and continent-wide. Mutual suspicions were replaced with mutual cooperation for the defence of North America.

The Ogdensburg Agreement largely rendered the Rush-Bagot Agreement superfluous as a political measure to protect Canada from its much more powerful neighbour. For all practical purposes the Rush-Bagot Agreement was now diplomatic symbolism, an exemplar of the peaceful intent of both countries towards one another but no longer necessary as a practical measure to maintain the continental peace. Yet the Agreement would continue to survive because in a world consumed by war there would be a perceived value in maintaining an international agreement that showed how states could limit warlike preparations and intentions for the benefit of peace.

The Ogdensburg Agreement now gave Canada the security that it would not stand alone if it was attacked in North America and it gave the United States the assurances of Canadian cooperation that it needed to ensure its own continental defence. In conjunction with the establishment of its temporary protectorate over Greenland, and the acquisition of bases in British possessions both in North America and the Atlantic, including Newfoundland and Bermuda, the Ogdensburg Agreement gave

33. McManus, "Stability and Flexibility: The Rush-Bagot Agreement and the Progressive Modernization of Canadian-American Security Relations" 89.

the United States the opportunity to prepare a defence perimeter for the war that Roosevelt knew was coming to the United States.

Canada had not been directly threatened in World War One by Germany. German submarines appeared off Canada's east coast in 1918 but merely transited Canadian offshore waters to and from Germany without undertaking offensive operations. In World War Two however, the impacts were different. While Canada was never threatened by Nazi Germany's small surface fleet, the threat from German U-boats was very real and it was sustained throughout the war. Great Britain's very survival depended on maintaining its maritime transportation links to the Americas, which provided everything from foodstuffs, to war materiel, to the oil that fuelled British ships at sea. The German Navy was determined to use its submarines to destroy those linkages and to starve Britain into submission. From the start of the war Canada began to play an enormous role in marshalling and protecting the ships and convoy routes from Halifax and St. Johns, Newfoundland to Great Britain. The Battle of the Atlantic lasted throughout the war and the outcome was ever in doubt despite the increasing technological advantages accruing to the allies, and a greater deployment of resources as the war progressed. Into 1943 it still remained the greatest military challenge occupying the mind of British Prime Minister Winston Churchill[34].

The Battle of the St. Lawrence, a subset of the Battle of the Atlantic, was fought from 1942-44 within sight of Canadian shores. German submarines *U-165*, *U-553*, *U132* and especially *U-517*, penetrated into the Gulf of St. Lawrence and then into the lower St. Lawrence River to attack shipping. Although wartime censorship minimized public knowledge of the fighting, Canadians who lived along the shores of the St. Lawrence River saw and heard the explosions, and found the bodies of dead

34. Allen, *Ordeal by Fire*, 390.

seamen washed up on the shore. For the first time since Great Britain's Royal Navy had penetrated the St. Lawrence River during the Seven Years War the country faced a maritime threat within its main riverine artery. For a time, the St. Lawrence River and the Gulf of St. Lawrence were closed to shipping, forcing war materiel onto the less efficient railway mode of transportation but ultimately Canada succeeded in keeping open the St. Lawrence route, albeit at a severe cost in lives and ships[35].

To counter the threat of U-boat depredations on allied shipping, it was essential to maintain the rate of construction of both merchantmen and warships in allied shipyards. Canadian shipyards played an important national role in this context and the Great Lakes shipyards were fully engaged in the war effort. One aspect of the now modernized Rush-Bagot Agreement that concerned Canadian officials was the need to avoid installing armaments on newly built warships on the Great Lakes until those ships reached the Atlantic. That meant having to send the warships into an Atlantic yard for completion which interfered with the efficient construction of naval vessels in Atlantic shipyards. To avoid that problem Canada approached the United States and asked for limited relief from the Rush-Bagot Agreement to make it possible for Canada to install armaments on warships being built in Great Lakes yards provided that Canada did not put the armaments into a state of readiness for immediate use while the new warships remained on the Great Lakes. That request, formulated in a letter from Dr. Skelton to US Minister Jay Pierrepont Moffat on October 30, 1940, proved acceptable to the United States since the Roosevelt Administration was acutely conscious of the depredations of the German U-boat campaign, and it was anxious to help the allies to maintain their transatlantic shipping links[36]. The new

35. J L Granatstein and Dean F Oliver, *The Oxford Companion to Canadian Military History*, 391-393.
36. Stacey, *The Undefended Border*, 16; Purver, "The Rush-Bagot Agreement: Demilitarizing the

formulation for the construction of naval vessels on the Great Lakes was:

1) The vessels are not intended for service on the Great Lakes,

2) Prior to commencement of construction, each Government furnished the other with full information about vessels to be constructed at Great Lakes ports,

3) The armaments of the vessels are placed in such condition as to be incapable of immediate use; and,

4) The vessels are promptly removed from the Great Lakes upon completion[37].

The year 1941 was crucial in determining the outcome of World War Two because the two major neutral powers, the Union of Soviet Socialist Republics, and the United States of America, both became embroiled in the war in that year. (However, previously, after the outbreak of the war, the United States had established a Neutrality Patrol in the western Atlantic which tended to benefit Great Britain and Canada more so than Germany, and within a year the United States Navy also began escorting convoys to Iceland, and actively engaged German submarines.) The Soviet Union was attacked by Germany in June 1941 and staggered under the assault until the eastern front was stabilized near years' end. In December 1941, Japan, which had been an ally of the west in World War One but which had subsequently allied itself to Germany and Italy in the 1930's moved against western colonial empires in the Far East, attacking the US-owned Philippine Islands after first destroying the US Navy's battleship squadron at the Pearl Harbour naval base on the island of Oahu in Hawaii. The Japanese also attacked

Great Lakes, 1817 to the Present," *Encyclopedia of Arms and Control and Disarmament, Vol. 1*, 590.

37. *Canada Treaty Series vol. 1940* (electronic version); www.treaty-accord.gc.ca (accessed October 21, 2015).

the British in Hong Kong (garrisoned in part by Canadian forces) and Malaya, as well as the Dutch in the Netherlands East Indies, where the Japanese hoped to obtain essential oil supplies. Japan quickly overran the dilapidated western defences in the Orient and the Pacific and a long struggle ensued both in the Pacific and in China, where the world war in the Far East had begun in 1937.

Those developments now brought to full fruition the defence plans initiated by the Ogdensburg Agreement for North America. US troops flooded into Canada to construct air bases for the ferrying of aircraft to Europe and Russia, and to build the Alaska highway to provide road communications between the lower 48 states and America's exposed far northern territory. When Japan attacked Alaska Canadian soldiers and airmen were sent there to help the US defend it, and to assist in the expulsion of Japanese forces. The United States quickly ramped up its industrial capacity, the greatest in the world, to support the war effort. Among the important industrial contributions to the war effort made by the United States was the construction of approximately 600,000 tons of warships in its Great Lakes shipyards.

US concerns about the German U-boat campaign in the St. Lawrence River prompted the American Minister, Pierrepont Moffat, to write to Norman Robertson, the Under Secretary of State for External Affairs, on February 26, 1942, with a suggestion that the two North American states allow for the complete readiness of armaments installed on warships being built on the Great Lakes, and that the testing of both guns and torpedo tubes while on the lakes should be allowed[38]. Moffat stated that the United States wished that any warships constructed on the Great Lakes be able to "combat enemy action upon their arrival in the open sea . . ." and that their armaments should be battle-ready ". . . and that all essential tests and trial

38. Ibid.

of machinery and armament, including submerged operations of submarines and test firing of torpedoes and guns be effected in Great Lakes waters[39]." The United States suggested that this arrangement should only be put in place for the duration of the war. Canada responded on March 9, 1942, agreeing to the entirety of the American proposals[40]. These wartime measures to relax some of the stringencies of the Rush-Bagot regime served to help both countries meet their immediate military needs during the war emergency.

Italy was defeated in 1943, and both Germany and Japan were defeated in 1945, ending the greatest cataclysm that the world had hitherto suffered. As in World War One, Canada made an enormous contribution to the success of the Allied war effort. Canadians served in all theatres of the war, eventually fielding a full army in northwest Europe, a full air bomber group in Europe, and the Royal Canadian Navy assumed full responsibility for one theatre of war, the Northwest Atlantic theatre, where Canadian Rear Admiral L W Murray served as the allied commander-in-chief. At war's end Canada possessed the third largest allied navy and the fourth largest allied air force. The army had reached a strength of almost 500,000 men. During the war the army suffered approximately 81000 casualties, including approximately 23000 fatalities. The Royal Canadian Navy suffered approximately two-thousand casualties, most of whom were fatalities. The Royal Canadian Air Force suffered approximately 18000 casualties, 17000 of which were fatalities[41].

With the coming of peace there was a new appreciation for the benefits and obligations of political and military alliance in North America. Unlike the end of World War One, after which

39. Ibid.
40. Ibid.
41. Ralph Allen (et al), "Return, The veterans come home to a country transformed and grown up" in *The Canadians at War 1939-45, Vol 2,* ed. Douglas How (Montreal, The Readers Digest Association (Canada) Ltd., 1969) 660-61.

both North American countries retreated from world affairs, in the aftermath of World War Two both the United States and Canada expressed their intentions to remain engaged in the world, and to continue and bolster their alliance.

1945-2015 THE POSTWAR WORLD AND THE MODERN ERA

As the guns fell silent in 1945, the world from a North American perspective looked much different then it did in the 1930's. The terrible toll of World War Two on Europe so soon after the losses of World War One had left Europe much diminished on the world stage. The major European powers were virtually bankrupt in 1945, and had lost significant stature because of their near defeat during the war. A new spirit of nationalism began to sweep over their colonial empires and the hostility of the major communist powers, the Soviet Union and (after 1949) China, to colonialism, was palpable. The European colonial empires began to dissolve as early as 1947[1], with the independence of the Asian subcontinent states of India, Pakistan, Burma, and Ceylon, and by 1980 the European empires were virtually gone.

The United States was now the predominant power in the world, although it faced a severe challenge from Soviet Union and its communist allies during the Cold War (1947-1991) which was fought largely through competing ideologies and small brush fire proxy wars in various parts of the world. Countries aligned themselves into formal competing blocs, although many of the newly independent countries sought to remain non-aligned. For Canada, the country in closest proximity to the newly-dominant

---

1. The United States also granted independence to the Philippines in 1946.

United States, relations with its southern neighbour became more important then ever before.

The political and military alliance formed between Canada and the United States at Ogdensburg continued into the postwar world with Canada and military questions relating to North American defence continued to be dealt with through the mechanism of the Permanent Joint Defence Board. In March of 1946 the US representative on the Board advised Canadian officials that the US Navy desired to maintain an additional number of naval vessels on the Great Lakes for training purposes[2]. Discussions between the United States and Canada within the Board led to a favourable result and formal letters on the subject were exchanged in late 1946. The initiating letter was sent by the Canadian Ambassador to the United States, Hume Wrong, rather than by the representative of the United States to Canada. It is unclear why Canada initiated the formal exchange of letters in this case when the original request came from the United States through the Permanent Joint Defence Board but perhaps there was a recognition of lingering public sensitivities in Canada with respect to the number of US Naval vessels stationed within the Great Lakes. Wrong's letter stated that both governments agreed that the stationing of naval vessels on the Great Lakes for the training of naval reservists would be valuable from the perspective of naval training, and that an acceptance of an unrestricted number of such vessels on the Great lakes was consistent with the intent of the Rush-Bagot Agreement[3]. A new arrangement whereby each country could station on the Great Lakes whatever number of training vessels it thought necessary was concluded subject to the conditions that each government must provide full details to the other government concerning the number, disposition, function, and armament of all such vessels.

2. Purver, "The Rush-Bagot Agreement: Demilitarizing the Great Lakes, 1817 to the Present," *Encyclopedia of Arms and Control and Disarmament, Vol. 1*, 590.
3. Canada Treaty Series vol. 1946 (electronic version) (www.treaty-accord.gc.ca, accessed October 21, 2015).

The United States formal response contained in a letter from Dean Acheson, the Acting Secretary of State, accepted the proposal. Acheson noted ". . . the historic importance of this Agreement as a symbol of the friendship between our two countries" and emphasized "that it is the spirit of this Agreement which guides our Governments in matters relating to naval forces on the Great Lakes[4]."

Cold war threats prompted a strong response from the western powers, beginning with the Soviet Berlin Blockade in 1948. The strength of the Soviet challenge to the western powers became increasingly apparent and Canada moved to strongly support the United States in resisting Soviet pressure. Canada had already become aware of the Soviet threat to its own national security when a cipher clerk at the Soviet embassy in Ottawa defected shortly after the conclusion of World War Two and disclosed a wide-ranging Soviet espionage effort against Canada. In April 1949 Canada joined the United States and European powers in the formation of NATO as part of a larger containment strategy orchestrated by the United States against Soviet expansion in Europe. Later, as technology rendered it possible for Soviet strategic bombers to cross over the Arctic Ocean to attack North America with nuclear weapons, Canada joined the United States in a continent-wide air defence initiative, the North American Air Defence Command (NORAD) which was designed to detect Soviet bombers crossing the polar route to North America well before they reached the centres of population.

Despite providing significant support to US-led western defence efforts in the Cold War Canada maintained an independent foreign policy and actively sought to limit both nuclear and conventional weapons through multilateral diplomatic processes[5]. Canada was a founding member of the United Nations in November 1945, and it was primarily through the

4. Ibid.
5. Canada, for example, was very prominent in the effort to ban landmines which resulted in

United Nations, and NATO forums, that Canada expressed its position in favour of nuclear arms control and disarmament[6]. Canada was a wartime participant in the Manhattan Project that led to the development of the atomic bomb and was one of only three countries in 1945 (along with the United States and Great Britain) that possessed the knowledge to construct such weapons. However, Canada became the first country possessing a knowledge of nuclear weapons technology to make a voluntary decision not to develop such weapons[7]. Canada was also a supporter of initiatives to ban or restrict the testing of nuclear weapons[8] and was the sole NATO member to challenge the United States when the Reagan Administration sought to unilaterally reinterpret the Anti-Ballistic Missile Treaty between the United States and the Soviet Union[9]. A Canadian Disarmament Ambassador was appointed in 1980 to promote arms limitation efforts[10].

Throughout the Cold War the Rush-Bagot Agreement was held up as an example of how a successful arms limitation regime could be put in place between nation-states. When Harold Stassen, President Eisenhower's disarmament advisor, testified in the US Senate with respect to President Kennedy's proposed Nuclear Test Ban Treaty with the Soviet Union in 1963, he pointed to the Rush-Bagot Agreement as a model for disarmament agreements. Stassen pointed out that the inclusion of a six-month termination clause in the Agreement served to allay the very real concerns of US military leaders at the time that the Agreement was entered into who worried about the

the Ottawa Treaty, more formally known as the Convention on the Prohibition of the Use, Stockpiling, Production and Transfer of Anti-Personnel Mines and on their Destruction.

6. John Lamb, John B A Macleod, "Canada" in *Encyclopaedia of Arms Control and Disarmament, Vol. 1*, Richard Dean Burns, ed. (New York: Charles Scribner's Sons, 1993), 45.

7. Ibid, 47.

8. Ibid, 48.

9. Ibid, 50.

10. Ibid, 55.

possibility of denuding the country's northern frontier of its necessary naval defences[11].

Eugene Rostow, President Reagan's arms control director, also thought highly of the Rush-Bagot Agreement as a model for arms limitation initiatives. Speaking to the US Senate in 1981 he said that although the Rush-Bagot Agreement was dull that was the basis for its success in the aftermath of the War of 1812. Rostow noted that there had been periods of political tension between the United States, Canada and Great Britain throughout the nineteenth century but that the Rush-Bagot Agreement had played an important role in enforcing restraint and diminishing the impetus for war[12].

In the postwar world peaceful and cooperative relations remained the norm between Canada and the United States. Though independent, Canada had moved from an alignment within the British political orbit to an American orbit; geography is its destiny. An important signal of the new level of cooperation between Canada and the United States was the completion of the St. Lawrence Seaway in the 1950's, which finally provided the long sought-after continuous maritime line of communication between the Atlantic Ocean and the continental interior through the Great Lakes. Canada had long sought American cooperation for this gigantic project involving the massive dredging of the St. Lawrence River and the construction of locks but a proposed treaty to jump-start the project was shelved during the Bennett Ministry when opposition from special interests in the United States, particularly the US railways, prevented Congress from approving the proposal. At the time lobbyists even raised the

11. William Lambers, "Nuclear Weapons, the Great Lakes and Lake Champlain", August 21, 2011 (www.williamlambers.com/category/rush-bagot-agreement, accessed November 6, 2012) 5.
12. Ibid, 7.

old American fear of Great Britain's Royal Navy penetrating the Great Lakes as a reason not to approve the project[13].

However, by the 1950's, political circumstances were much different and the Eisenhower Administration was keen to invest in massive infrastructure projects such as the St. Lawrence Seaway. In Canada, the St. Laurent Ministry proposed to build the seaway alone if US support was not forthcoming but economic needs for a navigable waterway between the ocean and US Great Lakes ports finally swayed US legislators and the necessary congressional authority was secured. Most of the cost was paid by Canadian taxpayers but the project proved to be of great economic advantage for both countries. The St. Lawrence Seaway was formally opened in 1959, in ceremonies presided over by Queen Elizabeth II, in her capacity as Queen of Canada, and President Eisenhower of the United States.

When the seaway was completed, a continuous line of marine communication was provided from the Atlantic Ocean to Duluth, Minnesota, a total distance of 3,701.4 kilometres. The system bypassed rapids on the St. Lawrence River near Montreal by raising westbound ships (or lowering eastbound ships) through the St. Lambert, Cote St. Catherine, and the Lower and Upper Beauharnois locks. Upon reaching the point where the US border meets the St. Lawrence River westbound ships proceed through the American Snell and Dwight D Eisenhower locks, which are joined by the Wiley-Dondero canal. A final lock at Iroquois, Ontario, allows vessels to proceed through the St. Lawrence River into Lake Ontario. At the Niagara Peninsula ships enter the Welland Canal where they proceed through eight locks which lift the ships up to the water level of Lake Erie and thus bypass Niagara Falls. Upon entering Lake Erie ships can pass through that lake and the connecting waterways of the Detroit River, Lake St. Clair, and the St. Clair River into Lake

13. Berton, *The Great Lakes* 155.

Huron. At Sault Ste. Marie ships must pass through the Soo locks on the St. Marys River to access Lake Superior. Most marine traffic proceeds through one of the two main American locks because the Canadian lock is restricted to smaller vessels, following the collapse of one of the Canadian lock walls in the 1990's.

The construction of the St. Lawrence Seaway was an important milestone in the economic development of the Great Lakes waterways but it also raised a new concern, which was muted for a time, around the security of the Great Lakes. With the completion of the seaway large oceanic ships for the first time could enter and sail within the Great Lakes thus opening up the waterway to ships from any corner of the world. Although Canada and the United States continued to control the waterway it was no longer exclusively used by Canadian or US-flagged merchant vessels.

The construction of the St. Lawrence Seaway was a reflection of the growing economic cooperation between Canada and the United States, and the warmth of their relationship. When President Kennedy spoke to the Canadian Parliament in 1961, he described this new-found relationship by stating: ". . . we share more than a common border. We share a common heritage, traced back to those early settlers who travelled from the beachheads of the Maritime Provinces and New England to the far reaches of the Pacific Coast . . . Geography has made us neighbours. History has made us friends. Economics has made us partners. And necessity has made us allies . . . [14]"

Warm relations between Canada and the United States continued throughout the latter part of the twentieth century, although in an age that gave greater weight to personal diplomacy by heads of government it was only natural that some Canadian and American leaders did not always share the same

14. John F Kennedy, "Address to the Canadian Parliament", May 17, 1961.

points of view. Nevertheless, the overall relationship between the two countries remained close.

The Rush-Bagot Agreement was of little concern during the Cold War owing to the close political and military alliance between Canada and the United States. Nevertheless, the Agreement retained its value as a symbol of the enduring peace between the two countries. When the 150th anniversary of the exchange of notes between Great Britain and the United States approached in 1967, Senator Everett Dirksen proposed in the US Senate that April 28-29 1967 be proclaimed as Rush-Bagot Agreement Days to commemorate the signing. The Senate report noted that the Rush-Bagot Agreement ". . . is one of the most significant steps in the development of peaceful relations between the United States and Canada[15]." Subsequently, President Lyndon Johnson issued a proclamation to commemorate the signing of the Agreement.

As the century progressed, the economic contradictions of planned economies that was characteristic of communist systems became glaring and the Soviet Union, in particular, began to fall significantly behind the United States and its western allies in the development of both better living standards for the Soviet people, as well as the development of the sophisticated weapons systems required to maintain the USSR's standing as a world superpower. When the Soviet Union tried to liberalize its economic structures to afford itself the capacity to catch-up to the west in technological terms, the economic contradictions in Soviet communism resulted in a level of political instability that the country's political structures could no longer withstand. The result was the collapse of the Soviet system and the dissolution of the Soviet Union in December 1991, thus ending the Cold War.

In the modern era that resulted the United States occupied the

15. 90th Congress, 1st Session, Senate Report No. 185, April 13, 1967.

most powerful position in world affairs although latterly it has faced economic and strategic competition from China, an ostensibly communist-governed state that in reality has transformed itself into a powerful market-based economy state. Although Russia, as a successor state to the former Soviet Union, has remained an important international actor, it is diminished in size and power from Soviet days.

The demise of communism as an ideological challenge to the west coincided with the rise of an ideological challenge from a violent brand of Islam, centred in the Middle East but with the capability to strike at western states with either trained Middle Eastern terrorists, or by inspiring Muslim youth in western countries to adopt the Islamic tactic of a violent *jihad*. Nowhere was this more apparent then on September 11, 2001 (subsequently known as the 911 attacks) when separate but coordinated groups of terrorists who had legally entered the United States from Saudi Arabia, or other middle eastern countries, commandeered several American civil airliners and deliberately crashed them into the World Trade Center in New York, into rural Pennsylvania, and into the Pentagon building in Washington, killing approximately three thousand people.

In the aftermath of those attacks the United States mounted both a foreign and domestic response. Canada supported the United States in its military intervention in Afghanistan, which had harboured the leaders of the attacks, and Canada cooperated with the United States as the latter thickened its border defences despite the fact that Canadian economic strategies favoured an open border with the United States. American citizens were understandably shocked by the 911 attacks and supported all efforts by the US Government to secure the American homeland from similar attacks in the future. Of necessity, Canada adapted itself to American requirements in relation to border security.

As the United States began to reassess its security profile in

North America, it began to closely examine the northern maritime border with Canada. American officials became concerned that security along the Great Lakes was lax, owing in part to the existence of friendly and peaceful relations between Canada and the United States, which encouraged the ease of entry into both countries. Despite the fact that there was no evidence that any of the 911 attackers had entered the United States from a Canadian origin, a heightened American concern about its borders was a consequence of the 911 attacks and it required an adaptive Canadian policy response. There was a perceived need to provide a stronger border to limit the possibility of cross-border infiltration by terrorists.

A key element of the new security approach, and one that caused considerable consternation in Canada, was a proposal to enhance the armaments on US Coast Guard vessels patrolling the Great Lakes. Like the Canadian Coast Guard, the US Coast Guard is a civilian agency but unlike its Canadian counterpart it automatically comes under military control and provides military services in the event of a war emergency. A number of US Coast Guard vessels are therefore ordinarily armed with weapons. In the years after the 911 attacks the United States sought to enhance the armaments on its coast guard cutters patrolling the Great Lakes and to ensure that all necessary resources, including live armament training, were available to US coast guard personnel.

Under the framework of the Rush-Bagot Agreement, vessels of the US Revenue Marine (the predecessor of the US Coast Guard) were not considered to be vessels of war, and therefore they were not regarded as falling within the restrictions imposed by the Rush-Bagot Agreement[16]. This principle applied as well to

16. In 1929 the US Legation in seeking permission for USCG cutter *Seminole* to transit Canadian canals, described the functions of the vessel as "assistance to vessels in distress, enforcement of the customs and navigation laws and patrol at regattas", (LAC, Despatch No. 374, May 27, 1929, RG-25-6-1, vol 1396, file 59).

armed Canadian fisheries protection vessels stationed on the Great Lakes, which were forerunners of the modern Canadian Coast Guard. However, as government-owned vessels, both coast guard and fisheries protection vessels of the United States or Canada were required to obtain permission from the other country before transiting foreign territorial waters, or a foreign canal, under the *Chicora* principle that was established at the time of the Red River Expedition.

The role and relationship of coast guard vessels to the Rush-Bagot Agreement had been reexamined by Canada in the 1930's when USCG vessel *G-106* transited Canadian canals without obtaining prior permission to do so from the federal government. In an exchange of memoranda between Dr O D Skelton, Under Secretary of State for External Affairs, and G J Desbarats, the Deputy Minister of National Defence, it was noted that US coast guard vessels were not part of the naval forces of the United States. Rather, they were (then) under the control of the US Secretary of the Treasury[17] at least until a war was declared, and thus did not fall under the terms of the Rush-Bagot Agreement as it had been interpreted and applied in the past. However, that result did not really satisfy the Defence Department with respect to the transiting of Canadian canals, as the Defence Department noted that in many previous occurrences US coast guard vessels, whether armed or unarmed, had sought permission from Canada for passage through Canadian canals. At the time, Deputy Minister Desbarats opined that all of the existing precedents should be maintained because of the possibility that US coast guard vessels would be taken under US naval control in wartime and that remained the view of the federal government[18].

17. Skelton to Desbarats, "Memorandum, October 23, 1931," (LAC, RG-25-6-1, vol 1396, file 59).
18. Desbarats to Skelton, "Memorandum, October 28, 1931," (LAC, RG-25-6-1, vol 1396, file 59).

Now, in the early years of the 21st century and in the wake of the 911 attacks the US Coast Guard sought to provide its eleven Great Lakes cutters with an enhanced armament in order to address terrorism, human smuggling, and customs violations[19]. Although past interpretation of the Rush-Bagot Agreement excluded coast guard vessels from the purview of the Agreement[20] the United States consulted Canada in 2006 on the installation by the US of enhanced armaments on its coast guard vessels operating within the Great Lakes[21]. The existing US standard armament on its Great Lakes cutters consisted of a 7.62 mm machine gun, which was considered to be a light-calibre weapon, although it was capable of firing 600 bullets per minute. Now, the United States sought to fit its coast guard cutters with machine guns with a range of sizes up to .50 calibres. Such a weapon could neutralize any likely marine terrorist threat and could possibly bring down a helicopter, or penetrate a lightly armoured vehicle[22].

Canada agreed to the US request. An official of the Department of Foreign Affairs stated that Canada considered the mounting of heavy-calibre machine guns on coast guard vessels to be a law enforcement weapon, rather than an offensive naval weapon, and therefore it fell within the accepted exclusion under the Agreement for law enforcement vessels. Canada agreed with the United States that this interpretation would be consistent with

19. The United States took the view that it was in a state of war following the 911 attacks and was engaged in warfare against international terrorists. Other countries did not accept this conception of international law however. Although, the US coast guard can be subject to military direction during wartime it is unclear whether that fact influenced the United States to seek Canadian concurrence to the proposed enhancements of its coast guard armaments. More likely, the United States consulted Canada on this matter as part of a broader range of border enhancements that it wished to undertake, and for which it sought Canadian cooperation.
20. Although they were not exempt from obtaining transit privileges and the right to use Canadian canals under the *Chicora* principle.
21. Canadian Broadcasting Corporation, "US puts machine-guns on Great Lakes coast guard vessels," (www.cbc.ca/news/canada/story/2006/03/15/coastguard-060315.html (updated Wed. March 15, 2006) [accessed 2011-07-15]).
22. Ibid.

the spirit of the Rush-Bagot Agreement[23]. The interpretation was consistent with the past practices in the administration of the Agreement, under which vessels associated with law enforcement had been excluded from the restrictions contained in the Rush-Bagot Agreement. As with other past mutually agreed-to interpretations within the framework of the Rush-Bagot Agreement, Canada reserved the right to equip its own coast guard vessels with the same size heavy calibre weapons that were permitted to the US Coast Guard. However, Canadian enforcement vessels on the Great Lakes, which include Canadian Coast Guard cutters, and Royal Canadian Mounted Police or Ontario Provincial Police small craft, are normally armed only with personal weapons, such as sidearms, and Canada indicated that it did not contemplate any changes to the existing weapons configuration on constabulary vessels as a result of the revision to American armaments carried by US coast guard vessels.

Further enhancements to the capabilities of the US Coast Guard in the wake of the 911 attacks included the creation of new maritime safety and security teams as rapid response forces located at key US ports, which are capable of deployments across the Great Lakes, or elsewhere. Those units are in addition to port security resources which provide both water-based and land-based security for US ships on the Great Lakes, and critical US Great Lakes infrastructure[24].

Canada also agreed to work with the United States on a wide range of other border security enhancements, and improved its own domestic national security mechanisms to counter the growing threat of terrorism. In addition to enacting new anti-terrorism legislation Canada reorganized its national

23. Ibid.
24. Herb Gray, P.C., Chair and Commissioner, Canadian Section, International Joint Commission, "Proceedings of the Standing Senate Committee on National Security and Defence" March 29, 2004; (www.parl.gc.ca/Content/SEN/Committee/373/defe/02evb-e.htm?Language=E&Par, accessed 2011-07-15).

institutions to mirror developments on the American side of the international border. A new Department of Public Safety was created to liaise effectively with the new US Department of Homeland Security. Canada also entered into new information sharing arrangements with US authorities and special programs were created to ease border congestion for truckers and people who frequently cross the US-Canadian border. Canada and the United States each posted customs inspectors in the other country to facilitate the inspection of marine containers in international trade. A unique ship-rider program was created that allowed American enforcement officials to serve on Canadian Coast Guard vessels and Canadian enforcement officials to serve on United States Coast Guard vessels to more effectively police marine traffic on the Great Lakes. The United States began to use aerial drones to monitor the US-Canadian border, including activities on the Great Lakes, and Canada enhanced its patrols by the Royal Canadian Mounted Police and Canada Border Services Agency on strategic waterways, such as the Detroit River. Above all, both Canada and the United States enhanced their intelligence-crunching capabilities to identify and mitigate potential threats to domestic national security. All of the measures represented the modern close cooperation between the Canadian and US governments with respect to the security management of the North American Great Lakes water basin.

In responding to the American concerns in the early twenty-first century the successive Chretien Ministry, Martin Ministry and the Harper Ministry were each careful to appease US concerns about national security. Any failures on the part of the federal government to support Canada's US ally as the US sought to increase its margin of safety in relation to asymmetrical warfare would have damaged Canada's participation in the continental defence of North America. References to the Rush-Bagot Agreement as part of the framework in which these modern decisions were undertaken have shown that the Agreement has a continuing, though largely symbolic relevance, in the context of Canada-United States relations[25].

Thus, when the US Coast Guard publicized its intention to conduct live-fire machine gun exercises on the Great Lakes considerable consternation resulted on both sides of the border but much more so in Canada. Although target practice had previously been recognized as a normal function of naval training vessels on the Great Lakes that question had not previously been raised in the context of civilian vessels operating in an enforcement capacity on the Great Lakes. It was acknowledged that nothing in the Rush-Bagot Agreement precluded the US Coast Guard from engaging in live-fire training exercises but some marine companies expressed anxiety about the proposal, and environmentalists objected to the use of lead bullets because lost lead bullets could be harmful to the marine environment[26]. The resulting hue and cry were sufficient to stop the exercises, as of December 2006[27].

As the two-hundredth anniversary of the Rush-Bagot Agreement approached both the United States and Canada remained committed to jointly managing the security environment on the Great Lakes, without contributing to the militarization of their joint maritime border. The validity of the Rush-Bagot framework for managing naval deployments on the Great Lakes is not seriously questioned even though its relevance in the context of the modern US-Canada relationship is now only symbolic. Nevertheless, the Rush-Bagot Agreement has a

25. McManus, "Stability and Flexibility: The Rush-Bagot Agreement and the Progressive Modernization of Canadian-American Security Relations," 132.

26. "Machine Gun Drills on Great Lakes Put on Hold," (http://torontoist.com/2006/10/ machine_gun_dri.php, accessed 2011-07-15; Toronto Star September 2, 2006; published in Canadian Canoe Routes@ Wilderness Canoe Association; http://myccr.com/phpbbforum/ viewtopic.php?f=21&t=17962&start=0; accessed 2011-07-15).

27. McManus, "Stability and Flexibility: The Rush-Bagot Agreement and the Progressive Modernization of Canadian-American Security Relations," 132.

continuing value in the context of US-Canadian relations, as an ongoing commitment of their peaceful intentions towards each other.

2016 - REFLECTIONS ON THE RUSH BAGOT AGREEMENT

The Great Lakes are quiet now. Squadrons of warships no longer patrol the Great Lakes and Lake Champlain as a potential threat to the inhabitants living along the banks of the lakes. In place of the enmity of recurring wars, insurgencies, and the suspicions that lingered for a century or so afterwards, there is now only shared peace, friendship between two countries, and a strong alliance that is dedicated to the protection of the North American continent. The Rush-Bagot Agreement has withstood the force of time. It remains the oldest arms limitation agreement in force in the world. After 200 years it is a symbol of both restraint in the creation and deployment of arms, and of friendship between two nations which grew up in its shadow.

Canadians, in 1817, could look back on more than sixty years of conflict with their southern neighbours through three wars. The Seven Years War led to an invasion from the south, the collapse of the French colonial state, and the transfer of sovereignty over Canada from France to Great Britain in 1763. The American Revolutionary War resulted in an unsuccessful invasion of Canada by American rebel colonists in 1775, and the resulting loss, following American independence, of all British colonial territory south of the Great Lakes. The final conflict, from 1812 to 1815, once again led to a military invasion of Canada from the south and the real threat of a second conquest. Although the military threat from the south was successfully blocked it remained a very real threat, and Canadians watched with some trepidation as the power of the United States grew throughout the nineteenth century. The growing economic and military power of the United States made it less and less likely that Great Britain would, or even could, effectively defend the country from a fourth attack from the south, as the century wore on.

The solution of Canadian leaders was to build sustainable political relations with the United States while the country could still shelter under the umbrella of Great Britain's declining but potent power in the nineteenth and early twentieth centuries. The Rush-Bagot Agreement remained an important part of the architecture of Canadian – American relations throughout the nineteenth and early twentieth centuries as both countries strove to consolidate their respective positions in the world.

In 1817 it was by no means clear that Great Britain and Canada would not have another hostile collision with the United States. There was antipathy on all sides. The United States had been redeemed of its strategic failures in the north and along the eastern seaboard by the great victory at New Orleans and it had no reason to feel that it had been worsted in the war. Meanwhile, the prize of Canada, an early object of the sentiment that would become Manifest Destiny, continued to beckon to those Americans who sought new fertile lands for the republic, or those who wanted to eliminate the threat that Great Britain was seen to pose to the security of the nation.

Canada had been invaded and Americans had devastated western Ontario, creating fear among the political elites that were prominent in the affairs of both Upper and Lower Canada. Treason trials following the conflict showed the elites at their most vulnerable, and their determination to adopt a hard line in protecting Canada from the southern threat. In Great Britain, the political class continued to view the Americans with disdain and Great Britain was particularly outraged by the temerity of the United States in creating a state of war at a time when Great Britain was engaged in an existential fight for survival against Napoleon's continental empire.

Credit must accrue to the four men who had the ability to see that a moment had arrived when their countries must choose to seek dominance on the Great Lakes of the North American interior or to forswear all but the minimum of naval armaments on North America's great inland seas. Those men, President James Madison, and Secretary of State James Monroe in Washington, and Foreign Minister Lord Castlereagh, and Prime Minister Lord Liverpool in London, were guided by national interests but were still able to see the futility of mounting a naval arms race for the control of the lakes. The US Secretary of State, James Monroe, who played a vital role in the negotiations, noted that if naval competition continued "the moral and political tendency of such a system must be to war and not to peace[1]." Of the four principals involved in the negotiations, it was Lord Castlereagh whose views were the most critical for the creation of the Rush-Bagot Agreement. It is true that he faced pressures in Great Britain for the reduction of expenditures on armaments but the strategies and actions of the government he served were not determinatively constrained by those considerations.

Despite an obvious concern with the ability of the United States to quickly increase the deployment of its naval resources on the Great Lakes and to launch a strike against Canada before the British could adequately respond to it, Castlereagh accepted the *beau risque* of a naval arms limitation agreement for the Great Lakes. Although initially suspicious of the original American proposal his views matured and he came around to the view that a ruinous naval arms race would not guarantee Canada's security and that it would be ridiculous to continue the policy of building larger and greater vessels on the landlocked lakes. Perhaps he

1. Quoted in Fitzpatrick, *An Address Delivered by the Rt. Hon. Sir Charles Fitzpatrick*, 6.

also had the historic imagination to foresee that the future paths of Great Britain and the United States would converge, rather than diverge, and that the shared culture of both countries would form the basis for a future friendship. Castlereagh's acceptance of the principle of naval arms limitation on the Great Lakes was essential to the formulation of the Rush-Bagot Agreement.

Of course, the creation of the Rush-Bagot Agreement was not the end but rather the beginning of the efforts to limit naval arms on the Great Lakes. That effort continued through an era of rebellions and border insurgencies, including an attack on Canada from the Patriot Hunters in the United States, an attack by the Confederate States of America from Canada on the United States, and finally attacks on Canada by the Fenians in the post-Civil War environment. These insurgencies placed great strains on the Rush-Bagot Agreement which each country violated during the successive crises, and sustained an environment of mutual suspicion that continued to affect their relations.

During the Patriot War, Captain Sandom of the Royal Navy, who was responsible for maritime security on the Great Lakes, was forced to exceed the limitations of the Agreement in order to respond to multiple threats from the major incursion at Prescott, Ontario, and to other attacks along the western frontier of the Detroit River, and in the Niagara region. Sandom was, however, careful to limit the need to exceed the Rush-Bagot Agreement only to the minimum force required to suppress the insurgent attacks, and to enforce the authority of the colonial government. Canada was also fortunate that US President Martin Van Buren desired peace along the border and took active and concrete steps to prevent the insurgents invading Canada from the United States. His despatch of General Winfield Scott to the frontier helped to calm the American population along the border, and the firm efforts taken by Scott and by other responsible US Army officers, including Colonel Worth, aided in stabilizing a critical situation.

At the time of the US Civil War imperial policy favouring the Confederacy conflicted with the views of most Canadians, who favoured the Union owing to the proximity of the northern states, the strong personal relations that transcended the border, and an aversion to slavery. Canada had no substantial history of slave-holding before imperial emancipation in 1833, and the sentiments of the Canadian public were aligned afterwards with the abolitionists on the issue of slavery south of the border. Many Canadians enlisted in the Union Army and actively participated in the US Civil War. Yet there were also some Canadians whose sympathies lay with the southern Confederacy, and a few, such as George Denison, who were prepared to actively aid the Confederate insurgents that were sent by the Richmond government to mount assaults against the US northern border from Canada.

The raising of the Confederate naval standard on Lake Erie caused great alarm in the northern states, and together with planned Confederate attacks on New York, led the United States to come close to repudiating the Rush-Bagot Agreement. It may have been only the sudden collapse of the confederate armies in the field that caused a change of mind in Washington, although renewed efforts by the colonial government in Canada led by the Governor General, Viscount Monk, and his ministers, to forestall confederate insurgents from mounting operations from Canada, no doubt helped.

So too did the efforts of Sir John A Macdonald to establish Canada as an autonomous state within the British Empire, which gave a framework for the policy of continental withdrawal by Great Britain, a fact which became established after the Treaty of Washington in 1871 when British military forces withdrew from Canada except for the garrisons at the coastal naval bases. Although the Fenian crisis which emerged in the aftermath of the US Civil War required the new Canadian federal government to rely on the Royal Navy once again for naval protection on the Great Lakes (and to also once again exceed the Rush-Bagot limits as an emergency measure) Prime Minister Macdonald was wise to let the naval defences on the Great Lakes run down and eventually disappear when the emergency passed.

The most critical period for the Agreement, other than the crisis at the end of the US Civil War, occurred in the 1890's and early 1900's as the United States began its rise to a predominant position in world affairs. A series of aggressive presidencies, particularly that of Theodore Roosevelt, led to a substantial increase in US naval units committed to the Great Lakes. Prime Minister Sir Wilfrid Laurier followed a policy of seeking to revise the Agreement to meet modern needs while maintaining the limitations that served the needs of Canadian security. When that policy approach failed because of a dispute over the Alaskan boundary he fell back on a strategy of accommodating American desires lest his opposition to naval increases on the Great Lakes led to the abrogation of the Rush-Bagot Agreement entirely. Laurier also embarked on a strategy of ensuring Canadian security by entering into diplomatic agreements with the United States that would establish a firm and friendly foundation for future Canadian – American relations. The International Boundary Waters Treaty of 1909 was one element of his approach, as was the Reciprocity Agreement that he attempted to negotiate with the United States in 1911. Laurier's conciliatory strategy improved Canada-US relations and Laurier was able to obtain some concessions in the practical implementation of the Rush-Bagot Agreement from US President William Howard Taft.

In his efforts, Laurier obtained considerable assistance from the imperial government's Ambassador in Washington, James Bryce, who worked assiduously to sustain the Rush-Bagot Agreement and who also sought its modernization. At times Bryce felt compelled to set aside some of the specific and less helpful instructions that he received from the Laurier Ministry in order to avoid jeopardising the Agreement. The Taft-Bryce understanding that he achieved with the American President stabilized the Rush-Bagot Agreement in the years before the outbreak of World War One, although Bryce's hopes for the creation of a new and modernized Rush-Bagot Agreement did not come to fruition.

In the aftermath of World War One Canada and the United States, allies in the war, reverted to a more distant political relationship and prompted a final Canadian attempt to formally update the Agreement to match modern conditions. However, the deal negotiated by the inexperienced Mackenzie King Ministry was unsatisfactory from a Canadian perspective and it was shelved. When the Americans sensed the gathering of war clouds in 1939 they sought to unilaterally rewrite the Agreement to suit their needs but through the efforts of Dr. Oscar Skelton, the Canadian Under Secretary of State for External Affairs, the United States was prevented from accomplishing a unilateral alternation of the Agreement. Both countries thereafter agreed to gloss-over any necessary exceptions from the Agreement through mutually agreed-upon and recorded diplomatic letters, treating the Rush-Bagot Agreement as a true framework agreement, rather than as a strict instrument of arms limitation. Skelton's approach ensured that Canada would continue to have the ability to influence how the Great Lakes were used by the naval forces of its much more powerful neighbour.

Within a short time both Canada and the United States were allied once again in World War Two and the Rush-Bagot Agreement was subjected to a number of changes mandated by wartime exigencies. Unlike the case in World War One however, the new alliance was a permanent one, orchestrated by President Roosevelt in 1940, who moved decisively to position the United States as the driver of a continent-wide defence structure in preparation for the world-girding role its political and military representatives would assume in the postwar world.

So what are the contemporary lessons, if any, to be gleaned from the British-Canadian and American experience with the Rush-Bagot Agreement? There are several points to consider. Firstly, it was important that the international actors who originally entered into the agreement, Great Britain and the United States, were part of the international concert of nations who had a shared perspective on the regulation of international affairs. Thus, there was a basic level of trust that each could rely on the other to make the requisite effort to abide by an agreement, thus giving the Rush-Bagot Agreement a high potential for success. Where states regularize their relations with one another it is possible for the parties to an arms limitation agreement to identify and accept the necessary political and military risks that are inherent in such an agreement. Where an arms limitation agreement is contemplated with an international pariah however, the likelihood that such an agreement will be sustainable for any lengthy period of time is probably remote, and such an agreement will be fraught with political and military risks.

Secondly, it was favourable to a successful outcome that Great Britain, the United States, and colonial Canada possessed common cultural linkages, and those linkages were well developed in the early nineteenth century[2]. Both Canada and the United States could point to Great Britain as the source of their common political culture, due allowances being made for the differences between them in the outward forms of government. That helped to ensure both that an agreement could be obtained and that the parties would have confidence in its sustainability. Nevertheless, common political or cultural antecedents are not necessarily prerequisites to the establishment of desirable arms limitation agreements. A more basic focus can also suffice.

2. In his diaries, Prime Minister Mackenzie King commented that "Had the Americans and ourselves not been virtually the same people the Rush-Bagot agreement might never have been made." (Mackenzie King, Diary, Friday, November 14, 1946, LAC "The Diaries of William Lyon Mackenzie King", Item No. 30221).

President Kennedy said as much in his famous American University speech in 1963 when he publicly stated the need for détente between the United States and the Soviet Union. In establishing common ground between the American and Soviet peoples Kennedy stated: "For in the final analysis, our most basic common link is that we all inhabit this small planet. We all breathe the same air. We all cherish our children's futures. And we are all mortal.[3]"

Thirdly, a framework agreement is preferable to one that imposes static requirements. Fixed or static requirements were almost the undoing of the Rush-Bagot Agreement because technological change rendered the strict terms of the agreement obsolete in only a few years after it was negotiated. The parties were subsequently able to begin treating the Agreement as a framework for managing naval relations on the Great Lakes, which allowed the Rush-Bagot Agreement to play a continuing role in the relations between Canada and the United States. Thus a framework agreement that places emphasis on the management of the relationship between the parties, as well as the establishment of the goals to be met, can assist the parties in keeping an arms limitation agreement relevant to current conditions. That is not to infer that an arms limitation agreement should lack specificity in its terms but rather it means that, where possible, an arms limitation agreement should be capable of being upgraded to take into account the pace of technological and other changes over time.

Fourthly, it is important to acknowledge that there will be suspicions from time to time of the motivations or perceived intentions of the other party to an arms limitation agreement. Therefore, exchanges of information will be crucial to the creation of the agreement and to is subsequent sustainability. During the negotiation of the Rush-Bagot Agreement it was

3. President John F Kennedy, "A Strategy of Peace," American University Commencement Address, June 10, 1963.

important that both Great Britain and the United States agreed to exchange information concerning the current strengths of their respective naval squadrons on the Great Lakes and agreed to temporarily halt new construction while the negotiations proceeded. A failing of the Rush-Bagot Agreement was the omission of continuing exchanges of information or monitoring, which sometimes led one or the other party to become suspicious of the intentions of the other party. Thus, in the mid-nineteenth century Great Britain periodically made a series of complaints to the US about the presence on the Great Lakes of the *Michigan* (which did exceed the strict limitations of the Agreement). When Canada became concerned about the intentions of the United States during a rapid run-up of US naval training vessels on the Great Lakes at the end of the nineteenth century the Laurier Ministry actually sent a spy to locate and observe the American training squadron during its summer manoeuvres. For its part, the United States kept its great three decker ship of the line *New Orleans*, which had been intended to defy the *St. Lawrence* in the War of 1812, on the navy list until long after the end of the US Civil War. Doubts among nations concerning their negotiating partners are natural, and can be addressed in an arms limitation agreement through confidence-building measures such as providing for regular meetings to discuss the joint progress of the state parties towards the implementation an arms limitation agreement. It is also desirable to ensure that effective monitoring is an accepted and recognized part of any arms limitation agreement – the "trust but verify" approach espoused by US President Ronald Reagan in his dealings with Soviet leader Mikhail Gorbachev near the end of the Cold War.

Fifth, the parties should accept that a violation of an arms limitation agreement does not necessarily mean that it has been repudiated. Both Great Britain and Canada, as well as the United States, violated the strict terms of the Rush-Bagot Agreement at various times in the nineteenth century. It would have been open to one or another of the parties to have concluded that the action of the other party in violating the terms of the Agreement was a possible repudiation of it. However, careful observation shows that suspicions mostly arose where one party was operating under the strain of responding to insurgencies, or where miscalculations of the other party's benign intentions (e.g., US naval training activities on the Great Lakes) or the effects of technological change in the marine environment, were present. Thus, in the absence of any clear indication of hostility, when an apparent violation of an arms limitation agreement arises a careful and thorough consideration of a party's intentions should always be undertaken before the observing state develops a response to that violation. In that event diplomatic discussions between the parties can be an important dispute prevention measure.

Lastly, the symbolism of an arms limitation agreement should not be underestimated. It can have a salutary effect on public opinion in the countries that are parties to the agreement and can help to foster increased trade and other relations between states which, in turn, can help to create or restore a virtuous cycle of state-to-state relations, and thus contribute to the general peace.

In the years following its negotiation of the Rush-Bagot Agreement ultimately obtained an iconic status in the relationship between the two states sharing North America's Great Lakes. Cordell Hull recognized the symbolic importance of the Agreement in the late 1930's, and its relative stature has not significantly diminished since. It remains firmly embedded in the consciousness of both populations, as shown by the alacrity with which it came to the fore of public debate when the US Coast Guard was considering new armaments and live-firing exercises on the Great Lakes early in the twenty-first century. While it is no longer the text of the Agreement that governs the naval relationship between Canada and the United States on the

Great Lakes the spirit of the Agreement has endured, and it is the spirit of the Agreement that continues to be adhered to by both parties.

The Rush-Bagot Agreement has been commemorated in both countries in a number of ways. Plaques commemorating the Agreement were erected in Washington, at the site of the former British Legation, and in Kingston, Ontario, on the grounds of the Royal Military College. A plaque containing a copy of the Rush-Bagot Agreement was also included in the Perry Memorial at Put-in-Bay, Ohio, where both Commodore Oliver Hazard Perry's notable victory at the Battle of Lake Erie, as well as the enduring peace on the Great Lakes which the Rush-Bagot Agreement brought about, is remembered[4].

The peaceful use of the North American Great Lakes by the populations of both Canada and the United States remains the enduring legacy of the Rush-Bagot Agreement. May it always remain so.

4. At the time of its dedication in the early nineteen-thirties President Hoover pointed to the Rush-Bagot Agreement as evidence of the ability of the United States to enter into a lasting peace with its neighbours.

BIBLIOGRAPHY

BOOKS

1.   Gardner W Allen, *A Naval History of the American Revolution, vol 1*, (New York: Houghton Mifflen Co, 1913)

2.   Ralph Allen (et al), "Return, The veterans come home to a country transformed and grown up" in *The Canadians at War 1939-45, Vol 2*, ed. Douglas How (Montreal, The Readers Digest Association (Canada) Ltd., 1969)

3.   Ralph Allen, *Ordeal by Fire Canada, 1910-1945* (Toronto: Doubleday Canada Limited, 1961)

4.   Fred Anderson, *Crucible of War: The Seven Years War and the Fate of Empire in British North America, 1754-1766* (New York: Vintage Books, 2001)

5.   Don Bamford, *Freshwater Heritage: A History of Sail on the Great Lakes, 1670-1918* (Toronto: Natural Heritage Books, 2007)

6.   John Bell, *Rebels on the Great Lakes: Confederate Naval Commando Operations Launched from Canada 1863-1864* (Toronto: Dundurn, 2011)

7.   Pierre Berton, *Niagara: A History of the Falls* (Toronto: McClelland & Stewart, 1992)

8.   Pierre Berton, *The Great Lakes*,(Toronto: Stoddart Publishing, 1996)

9.   Pierre Berton, *The Invasion of Canada, 1812-1813* (Toronto: McClelland and Stewart, 1980)

10.   Jeremy Black, *Fighting for America* (Bloomington (Ind.): Indiana University Press, 2011)

11.   Robert Bothwell, *Your Country, My Country: A Unified History of the United States and Canada* (New York: Oxford University Press, 2015)

12.   A L Burt, *The United States, Great Britain and British North America*, (New York: Russell & Russell, 1940, 1961)

13.   James Morton Callahan, *The Neutrality of the American Lakes and Anglo-American Relations* (1898; repr. New York: Johnson Reprint Co., 1973)

14.   Rene Chartrand, *British Forces in North America 1793-1815* (Oxford: Osprey Publishing, 1998, 2005)

15.   Catrine Clay, *King, Kaiser, Tsar, Three Royal Cousins Who Led the World to War* (New York: Walker Publishing Co., 2006)

16.   Thomas B Costain, *The White and the Gold* (1954; repr., Toronto: Popular Library,1965)

17.   Donald Creighton, *The Empire of the St. Lawrence*,(Toronto: MacMillan and Company, 1956)

18.   Yvon Desloges, *From a Strategic Site to a Fortified Town*, (Quebec: Septentrion, 2001)

19.   George C Douglas, *1812: The Navy's War* (New York: Basic Books, 2011)

20.   Gwynne Dyer and Tina Viljoen, *The Defence of Canada; in the Arms of the Empire, 1760-1939*, (Toronto: McClelland & Stewart, 1990)

21.   Charles Emmerson, *The Future History of the Arctic* (New York: Public Affairs, 2010)

22.   Barry Gough, *Fighting Sail on Lake Huron and Georgian Bay: The War of 1812 and its Aftermath* (St. Catharines (Ont.): Vanwell Publishing, 2002)

23.   J L Granatstein and Dean F Oliver, *The Oxford Companion to Canadian Military History* (Don Mills (Ont.): Oxford University Press, 2011)

24.   Leslie Hannon, *Forts of Canada: The Conflicts, Sieges, and Battles that Forged a Great Nation* (Toronto: McClelland and Stewart, 1969)

25.   Donald E Graves, *Guns Across the River: The Battle of the Windmill, 1838* (Montreal: Robin Brass Studio Inc., 2001, 2013)

26.   Donald R. Hickey, *Don't Give Up the Ship: Myths of the War of 1812* (Champaign (Ill.): University of Illinois Press, 2006)

27.   J R Hill, ed., *The Oxford Illustrated History of the Royal Navy*, (Oxford: Oxford University Press, 1995)

28.   William Johnston, William G P Rawling, Richard H Gimblett, John MacFarlane, *The Seabound Coast: The Official History of the Royal Canadian Navy 1867-1939* (Toronto: Dundurn Press, 2010)

29.   Richard Kluger, *Seizing Destiny: How America Grew from Sea to Shining Sea* (New York: Alfred A Knopf, 2007)

30.   Angus Konstam, *Confederate Raider 1861-65* (Oxford, Osprey Publishing, 2003)

31.   Ernest J Lajeunnesse, *The Windsor Border Region: Canada's Southernmost Frontier* (1960 repr. Toronto: Essex County Historical Association, 1972)

32.   W Kaye Lamb, *The Hero of Upper Canada* (Toronto: Rous & Mann Press, 1962)

33.   Mark Lardas, *Great Lakes Warships 1812-1815*, (Oxford: Osprey Publishing, 2012)

34.   Stephen Leacock, *Canada and the Sea* (Montreal: Alvah M. Beatty Publications (1943) Ltd., 1944)

35.   Robert Malcolmson and Thomas Malcolmson, *HMS Detroit: The Battle for Lake Erie* (St. Catherines (Ont.): Vanwell Publishing, 1990)

36.   Robert Malcolmson, *Lords of the Lake: The Naval War on Lake Ontario 1812-1814* (Toronto: Robin Bass Studio, 1998)

37.   Robert Malcolmson, *Warships of the Great Lakes 1754-1834*, (Annapolis: Naval Institute Press, 2001)

38.   Daniel Marston, *The French and Indian War 1754-1760*, (Oxford: Osprey Publishing, 2002)

39.   Philip P. Mason, *Detroit, Fort Lernoult and the American Revolution* (Detroit: Wayne State University Press, 1964)

40.   Phillips Payson O'Brien, *British and American Naval Power, Politics and Policy, 1900-1936* (Westport (Conn.), Praeger, 1998)

41.   Bradford Perkins, *The Great Rapprochement, England and the United States, 1895-1914* (New York, Athenaeum, 1968)

42.   Don Courtney Piper, *The International Law of the Great Lakes: A Study of Canadian-United States Co-operation* (Durham (N.C.): Duke University Press, 1967)

43.   Richard A Preston, *The Defence of the Undefended Border: Planning for War in North America 1867-1939* (Montreal/London: McGill-Queen's University Press, 1977)

44.   Bradley A Rodgers, *Guardian of the Great Lakes: The US Paddle*

Frigate Michigan (Ann Arbor (Mi.): University of Michigan Press, 1996)

45.   J B Priestly, *The Edwardians* (London: Sphere Books Ltd., 1972)

46.   Theodore Roosevelt, *The Naval War of 1812* (1882; repr., New York: Modern Library, 1999)

47.   David Ross and Grant Tyler, *Canadian Campaigns 1860-70* (Oxford: Osprey Publishing, 1992)

48.   K E Shewmaker (ed.) *The Papers of Daniel Webster: Diplomatic Papers, vo. 1, 1841-43* (Hanover (N.H.): Dartmouth College Press, 1983)

49.   George F G Stanley, *Toil and Trouble: Military Expeditions to Red River* (Toronto: Dundurn, 1989)

50.   Victor Suthren, *The Island of Canada: How Three Oceans Shaped Our Nation* (Toronto: Thomas Allen, 2009)

51.   Orrin Edward Tiffany, *The Canadian Rebellion of 1837-38*, (1905; repr. Toronto: Coles Publishing Co. Ltd., 1980)

52.   Robert B. Townsend, *The Story of HMS St. Lawrence* (Carrying Place (Ont.): Odyssey Publishing, 1998)

53.   Gilbert Norman Tucker, *The Naval Service of Canada* (Ottawa: King's Printer, 1952)

54.   Various Authorities, *Canada in the Great World War, Vol. 6* (Toronto: United Publishers of Canada, 1921)

55.   H.M. Queen Victoria, *The Letters of Queen Victoria – Vol 1*, (ed) George Buckle (New York: John Murray, 1926)

56.   Patrick A Wilder, *The Battle of Sackett's Harbour: 1813* (Baltimore: Nautical and Aviation Publishing Co., 1993)

57. Mark Zuehlke, *For Honour's Sake: the War of 1812 and the Brokering of an Uneasy Peace* (Toronto: Alfred A Knopf Canada, 2006)

MANUSCRIPT

1. Carol MacLeod, *The Tap of the Garrison Drum: The Marine Service in British North America 1755-1813* (Ottawa: Parks Canada, unpublished, circa 1974)

RESEARCH PAPERS AND DISSERTATIONS

1. Terence Fay, *Rush-Bagot Agreement: A Reflection of the Anglo-American Detente, 1815-1818* (Washington: Georgetown University (PhD diss.), 1975)

2. Alvin C Glueck, "The Invisible Revision of the Rush-Bagot Agreement, 1898-1914," in *The Canadian Historical Review Vol LX (1979)* (Toronto: University of Toronto Press, 1979)

3. Patrick McManus, *Stability and Flexibility: The Rush-Bagot Agreement and the Progressive Modernization of Canadian-American Security Relations* (Ottawa: University of Ottawa (PhD diss.), 2009)

4. Rear Admiral H F Pullen, *The March of the Seaman, Occasional Paper No. 8 of the Maritime Museum of Canada* (Halifax: Maritime Museum of Canada, 1961)

5. Charles P Stacey, *The Undefended Border: The Myth and the Reality* (Ottawa: Canadian Historical Association, 1953, 1996)

6. Ronald L Way, *The Day of Crysler's Farm*, (Repr. Toronto: The Ontario-St Lawrence Development Commission, 1961)

ARTICLES

1. John R. Grodzinski, "April 1813: Naval Base, Point Frederick", in *Veritas*, (Kingston (Ont.), Summer 2012, 22)

2. Robert Malcolmson, "Not Very Much Celebrated: The

Evolution and Nature of the Provincial Marine, 1755-1813", in *The Northern Mariner/Le Marin du nord, No. 1*,(Ottawa, Canadian Nautical Research Society, January, 2001, 25)

3.   New York Tribune, "Re Rush-Bagot Agreement, July 13, 1922," (Library and Archives Canada, Department of the Naval Service, Inland Waterways and Canals, Naval Control of the Great Lakes, 6287)

PAMPHLETS

1.   Minister of Indian Affairs and Northern Development, *Fort Malden National Historic Park*, (Ottawa: Queen's Printer and Controller of Stationary, 1966)

2.   Parks Canada, *Fort George National Historic Site of Canada: Walking Tour*, (Gatineau (Que.): Parks Canada, 2002)

3.   Parks Canada, *Shipbuilding at Fort Amherstburg 1796-1813*, (Ottawa: Minister of Indian and Northern Affairs, 1978)

ENCYCLOPAEDIC SOURCES

1.   Yvon Desloges, "LaForce, Rene Hippolyte," *Dictionary of Canadian Biography, Vol. V* (Toronto/Quebec: University of Toronto/ Universite Laval, 1983)

2.   W.A.B. Douglas, "Bouchette, Jean-Baptiste," *Dictionary of Canadian Biography, vol V* (Toronto/Quebec: University of Toronto Press/Les Presses de l'universite Laval, 1983)

3.   Jacques Monet, "Bagot, Sir Charles," *Dictionary of Canadian Biography, Vol VII*, (Toronto/Quebec: University of Toronto Press/ Les Presses de l'universite Laval, 1988)

4.   Ron Purver, "The Rush-Bagot Agreement: Demilitarizing the Great Lakes, 1817 to the Present," *Encyclopedia of Arms and Control and Disarmament, Vol. 1* (New York: Charles Scribner's & Sons, 1993)

ON-LINE MATERIALS

1.   Cecil Adams, "Did Chicago Once Have a Brick Battleship?", *Chicago Straight Dope*, April 22, 2010 (http://chicago.straightdope.com/sdc20100422.php, accessed 2011/07/15).

2.   Author Unknown, "Battleship Illinois (replica)," *Wikipedia: The Free Encyclopedia*, (http://en.wikipedia.org/wiki/Battleship_Illinois_replica accessed 2011-07-15).

3.   Author Unknown, "French and British Military Conflict (1664-1763)," Lake Champlain Maritime Museum (http://www.lcmm.org.)

4.   Department of Global Affairs Canada, *Canada Treaty Series* (Ottawa: http://www.treaty-accord.gc.ca/cts-rtc.aspx?lang=eng.)

5.   William Lambers, "Nuclear Weapons, the Great Lakes and Lake Champlain", August 21, 2011 (www.williamlambers.com/category/rush-bagot-agreement, accessed November 6, 2012)

6.   William Lyon Mackenzie King, *Diaries of William Lyon Mackenzie King* (Ottawa: Library and Archives Canada, http://www.bac-lac.gc.ca/eng/discover/politics-government/prime-ministers/william-lyon-mackenzie-king/diaries.aspx.)

7.   William Wood, "The Fight for Overseas Empire: The Declaration of War" in Adam Shortt and Arthur G. Doughty, eds., *Canada and Its Provinces, Vol. 1* (Toronto: Glasgow, Brook & Company, 1914) 246-254; repr. *L'Encyclopedie de l'histoire du Quebec/The Quebec History Encyclopedia*, C. Belanger, ed. (Montreal: Marianopolis College, 2005) (http://www.faculty.marianopolis.edu /c.belanger/ quebechistory/ encyclopedia/ TheSevenYearsWar.htm., accessed 2015-05-21)

8.   Yale University, Lillian Goldman Law Library, *The Avalon*

Project: Documents in Law History and Diplomacy (New Haven (Conn.): http://avalon.law.yale.edu/.)

PUBLIC ADDRESSES

1.   Rt. Hon. Sir Charles Fitzpatrick (Chief Justice) *An Address Delivered by the Rt. Hon. Sir Charles Fitzpatrick Before the Lawyers Club, New York City, March 17, 1917* (Address privately published, 1917)

2.   President John F. Kennedy, "A Strategy of Peace," American University Commencement Address, (Washington, D.C,: June 10, 1963)

3.   President John F. Kennedy, "Address to the Canadian Parliament" (Ottawa: May 17, 1961)

GOVERNMENT DOCUMENTS

1.   Library and Archives of Canada, Ottawa, Ont. The sources accessed are mainly in the Rush-Bagot Political Series, and in the Department of the Naval Service, Inland Waterways and Canals, Naval Control of the Great Lakes files. References to specific documents are contained in the footnotes in the various chapters within the text.

2.   Parliament of Canada, Ottawa, Ont., "Proceedings of the Standing Senate Committee on National Security and Defence" March 29, 2004; Testimony of the Rt. Hon. Herb Gray, P.C., Chair and Commissioner, Canadian Section, International Joint Commission, March 29, 2004

3.   United States of America, 90th Congress, 1st Session, "Senate Report No. 185", April 13, 1967

www.ingramcontent.com/pod-product-compliance
Lightning Source LLC
Chambersburg PA
CBHW031536260326
41914CB00032B/1824/J